Joy in the Journey

365 Whispers of Hope

Laurie Schwartz

From Amish to Author

Email: laurieschwartz111@gmail.com

Table of Contents

Introduction

Through a daily journal, jotting on a notepad, I journeyed 365 days to create this devotional. As I wrote snippets of my current life season, I remembered growing up a modest Amish girl. I never imagined the amazing things God would call me to later in life. My teen years were rough, running with the wild crowd, rebellious towards the church and, at times, my parents. At 18, God radically got my attention, and everything changed. Unfortunately, as I got older, I became overly strict and religious, thinking I could earn my salvation. God had a remarkable plan for my life; becoming born-again was only the beginning. My journey has been exhilarating and excruciating, scary yet exciting. In the following pages, you will find sprinkles of my Amish background and the current life I now live.

My daughters and I had planned a road trip to Atlanta, GA. Daughter Luanne drove. As she played her worship music my 'word of the year' came to my mind. It was simply 'restore.' My heart leaped a little with joy as I thought it could mean: Would it be certain relationships, my health, or broken dreams? The possibilities are endless, not just for me but for you, too, friend. Now I see it through this book. God has opened many doors. He is a God of restoration.

He changed our broken pieces into something beautiful. When we surrender our broken dreams, hopes, health, bodies, or whatever we need healing from, He is faithful to restore us. Joel 2:25 says, "I will restore the years that the locust have eaten." God will restore what was stolen and lost. Deuteronomy 30:3 says, "The Lord your God will restore your fortunes and have compassion on you." Verse 9 says, "The Lord God will make you prosperous in all the work of your hands and in the fruit of your womb...He will again delight in you and make you prosperous."

Prayer declaration:
God, I come to you in Jesus' name; I dare dream once again. I bring that dream you instilled in me to your feet. You see my tears and hear my every prayer. You're a good Father, and in You alone is my healing and hope. Amen.

Pursuing God

We arrived safely in Atlanta last night, just in time to get some food, unpack, and find our room on the 30th floor of the Marriot. It felt absolutely wonderful to relax and stretch out after 14 hours in the car. My husband called and said we'd just missed a snowstorm – we were ahead of it! Except for the gently falling rain, our drive was perfect. Thankful to be able to sleep a little longer this morning, we finally ventured down to Starbucks inside the hotel because, you know, first, coffee.

Slowly, as we got ready, chatting up a storm as only a mom and daughters can do, changing outfits a few times. We set out early with our umbrellas in tow. It was raining again, and we had a mile to walk to the Mercedes Benz Center. We explored the city a little, stood in long lines for food, and had more coffee. We stopped to enjoy the beautiful Centennial Park in the heart of the city, taking some pictures and getting wet. We finally arrived at the Benz Center along with about 65,000 other people for the Passion Conference. We stood in line again for an hour or more until the doors opened. It was absolutely worth the wait! We listened to some of our favorite speakers and singers until midnight. We walked the mile back to our hotel in the dark with many others. Our hearts and spirits were fed. The pure joy of worshiping alongside so many other believers was incredibly powerful.

Going to church is amazing, but for me, sometimes I need that overflow, being poured into for several days on end, seeking God, resetting my heart, and restoring my soul and spirit. Jeremiah 29:13 says, "You will seek me and you will find me when you seek me with all your heart." Sometimes that means getting out of our comfort zone. Sometimes that might even look like driving 14 hours across the country where you know God is moving mightily. Whatever it looks like for you, go after it! Don't settle for mediocre. What makes you come alive? Where do you find God's presence on a daily basis?

Prayer declaration:
Jesus, thank you for filling me up today. Show me where to find fresh manna every day. You alone are the food that will truly satisfy and sustain me. Amen.

January 3
Heavenly Seats

It's my 51st birthday today, and once again, the alarm clock jars me awake early. Going on about four or five hours of sleep, we get up and quickly get ready and set out toward the Benz Center again. Our plan was to grab a coffee from Starbucks, but the one wasn't open yet; the other one had a line wrapped all the way around the corner of the hotel. So much for that! We knew the doors opened at 7, and seats were first come, first served. The wind was ferocious that morning, and our mile walk was cold and miserable, *with no coffee.* We made it pretty close to the front of the line, happy we left early. We stood in line for another hour. By the time the doors opened, we were very cold, but we got front-row seats on the bleachers right across from the stage. We were allowed to keep our seats for the rest of the day, and even in sessions, which, once again, lasted until midnight.

Sandwiched in between my daughters, worshiping with arms stretched to heaven, with our 65,000 new friends, it was a heavenly experience. It got me thinking: are we as willing to push through the hard stuff in life, the uncomfortable and even painful things, to secure our seats in heaven? The Bible says, "No eye has seen, no ear has heard, what God has prepared for those who love Him," in 1 Corinthians 2:9, to lay down our pride and ask Jesus to come into our hearts and let him be our Lord and Savior. Remember, we don't wait to come to Jesus until we are cleaned up, but we come to him to be cleaned up. Jesus said himself, "It is not the healthy who need a doctor, but the sick. I have not come to call the righteous, but the sinners," Mark 2:17. Will you secure your front-row seat in heaven today? If you haven't done so, you are welcome.

Prayer declaration:

Jesus, today, I repent of my sins and self. I ask you to come into my heart and save me. Jesus, I believe that you are the Son of God, and that I am now saved by the blood you shed for me on the cross. Hallelujah!

January 4
The Right Way

On the way home from the Passion Conference, I set the directions into the GPS. I have double and triple-checked our route home. When it was my mother's turn to drive, I plugged the route into her phone and rechecked it again, yet she asked, "Is this the way? Which way do I go? Left, or right? Now which way?" When my sister-in-law drove, she too, asked, "Is this the right way? Are you sure? It looks like we're headed to Chicago. Are you *100% sure*?" At this point, I was growing frustrated. All I wanted was to sleep after my shift of driving since early that morning. I checked the route so many times. I planned it before we left. I knew our destination was ahead; all they had to do was follow the path the GPS was showing: That was all. No matter what it said, it was taking us home. It knew our destination, no matter what it *looked* like. We were not headed to Chicago, but to our final destination – *home.*

I think God has some experience with this. He creates a roadmap for us, a path, a plan, a purpose, and He says, "Follow me, and I will show you." Yet we say, "Is this right, God? This doesn't feel right. This doesn't look right. It's taking me here, God, and I don't want to go there. Are you sure, God? Are you sure?" I imagine God is saying, "Stay on my path. It's right in front of you. It doesn't need to make sense to you right now, but you will see. Stay on my path. Trust in me and you will get there."

My mother and sister were confused because the Chicago Road signs kept popping up. Everything around us seemed to be pointing us in that direction; it was distracting them. It clouded their vision causing confusion, and they lost sight of the path. Rest assured; God is in control.

Prayer declaration:
May we always keep our eyes on You. May you lead us on the right path when we trust in you. "Trust in the Lord with all your heart, and lean not on your own understanding." Proverbs 3:5-6.

(Chapter written by my daughter Luanne)

January 5
Resting Well

Do you rest well? I mean complete rest. Have you ever allowed yourself a day in the middle of the week to rest and restore your body and spirit? Getting enough rest and sleep are essential for our overall health and well-being. Especially after a week of travel, it's important to give yourself some downtime, which is exactly what I'm doing today after being gone all weekend.

Let's face it. Sunday isn't always a day of rest as it could or should be. By the time you get your family out the door for church and everyone gets lunch, if you are lucky, you might get a nap in the afternoon. I personally don't believe it has to be on Sunday, as long as you still make time for a Sabbath in your daily life, occasionally. Sabbath, to me, means resting from your normal work and connecting to God. Whatever way that looks for you, maybe you find it in nature. Maybe you find it in the Bible or a book that points you to him. Maybe it's worship or creating something with your hands.

Even Jesus needed to get away from the crowds and the needs of the people sometimes, to be alone and connect with his heavenly father. How much more, then, do we, too, need it in our fast-paced world today? So why not plan yourself a pajama rest day soon? Silence your emails, mute your phone, and do something that recharges you. In Matthew 11:28, Jesus gives us a wonderful invitation, "Come to me all you who are weary and burdened and I will give you rest." Hebrews 4:10 says, "For anyone who enters God's rest also rests from their works."

My favorite says, "In repentance and rest is your salvation. In quietness and in trust is your strength," Isaiah 30:15.

Prayer declaration:

Jesus, thank you for the rest we will find in you alone. Show us how to rest in you, our rock. Thank you for helping us let go of unrealistic expectations and entering into your rest. Amen.

January 6
Beauty All Around

Beauty. What comes to mind when you think of that word? Do you think of physical beauty in people, looks, and actions? Do you see it more in nature? In a beautiful sunset or sunrise? Those are two of my personal favorites. Did you know there is beauty *all around us, all the time*? When we open our eyes to see it, it's there. Beauty is, therefore, much more than physical appearance. We can cultivate and have a beautiful, tender spirit that draws others to us. We can see it in the sunshine, after the rains and storms, in nature, and also in our lives because often, the very storms that come crashing into our lives have a way of pruning us and turning our ashes into beauty.

When we surrender our ashes, he makes beauty from them. There is a song by Tenth Avenue North – "He makes beautiful things out of the dust. He makes beautiful things out of us." What do you need to surrender today to Jesus, so he can start putting the pieces back together again? Isaiah 61:3 says, "To bestow on them a crown of beauty for ashes, the oil of joy for mourning." Ahh! Who doesn't want that? I know I do! A crown of beauty! I don't think we have to wait for heaven for that. I believe the more we let Jesus sanctify and purify our hearts, the more we will radiate true beauty that comes from the inside out. Beauty will show up even in our physical appearance.

Prayer declaration:
Jesus, thank you for creating so much beauty for us to enjoy in your creation. Thank you for opening our eyes to the beauty around us in people, places, and things. Give us your eyes to see. Thank you for pruning and purifying us and making beauty out of the ashes of our life.

January 7
Date Your Spouse

If you are married, did you date your spouse first? Did you know the person you were going to marry before your wedding day? My husband and I hardly did; we grew up in a strict community where we were only allowed to see each other a few hours a week. Of course, we broke the rules often, which made us feel guilty at times. For us, those few hours just weren't enough!

We went through some hard times and did get into trouble with the church at different times. However, God is a God of redemption, and our relationship now has a solid foundation. One thing we do now, on a weekly basis, is date night. Sometimes I feel like, even after 30 years of marriage, we are still getting to know each other.

What do you do to keep the spark alive in your marriage? Do you know your spouse's love language? If not, you can google it and take a simple test that's very easy (lovelanguages.com). I love gifts and surprises, and my husband is great at both. For my 51st birthday, he sent five dozen roses to the hotel I was staying at for the weekend. He loves quality time and touch. We are complete opposites in almost everything, but this is our mantra: "What God has joined together, let not man put asunder," Mark 10:9. Of course, there are exceptions, like abuse and unfaithfulness, etc., but hold on to your faith. If you are single, let God be your partner and help you find the one He has for you.

Prayer declaration:
Jesus, thank you for your plan for marriage. Thank you for helping us to love like you do, and to never stop dating each other. (To the singles, "Lord, help me find the one you have chosen for me; I trust in you to guide me.") Help me know my own love language.

January 8
Trustworthy Friendship

Do you have someone you don't worry about letting it all hang out, so to speak: The kind of friend that you know will not judge you no matter what you tell them? Do you know someone who will actually take your requests and truly pray for them? I always told my children, you don't need a lot of friends; you only need a few you can trust. These types of friendships are truly precious. Even the Bible has something to say about this subject. Proverbs 18:24 says, "One who has unreliable friends soon comes to ruin, but there is a friend that sticks closer than a brother."

I met some of my closest friends through my children and their friends. Other mamas from school, two in particular, one of them is my friend Ann. She is a prayer warrior. I have often felt the power of her prayers. What a blessing!

Do you have this type of friend? If not, you can simply ask God for one. You might be surprised where you find one. Mine came through public school, but it was our faith that connected our hearts to each other. Ann came over this past Saturday, and we worked on a very difficult puzzle together. We listened to worship music, had coffee and chocolate and wine, and caught up on each other's lives – the good, the bad, and the ugly – because that's what true friends do. Proverbs 27:9 says, "Perfume and incense bring joy to the heart, and the pleasantness from a friend springs from their heartfelt advice."

Prayer declaration:
Jesus, thank you for like-minded friends that encourage and upbuild me, help me grow in my faith, and bear the burdens of life.

January 9
Making Assumptions

Have you ever made assumptions about people or situations only to find out later how wrong you were? Webster's dictionary defines assumption as a noun meaning *the act of assuming or taking for granted.* I have done this too often in my life, judging and condemning people without knowing their side of the story. It's such an easy trap to fall into. *(Lord, forgive me.)* The last three big assumptions I made, however, turned out to be funny, but there is still a lesson attached to them.

Take this past Sunday evening, for instance. In my 51st birthday month, I assumed because I had been gone for my birthday and my husband had sent me the beautiful rose bouquet that nothing else much would happen. Even though I love having my family around me for my birthday, I knew they were busy; it was only a few digits above zero, yet my husband told me to be ready to leave the house by 6 pm Sunday night. I assumed we were going somewhere to eat, maybe, but he said, "Dress warm." I assumed again, "Oh! He's taking me on a sleigh ride at my friend's house!" We had done that before as a family; he knew how much I enjoyed that.

Imagine my huge surprise, then, when he took me on a moonlit walk back into our woods. All of a sudden, several strings of lights flashed on, and I saw a roaring fire. Next, I heard someone singing "Happy Birthday;" here were my precious children gathered in the woods to surprise me! My heart leaped; I felt loved and celebrated and was so glad I assumed wrong once again!

Prayer declaration:
Jesus, thank you for your forgiveness when we make wrong assumptions about people or situations. Give us hearts to always see and believe the best about people and situations. Amen.

January 10
Love Yourself First

In today's culture, there are mixed messages about self-care. Some people say you absolutely should take care of yourself first. Others think everyone else should come first and you should always come last. Their thinking is that would be the selfless way to live, but let me ask you a question. Can a person pour from an empty cup or an empty heart? Can you love someone if you don't love yourself? The Bible says, "Love our neighbors as ourselves." Mark 12:31. However, the verse above continues, "Love the Lord your God with all your heart, soul, all your mind and strength. "There is no greater commandment than these two." Mark 12:30-31.

I think it's safe to say we definitely can't love others well if we aren't first filled up to the brim with God's love ourselves. So often, though, we run, and we run, and we run, trying to get our worth and fulfillment out of doing for Jesus. When what if He really would want us to slow down and just be more in his presence? What if we slowed down enough to truly love ourselves enough to take care of ourselves? When we are exhausted, to rest, instead of continuing to push ourselves to the breaking point? It's okay also to do things you truly enjoy when you need to recharge. What is it for you, coffee with a friend, a funny or heartfelt movie, or a good book? One of my personal favorites is a massage, it was my treat to my aching back just this week. Take care of yourself and you will have more and richer substance to give away, giving out of your overflow instead of your lack.

Prayer declaration:
Jesus, show us where we need to slow down and take care of ourselves. Thank you for loving us so we can love others with your abundant, overflowing love.

Mental Self Care

Another form of self-care is to allow yourself to be poured into by a mentor or therapist. Let me guess. Instead, you are always the one giving. I, too, did this for years, often pouring, giving out of my own lack, trying to give what I didn't always have to give. This worked for a season, but like anything, when things aren't in alignment with God's heart, they are not sustainable.

I was always the listening ear for everyone else all through my 20s and 30s. When I turned 40, it felt like all hell broke loose physically, emotionally, and spiritually. I felt like I was at a breaking point in my life and for a season. I could hardly even be around people other than my family. Depression set in, and the doctoring began. She told me my stress hormones were completely depleted. In fact, they didn't even show up on the charts of my tests. I started making changes that day, in every way!

My mentor told me the healthiest way to be is to pour into others while being poured into by someone I trust. Think of a river. It constantly has fresh water pouring in and out of it. How different than a stagnant farm pond? Which one do you want to be – fresh and flowing with life or stale and stagnant and not growing? There's a verse in the Bible that says, "Let the older women [or men] teach the younger." Titus 2:3. I love this. Receive your advice/mentorship from those older than us and pass it on to those younger than us.

Prayer declaration:
Jesus, today I thank you for counselors, mentors, and therapists. Thank you for healing us first so that we can heal others. Heal us from the inside out, Jesus. Amen.

January 12
Dare to Dream

Dreams actually do come true. I experienced this first-hand. After we left our strict Amish community, where dreaming was not encouraged at all, my husband and I had to learn how to dream. Do you know how? One of the best ways to start dreaming is to ask yourself, "If time and money wouldn't be an issue, what would I do or be?" I encourage you to start a dream journal today. Even if it seems impossible to you, write it down. Actually, if you can make it happen with your own strength, you are probably dreaming too small. Write those dreams down and ask God to breathe on them, and then watch what He can do! If God could bring dry bones back to life, in Ezekiel 37:1-14, then He certainly can bring your dreams to life, too, especially if they line up with His word and His will. There's another verse I love. It says, "...with thanksgiving, present your requests to God." Phil. 4:5

Some of my personal dreams that are coming true are: Making a difference in Africa; building our dream house close to a wooded area; having all our children love and serve Jesus. There's no limit to our dreams. When they come true, you dream even bigger. It's wonderful to remember and thank God for every dream that comes true for you. It also builds your faith as you watch and do the things that once seemed impossible. Our God specializes in the impossible. What forgotten dreams do you need to rekindle in your heart? If it matters to you, it matters to God.

Prayer declaration:
Jesus, will you help us to dare to dream again? Will you fill us with your visions for our lives? Jesus, thank you for giving us fresh dreams, and thank you for all the dreams that have come true.

More Dreams

Recently, I traveled to Madison, Wisconsin, to visit my doctor. As I was driving home on the busy beltline Highway, in the flow of the traffic, suddenly I thought of how dreams come true. Growing up driving a horse and buggy, driving a car was considered wrong, even though the Bible says, "A horse is a vain thing for safety." Psalm 37:17. I agree. Of course, my brother always had the wildest horses, and later, my husband did too. However, he did buy me a wonderful horse named Stella that was safe and fast! I loved her and felt sad the day we had to sell her. She got sick and couldn't run anymore.

In those days, I never dreamed I would be able to drive a car. Fast forward about 25 years plus, here I am, cruising along with everyone else. It started me thinking and dreaming again. What else does God have in store for me that I don't even know about yet?

What about you? What is something you have accomplished that you never thought possible? Remember it! Bask in it! It's so good to look back sometimes and remember what God has done. Thank Him and praise Him and ask Him to do even more in your life!

Psalm 126:3 articulates, "The Lord has done great things for us. We are glad." We should be glad when we remember where we have been and where God has brought us. He brought us into freedom in Him through this whole process.

Prayer declaration:
Jesus, today I thank you for what you've done, and what you are going to do. Thank you for giving us willing hungry hearts, eager to grow with you.

January 14
Protection in the Storm

Snowstorms in Wisconsin are not uncommon, especially in January, February, March, and sometimes even May. This used to be a struggle for me. All the snow and the cold – I hated it! Eventually, though, I figured out, like anything else in life, if you are equipped and prepared for it, you can handle it. Since then, I have bought two thick winter jackets, several pairs of warm boots, hats, gloves, and scarves. I've learned to embrace what I can't change.

This past Friday, my daughter and I had planned a dinner date with friends in my daughter's town, an hour away from me. Not only was it a cold day, but it snowed most of the day. I debated not going out that night – even called my daughter and discussed the pros and cons. She said, "Just come, Mom. You can stay at my house for the night if the weather gets worse." Oh, the things we do for our kids at times! It took me longer than normal because the roads were bad in some places, but I prayed for protection as I drove.

I comforted myself with a verse from Deuteronomy 31:8, "The Lord himself goes before you and will be with you." I truly felt it during the drive that night as the snow continued to come down. The rest of the verse says, "He will never leave you nor forsake you. Do not be afraid or discouraged." I did have to face some fear because of a previous accident about five years earlier that I had, but God is faithful to his promises, and he protected me, and by the time I came home, the snow had quit, and the roads were much better. We had a wonderful dinner date with our friends.

Remember, God is there even when you're not aware.

Prayer declaration:
Thank you for caring about every detail of our lives, even dinner dates. Thank you for your protection and peace, even when the wind howls and the snow flies.

Forgive Like Children

"Do you want the boys for a few hours today, Mama?" Our sweet daughter-in-law asks a question I never get tired of hearing. Daddy is sick, and she's under the weather herself, and she's exhausted from doing it all alone. Of course, I say yes. Even though my week has been extra busy and I'm feeling tired myself, there is something about having the boys that energizes and invigorates me, so I say yes whenever I possibly can. Maybe it's just their pure sweetness. Maybe it's their innocence and how they say my name, "Gramma." It melts my heart, and it's one of my absolute favorite names. Maybe it's the way they sing along to their little favorite songs, "Jesus Loves Me" and many others.

All I know is they fill my heart and make me happy and make me want to become more like a child. Matthew 8:3-4 says, "Unless you change and become like little children, you will never enter the Kingdom of God. Therefore, he who humbles himself like this child is the greatest in the Kingdom of heaven." Wow! Isn't that sobering? What if we forgive as quickly as children? What if we love and trust as children do? I do believe our world would be a better place. Think about when children fight or have a disagreement. As soon as it's cleared up and they express their emotions, they often go right back to playing with no hard feelings toward each other. In Mark 10:14, Jesus said, "Let the little children come to me and do not hinder them, for the Kingdom of God belongs to such as these."

Prayer declaration:
Jesus, thank you for sweet innocent adorable children. Thank you for the example children are for us as adults. Thank you for making us more like these little ones.

January 16
Believe and Receive

It's Sunday. Looks like it will actually be a day of rest for me today. I dig out my stack of old journals and start reading through them. I bring a stack of sticky notes and a red pen. Every time I read a dream or prayer that God has answered, I write it on a sticky note. I can't tell you how satisfying that is to me seeing heart cries and fasts of the past, and what came out of that is a wonderful way to stir up your faith. Jude 1:20 says, "You dear friends, building yourselves up in your most holy faith, and praying in the Holy Spirit."

When I look back over my life and see all that God has done, it does just that; it stirs up my faith. It also fills me with gratitude and helps me know that he will do it again and again. Another of my favorite verses says, "If you believe you will receive whatever you ask for," Matthew 21:22. Now, do my answered prayers always look like I thought they would? Sometimes, but not nearly always, and some prayers have not been answered at all.

As I keep stirring up my faith, it's easy to keep believing that God is good and has the best plan for my life! Do you keep a prayer journal, a dreams or goals journal, or maybe all three? I've even started my own version of a prayer closet. The current prayer requests go on the inside of my one closet door. All the answered requests and dreams, and goals achieved go inside the other closet door on a different color paper. It's so easy to open that door and see all the requests and start praying or see all the answered prayers and start praising.

Prayer declaration:
Jesus, thank you for your faithfulness. Teach us how to stir up our faith. Thank you for all your good gifts and answered prayers.

January 17
More of God

One theme I see all throughout my journals is the cry for more of God. Over and over, that's been my heart's cry. I clearly remember when I first started praying that prayer, about twenty-five to thirty years ago. My husband and I had met and married in the Amish church. We had three little boys, and life was fairly good but boring, mundane, and with no adventure in sight. God was there, but often distant and very hazy, through the eyes of a religious spirit and setting; that's when I first started breathing this prayer, "God, if there's more of you to be experienced and discovered, I want it." Wow! Unless you are ready for a grand adventure with Jesus, be careful what you pray for. I still pray that prayer today, though.

I, for one, don't ever want to settle for less than all of what God has for me to experience in this life. One of my favorite verses is found in Matthew 7:7, "Ask and it shall be given to you, seek and you shall find, knock and the door will be open to you." This has been another one of my life verses, and it's so powerful! We have permission to ask! Our lives have completely changed since that prayer first escaped my lips. My husband and I and our six children ended up leaving our Amish culture. Yes, we had three more along the way, over a period of ten years, slowly, as God opened our eyes and hearts and doors in our lives. Was it always easy? Absolutely not, but God was faithful through hell and high water, tears and joys beyond measure. "It is for freedom he has set us free," Galatians 5:1.

Prayer declaration:
Thank you, Jesus, that you have set us free. Thank you that you are faithful to hear our heart's cry. Thank you for continuing to lead us into the more of you.

January 18
Around the Table

One thing I love about community is sharing not only the highs but also the lows of our lives. One of the things I miss the most about my Amish culture is the gathering together for home-cooked meals. It was such a big part of growing up that I didn't realize what we had until we didn't. It is something we still enjoy doing. My husband and I invite someone over and make delicious food. Maybe it's still in our DNA. As the saying goes, "You can take the girl out of the Amish, but you can't take the Amish out of the girl."

My husband and I both enjoy cooking. He is famous for his big breakfasts, which he loves to cook, whether it's for our family only or for friends from out of town. I also like to incorporate meals at our monthly Bible studies. Some conversations are just the best around the table. Even Jesus and his disciples often gathered around food.

Another way I do this is to meet other mamas for a meal or even just coffee at a cozy restaurant. It's the perfect atmosphere to bear one another's burdens. Galatians 6:10 says that, and the verse ends with, "...and so and so fulfill the law of Christ." How beautiful is that? That, too, can become a lost thing in a world of social media, where people, more often than not, only post their highlights. What about you? Do you have a community? Do you have friends to bear each other's burdens with, to eat with, to laugh with, to pray and cry with?

Prayer declaration:
Jesus, thank you for your plan for community. Help us make time for others. Bring our community around us so we can grow and do life together. Amen.

January 19
Naps Are Necessary

What do you do when your To-Do List is overwhelming and you are tired inside and outside? Are you working harder and faster, hiring help, or getting stressed out? Believe me; I've done all of the above. Sometimes, some of those work, but sometimes you might just need a nap. That's right; a nap can be the most rejuvenating thing ever as long as you don't sleep so long you ruin your bedtime sleep schedule. Even Jesus took a nap. He, too, must have gotten tired and needed to rest from it all. We read about this in Matthew 8:24.

Suddenly a furious storm came up on the lake so that the waves swept over the boat, but Jesus was sleeping! I just love that! It's all the permission I need to take a nap! It's also something I'm so grateful my mother taught me growing up. We always got up early to milk cows by hand and do a host of other chores on the farm, so after lunch, we were allowed to go read, nap, or rest, for at least one hour.

This was always a special time of day, our free time. It's a practice I still incorporate into my schedule whenever I can. One of my favorite ways to nap is to put on some soft worship music and let that lull me to sleep. It helps me fall asleep quickly instead of thinking about all I should be doing. Getting enough sleep is very important for our overall health, and that's why I believe naps are straight from heaven.

Prayer declaration:
Jesus, thank you for teaching us the benefits of naps and getting enough sleep. Teach us how to do this instead of letting our to-do lists and schedules overwhelm us. Amen

January 20
It's the Little Things

Sitting in a coffee shop today, thoroughly enjoying my cheesecake latte and writing – two of my favorite things. I love coffee shops! What is it about them that's so delightful and inviting? For me, it's the smell first of all, and sometimes they have a cozy fireplace space. This one today is inside a bookstore which is so fun because books are another thing that makes me so happy. Can one have too many books? I think not.

Books, coffee, and, later, a pedicure are some of the little luxuries of life – things we don't need but get to enjoy every so often. It's the little moments like these that remind me of how blessed I am, especially when I reflect back to our earlier days of marriage. We often had barely enough money for the bare necessities. Spending $5 on a latte would have been out of the question. We did have some basic books, though. Even as a young Amish girl growing up, if we got any kind of gift, it was usually a book. Maybe that's why I still love books, because of previous memories.

Now a pedicure would have been completely off limits – too worldly and too expensive, plus Amish ladies just don't paint their toes. So as I sit here and reflect today, I am filled with gratitude – gratitude for these little gifts God allows me to enjoy every now and then, still in moderation, lest we take it for granted. Psalm 136:1 says, "Give thanks to the Lord for he is good, for his steadfast love endures forever." Sometimes the best prayer we can pray is, "Thank you, Jesus."

Prayer declaration:
Thank you, Jesus, for what you've done, for what you are doing, and for what you will do.

January 21
You Be the Change

Yesterday, our house was packed with extended family. This is a huge and long-time-prayed-for answered prayer, one I do not take lightly. My sisters, a bunch of my nieces, and a few of the husbands came to spend the day with us. We were celebrating my birthday late and two of my nieces' birthdays, as well. It was a wonderful day of laughing, storytelling, eating too much food, drinking too much coffee, singing, and music. All too soon, the day ended, and they had to go home again, two and half hours away. Most of them are still Amish. In fact, I am one out of nine siblings (I have four brothers and four sisters), and I'm the only one who isn't Amish anymore.

I'm so very thankful to say we have a pretty good relationship twenty years after leaving. It wasn't always like this, though. For ten years, there was very little relationship, partially due to the fact that we lived in the West, far away from my family. I always miss them, and the thought of them getting together for holidays and weddings without us was hard and cost some tears. At times we were shunned. In that way, I have no ill feelings; it's just what most Amish do when you leave their church and way of life. They don't know anything else. Imagine with me how very sweet and healing days like yesterday are. Only God can do these kinds of things. He loves to restore relationships! If there are broken relationships in your family today, **you** step out in faith, **you** be the change, **you** make the first effort. Ask God what you can do. Psalm 68:6 says, "God sets the lonely or solitary in families." That was me for many years.

Prayer declaration:
Jesus, thank you for redemption and restoration in my family. Thank you that family is important to you. Help us to be brave and make the first step towards healing when possible. Amen.

January 22
Puzzle Pieces and Us

Our house was filled again Saturday night, not only our own children but friends of our children, which is just really special. My husband and I host a lot. We both love it when our schedule allows us the time to do so. Saturday night's occasion was our weekly family night, and also to watch the Packers. Unfortunately, they lost by like a minute, but we had a win when the guests and our children finished a very difficult 1000-piece puzzle our family and others had been working on for over three years. This was an extra special puzzle given to us as a Christmas gift from our daughter-in-law's parents, who are artists and painters and very talented. They painted the picture this puzzle was made of, so there was no way we were going to give up on it.

Don't you think that's how God feels about us? He won't give up on us even when our life feels and seems like a puzzle at times. He sees the finished product of us. I imagine him seeing us through his eyes of love and saying things like, "Don't give up! Eventually, the pieces will all fit together." Bit by bit, one piece at a time, He is creating a masterpiece out of us.

We were not surprised when one piece was missing after many times of moving the puzzle around, even from house to house, but we have a plan for that from our artist friends, just like God has a plan for us. Remember Romans 8:28, "All things work together for good for them who are called according to his purpose." Yes, even the puzzling missing pieces.

Prayer declaration:
Jesus, thank you that you care about every piece of our lives. Help us trust you. Even when the pieces don't fit or one seems lost, you still have a plan.

Grandchildren Are Our Crown

"Were you planning to come to church, Mom, or would you mind keeping the boys for us?" I received this text from my son Saturday. He and his wife were scheduled to play on the worship team the next day, and now the boys were under the weather. For me, it was a no-brainer. Of course, I will choose the boys over going to church! In my mind, I was already thinking of what I could do to doctor them up and make them feel better.

Sunday morning, they dropped the boys off bright and early so as to get to worship practice on time. We started the day with our little worship songs they love and can sing word for word. Little Zander, almost two, doesn't know quite all the words yet, but he makes up for it in volume with the words he does know! To see the little ones singing, "How Jesus loves me," does my heart good, like a church service. I love the church, so that's saying a lot! Later, we played, had breakfast, and then they took long soaking baths, and I did home remedies for their colds.

Next, we had snacks, snuggles, and naps until Mommy and Daddy came to pick them up after lunch. Our grandsons bring us so much joy! Is it any wonder the Bible says, "Grandchildren are the crown of the aged and the glory of grandchildren is their fathers," Proverbs 17:6 says this. It's so true for us. Also, like someone once said, "If we would have known how fun it is to be grandparents, we would have skipped straight to grandchildren!" A joke, of course. We love our six kids tremendously!

Prayer declaration:
Jesus, thank you for giving us grandchildren! What a reward! Thank you for helping us guide and teach them about you and your love for them. Protect their little hearts from the darts of the enemy.

January 24
New Mercies

Do you love or hate Mondays? Me? I love them, but it wasn't always like this. There was a time when, for me, Mondays meant going down to a basement to do a large laundry with an old-fashioned wringer washer. With six children, this was no easy task. It didn't work to take them down there with me, so it involved a lot of running upstairs to check on them. At one brilliant point, I would get up at four o'clock am, when the children were still all sleeping, and before my husband went to work, and got it done by seven am. It was such a good and accomplished feeling.

These days, though, I am so very grateful for a washer and dryer! No more cold and frozen fingers hanging laundry outside in the winter. I never did enjoy that. Never will I take my washer and dryer for granted. Now I love Mondays. I still do laundry sometimes but, in the warmth, and comfort of my laundry room. What I love most about Mondays now is the fresh beginning to a new week, back to my workouts, clean eating, and routine; a new week to accomplish goals and become a better person. I love, though, that we don't have to wait for a certain day to do that because the Bible says, "God's mercies are new every morning and his faithfulness is great," Lamentations 3:22-23. So, you can start over today and receive his love and his mercy. Where do you need to apply it to your life? Mondays and every day are a brand-new start.

Prayer declaration:
Jesus, thank you for your grace and mercy and your unfailing love. Help us to forgive ourselves and start over with fresh mercy you so freely give us. Show us what we need to let go of to become better humans and more like you.

January 25
Snow Days

Another fresh layer of snow is a common winter occurrence here in Wisconsin. It looks fresh, beautiful but it's oh so cold. This morning it was once again close to thirty below zero. However, when the sun shines and warms things up, it really isn't that bad. Just like life, right? It can seem pretty cold, frozen, and dreary, but when we allow the SUN to shine on our situations, pain, and disappointments, we will often begin to see the silver lining; every cloud has a silver lining: Plus, we have a promise from Jesus that he will never give us more than we can bear, "He will not let us be tempted beyond what we can bear," 1 Corinthians 10:13. So, whether you are in a cold season physically, emotionally, spiritually, or in the natural, the sun will shine again. Whenever I see the fresh white snow, it reminds me of two things: beauty and purity.

I'm reminded of this little verse from my childhood: "The future lies before us, like newly fallen snow, be careful how you tread it, for every step will show." The best thing about snowy, cold days for me now is the blessing of being inside, where it's nice and warm. I work from my home office, so it is very different from my childhood of being outside and doing chores, walking to school, etc. I'm grateful for that season of my life, too. Can you identify what season you are in today and ask the SUN to shine on it?

Prayer Declaration:
Jesus, thank you that you have the ability to thaw our frozen places. Thank you for ordering our steps and constantly tenderizing our hearts for you.

January 26
Choose Your Attitude

As I ventured outside to get the mail last night, it had warmed up considerably. I couldn't help but bask in the beauty of the magnificent sunset, a beautiful backdrop against the crystal-cold white snow. I was reminded of something my husband read to me a few mornings ago. It went something like this: "Whether you grumble and complain about the snow and cold, it won't change the amount of snow and cold that we have. So, we may as well choose to see the beauty, choose to be thankful, thankful for a warm house, a warm car, plenty to eat, and the list is endless.

The point is, we get to choose our attitude every single day, in every situation, even minute by minute. How we respond to what happens to us is our choice. Our attitude is the only thing we have power over. Philippians 2:14-15 says, "Do all things without grumbling or questioning, that you may be blameless and innocent, children of God without blemish in the midst of a crooked and twisted generation, among whom you shine as lights in the world." Wow! Don't you want to live like that? Where do we need to change our attitude and the words that come out of our mouths? Are we being a light to those around us, or are we adding to the darkness?

Prayer Declaration:
Jesus, convict each one of us in the areas we need to change. Help us to have your humble and grateful attitude. Help us to radiate your love, your peace, and your hope to those around us every day.

January 27
My Tribe

I woke up early this morning, went to the kitchen quietly, made my coffee, turned on the fireplace, grabbed my Bible, and snuggled in for some early morning bliss. Today is the monthly ladies' Bible study here at my house. My heart beats with excitement! It's always such a good, rich, and encouraging time. These ladies are my people. We all come from either Amish or Mennonite backgrounds, so we all have that in common. We love to study the Bible together and examine our lives, our hearts, and our motives. We often discuss where we came from and what we were taught. A lot of it was solid and good teaching, but the common theme we all have and still struggle with at times is to see God as a loving father.

Yes, even when we make mistakes, we tend to still sometimes see God as a God of punishment. We discussed verses like Romans 8:31, "What can we say then? If God is for us, who can be against us?" just reminding ourselves that God is for us. He knows, he sees, he cares, and he always, **always** welcomes us with open arms, no matter what we have done or what we are going through. My beautiful daughter-in-love led us in worship, and we lingered a long time in the *Way Maker Miracle Worker* song, bringing the areas of our life that needed a miracle to the feet of Jesus. Oh, we ate good food. We always share a meal; it's part of our roots.

Prayer Declaration:
Jesus, thank you for bringing my tribe to me. I pray you do that for everyone reading this book – to find their tribe who does life with them, a safe place where they can just laugh and cry together.

January 28
Pajama Day

Throughout this book, I will continue to write about the rhythms of rest I incorporate into my busy schedule. Today was a pajama day for me. My week was very busy up until yesterday. I could feel myself getting edgy and overwhelmed, getting short with those who are closest to me, which is always a sign that I need to slow down and rest. What about you? Have you learned to be aware of the red flags or warning signs that pop up when you are overwhelmed or said yes one too many times? Maybe you said yes to someone to make them happy when deep down you knew you should be saying no.

That's a never-ending one for me. Part of it is my personality. I love to serve and please people. That might be you, too, but we cannot do more than grace allows us to do. Learning to listen to our hearts, the Holy Spirit, and our bodies is a challenge, and it takes time to do it well or consistently. My day of rest consisted of doing only what needed to be done. Worship and prayer, my workout, reading, and then a massive nap in the afternoon while the worship music continued to play and wash over me. Psalm 62:1 says, "Truly my soul finds rest in God; my salvation comes from him."

Prayer Declaration:
Thank you, Jesus, that true rest comes from you alone. Teach us to learn the rhythms of rest that will heal us.

January 29
Weekend Wonder

Ah! Finally, a slower, more relaxing morning. I love weekends; my husband cooking breakfast, getting to sleep without an alarm in the morning, lingering a little longer over our coffee, and catching up over our busy week. Taking a break from working out, too, because our bodies need to rest from that too. Three to five days a week is a good average. It's a beautiful sunny day and actually about twenty degrees above freezing, above zero; a very welcome change! Our son is still not feeling the best, and his wife, too, has been battling some health issues. It seems they have had too much sickness lately. I cover them with prayer.

Our grandsons had been cooped up inside with colds, so I asked my son if I could come over and just help out a bit this afternoon. Of course, he says yes. The boys' delight in seeing me is always so rewarding! First, we need hugs and snuggles, stories, and snacks. Next, we get bundled up and go outside. They love this, and seeing the wonder in their eyes always brings me back to seeing things through the eyes of a child. They love the snow, and trying to ride through it with their trikes, getting stuck, and having grandma push them out makes them so happy. I'm reminded again it's truly the simple things in life that bring the most joy when we pause in wonder and see things from a child's perspective. Luke 5:26 speaks about amazement and wonder, "And wonder seized them all and they glorified God and were filled with awe saying, 'We have seen extraordinary things today.'"

Prayer Declaration:
Jesus, help us to never lose our childlike wonder, thanking you for all the good gifts you let us enjoy, the simple things that bring great joy.

January 30
More Wonder

So quickly, Sunday came, and another week passed. Sunday afternoons are a wonderful time of reflecting. What went right in your week? Notice that goodness and thank God for it. Celebrate your victories, and anywhere you see growth. Rest in it, or one of the words I like to use is bask in it. Often a nap is a part of my Sundays. There's something about getting rested up and refreshed after a busy week. What gets you ready for a new week? Do you meal prep? Some people do. I wish I would. Do you go to church or fellowship with other people in some way?

We fellowship most times one way or another Sunday. Occasionally we drive an hour to a church we really enjoy and meet up with our twin daughters who live in that area, and our son-in-law, of course. After church, we love going out for lunch together. Our oldest and youngest son often go with us, and time spent with our young adults is always so special. I'm filled with wonder at what they are accomplishing with their young lives. Other times the children all come home on a Sunday night.

It's wonderful, chaotic, fun family time, and I love every minute of it! The fact that we all love each other after going through an entire culture change together is a wonder. I guess what doesn't kill you makes you stronger, as the song goes! Waking up from a nap today just in time to drink in an extravagant sunset completed my day. I sit and wonder and thank God. Psalm 10:32 says, "Bless the Lord, oh my soul, and forget not His benefits.

Prayer Declaration:
Yes, Lord, thank you for all your benefits and good gifts you shower us with daily. Give us eyes and hearts to see them and not take them for granted.

January 31
Connecting Conversations

Another new day, another new week coming up. This day is so full of things we must get done before leaving for the rest of the week, yet my husband and I lingered longer over our coffee this morning. We are feeling a little bit disconnected after, especially me, having bit off almost more than I could chew the previous week. It's something I still tend to do way too easily, still learning how to pace myself and make good boundaries.

It's so easy to not save the best for our spouses and families, to give our best to our jobs, or hobbies, or clients, then be too exhausted to have anything left for our family or our spouse. Instead, we need to first be connected to our closest and foremost relationships – our marriage, our children – to remember to give and minister out of our overflow and not out of lack, not just giving them the scraps of what is left. The Bible says, "Two is better than one," when referring to marriage (Ecclesiastes 4:9). This is true in so many ways. We can keep each other grounded, among many other things. This morning, as we talk and process, and even apologize, our connection starts to be restored. Verse 10 says, "If either of them falls down, one can help the other up." Marriage takes humility, grace, and the pure love of Jesus. Verse 12 is my favorite, "Though one may be overpowered, two can defend themselves. A cord of three strands is not easily broken."

Prayer Declaration:
Thank you, Jesus, for your perfect plan of marriage. Thank you for helping us to keep first things first. Thank you for restoring our signal and connection when we lose each other.

February 1
Time Freedom

A new month lies ahead of all of us. We will all get the same number of minutes, hours, and days to accomplish whatever it is we are pursuing in life. Do you know what that is? One way to make goals is to dream of where you would like to be in five years. Now break that dream into bite-sized chunks over five years and go after it. My husband and I are reaping the benefits of some goals and dreams we made about twenty-two years ago. We started our own business.

Today, we traveled to Branson, Missouri, for the week to celebrate not only our achievements but those of our team as well. Not only do we celebrate, congratulate and reward each other, but we make bigger goals and dreams. We are so blessed to be a part of something we could never achieve with our own strength or efforts! We pack up the car and leave early. As we take turns driving, we talk and reminisce about where we've been and where we want to go. We listen to music, read books, have quiet moments in between phone calls, and work from our phones.

A good breakfast is in order, so at one point, we stop at my husband's favorite place – the Cracker Barrel. We were able to easily leave a day early this time. We both are our own bosses, which we totally enjoy. Driving through rain feels cozy. Car naps are the best. Colossians 3:17 says, "Whatever you do, whether in word or deed, do it all in the name of the Lord Jesus, giving thanks to God the father through him." That is a good verse to live our lives by.

Prayer Declaration:
Jesus, thank you for your word and your wisdom to live our lives accordingly. Thank you for helping us to grow into and become the men and women you have destined us to be. Amen.

February 2
Company Culture

It's so wonderful to be here, settled in and unpacked, to have quality time as a couple before our team arrives and our convention starts. It's always such a full, fun, faith-filled time and feels like a big family reunion. God dropped this business opportunity into our laps twenty-three years ago, and we have been very blessed by it. The owner of the company is a God-fearing man, something we don't take for granted. He often quotes this verse to us and encourages us to read the Bible for ourselves. Psalm 37:23-24 says, "The steps of a good and righteous man are directed and established by the Lord. He delights in his way and blesses his path. When he falls, he will not be hurled down because the Lord is the one who holds his hand and sustains him."

We saw him rise up out of deep sadness and grief after his wife passed away unexpectedly from a heart attack several years ago. His faith sustained him. We all miss his wife and partner in the business. She was one of the kindest souls, and everyone loved her. She loved children just like Jesus did and often took time to stop and talk to them and hold our children. Yes, we miss her dearly. The theme for this convention is Rise Up. It was fitting after the turmoil the world has been in since 2020 with the pandemic. What do you want to rise up out of or into this year? "We have the same power that raised Christ from the dead if we are saved," Romans 8:11. Find a coach, a mentor, a counselor, or whatever you need to rise up and become all that God has ordained you to do. No one else can take your place, your life calling, or your assignment. You are needed. You are wanted and important. Rise up!

Prayer Declaration:
Jesus, help us to know and trust that you order our steps as your sons and daughters. Thank you for helping us to rise up to all that you have for us to do and make a difference.

February 3
Laugh a Little

Morning coffee with some of our team at Starbucks. We all live in different parts of the US, so it's always so good to be together; it feels like family. I'm reminded of the thought that family isn't always flesh and blood. Since leaving our Amish culture, my husband and I have made many friends. Some are closer to us in some ways than we are to our own blood families. We also have met many amazing and wonderful people through our business, and it has changed our lives so much for the better. We were served a delicious lunch today and given small gifts.

Tonight, we attended our first session. They kicked it off with a comedian. He was formerly born and raised in Russia, so not only did he make us laugh until we cried, it was wonderful to hear how he sees America. He reminded us how blessed we still are, things we tend to take for granted so easily, and sometimes it's good to see things through the eyes of someone else. He also stressed the importance of laughter in our lives and especially in our marriages. When you laugh together, it is bonding, and he admonished us to notice if the laughter stops, it's a good indication that something is wrong or missing. It was such a good reminder for me because I tend to be pretty serious about life in general. My husband is the complete opposite, though, and one thing that attracted me to him early on was his ability to make me laugh. No joke is too corny for him, and he often sends me jokes via text or Facebook. The Bible backs this up. Proverbs 17:22, "A cheerful heart is good medicine, but a crushed spirit dries up the bones."

Prayer Declaration:
Jesus, let us be people of laughter and cheerful hearts. Increase our ability to see the good and humorous things in our lives.

Leadership Is Influence

Coffee on the 9th floor at the Hilton Convention Center. Branson and the Ozarks are beautiful even in the winter. They are having a snowstorm here which is unusual, and they aren't totally prepared for it, which causes a bit of chaos. I'm thankful we brought our own coffee. Our session starts at eight in the morning. We get to hear amazing speakers and lots of awards being handed out, anything from personal growth to business advice to our walk and faith in God. It was very inspiring, and it always is when people of one heart and mind gather together and are hungry for more. One of the speakers talked about leadership and what it means. Leadership is not a position, it's influence. Leadership is also serving others.

Didn't Jesus himself model that so well when he was here on earth? Another speaker talked about if we wait for everything in our lives to be perfect, that will never happen because our lives here on earth will probably never be perfect. Everyone we meet on a daily basis is fighting their own battles and struggles. None of us have it all together. One of the speakers spoke from her home in her wheelchair. She is paralyzed from the neck down, and yet she is speaking and bringing hope to others. How incredibly inspiring! The President's Club dinner tonight is incredibly beautiful, and they treat us like royalty! Again, I think it's only a tiny little taste of what heaven may be like. The Bible says, "No ear has heard, no eye has seen, no mind has imagined what God has prepared for those who love him" 1 Corinthians 2:9.

Prayer Declaration:
Jesus, thank you for the glimpse of heaven you allow us to experience on earth. May we have your influence everywhere we go and lead more people to you, Jesus.

February 5
Giving God Glory

Saturday, we got up early and made coffee in our room overlooking the Branson River. It's so breathtakingly beautiful. The fresh layer of snow and ice adds to it. Our meeting starts at eight in the morning. We see many well-deserved awards being handed out all day and evening again. Many of them have been our friends for a very long time, and we are so thrilled for them. We get to listen to more inspiring keynote speakers. After that, we gather for our personal team lunch, and we treat everyone to pizza, lemonade, and iced tea. We reward our team with gifts for their accomplishments. One couple got a cake for achieving President's Club status, quite an accomplishment. We are so proud of them.

All through our awards banquet, I see people receiving awards they didn't expect. Many of them are moved to tears in sheer gratitude and humility, thanking God and their peers for helping them, not taking the glory to themselves, which is so refreshing in the "me, myself, and I" culture we live in. Seeing them receive their awards reminds me of the verse where it says, "Let someone else praise you and not your own mouth" Proverbs 27:2. Don't you just love that? We all probably know people who love to boast about themselves, which reminds me of another verse that says, "Let him who boasts boast of the Lord" 1st Corinthians 1:31. It's so refreshing to see people giving each other and God the glory instead of themselves. Our gala banquet was elegant and so touching, with, at times, the entire ballroom worshiping together, from all different cultures, as a wonderful band *Cain* led us. It was a taste of heaven.

Prayer Declaration:
Jesus, again, I thank and praise you for a God-centered company. Teach us to always give you the glory you deserve and to be obedient, willing vessels in your hands, sharing the good news wherever we go.

February 6
Glow and Grow

Vacation is over; we roll out of bed and pack up our suite. It takes a while, having been here for the past week. We didn't get much sleep last night either, so we move a little slower, no coffee, mind you, until we get to Lambert's in Springfield. Our annual tradition is to stop at Lambert's for lunch on our way home from the convention. If you've never been there, you need to put it on your bucket list. They throw hot rolls at you and come around with fresh sorghum. The cups of coffee are bottomless. By the time your meal comes, you are already full, so we always bring home lots of food. It's always a good time with family and friends.

As we travel back home, my husband and I start writing down our business goals for 2022. Having been poured into all week and celebrated, we feel so inspired to do more than ever before. As I'm thinking over the week and just all the good people we get to do this business with, I'm reminded of the verse where it says, "Behold how good and pleasant it is when God's people live together in peace." We all have the same end goal in mind, and it's truly a beautiful thing to be a part of it. There's also this saying I love, "You glow differently when you have good people with good intentions in your life." Do you have good people around you who have good intentions for you? People who want you to win and see you succeed? If not, maybe you need a new tribe to come alongside you. What could that look like for you?

Prayer Declaration:
Jesus, thank you for the people you have placed in our lives to make us glow and help us grow. Thank you for helping all of us find those people whose end goal for us is to point us to you.

February 7
Choose Jesus Today

My alarm didn't go off this morning, so I accidentally slept in, but I needed it. We got home late last night, and as the saying goes, there truly is no place like home, even though we had a wonderful week of vacation in beautiful Branson, Missouri. I'm thinking this morning of how very blessed we are to be part of a Godly Christian company. Their mission statement is to bring Christ back to the business world/ marketplace. My husband and I love this company and what they stand for, and how they always preach salvation at our events. Every business meeting we go to, the owner of the company openly talks about the importance of having a personal relationship with Jesus Christ.

To me, that's pretty special, and people who may never step foot into a church have an opportunity to hear about Jesus. Even though this is a business with the potential to accomplish a lot, there is a verse in Matthew 16:26 that says, "For what shall it profit a man if he gains the whole world but loses his own soul?" Choosing Jesus is the most important decision you will ever make in your life. Out of that, you can accomplish whatever else you set your mind to do. The sky truly is the limit with Jesus. Surrounding yourself with people who will call you to your full potential, you will accomplish much. We all have equal choices in Jesus.

Prayer Declaration:
I thank you for a Christian company to be a part of. I pray for everyone reading this to find their tribe of good-hearted people to run with. Thank you for your favor and blessing on each one of us in our families.

February 8
Give Thanks

It's Tuesday. My alarm didn't go off this morning. My husband is usually up hours before I am, but I've come to realize women, as a whole, I believe, need more sleep than men do. At least, that's the case in our marriage. Another fun fact is my husband is a better cook than I am, so he takes on the role of cooking up a big delicious breakfast most mornings. I'm very grateful for this! In the culture, we grew up in, all cooking and housework was considered women's work only. I'm so thankful that the mindset has shifted in my husband and sons. They all do their own laundry and help with the housework in general. I feel very blessed and thankful for this.

It's cold again this morning. I feel great gratitude that I don't have to go outside and do chores, milking cows by hand or gathering eggs. You name it, and I don't miss it. Instead, I get to stay in my warm and cozy home office most of the day, counseling, coaching, and mentoring from my home, both in person and virtually. I also help my husband with our business. We work with our team of amazing people who are growing daily.

My heart overflows with thankfulness at times to have jobs that we love and which allow us to make a difference in people's lives. Psalm 9:1 says, "I will give thanks to you, Lord, with all my heart; I will tell him all your wonderful deeds." What about you? Do you take the time to look back and see what God has done for you? Praise Him, give Him thanks, and invite him to do even more. He is able. He loves giving good gifts to his children. Open your heart to Him and let Him.

Prayer Declaration:
Jesus, thank you for all you have done in our lives, help us to continually praise and worship, thank you for helping us live with an attitude of gratitude.

February 9
Self-Care

I woke up to one of my clients rescheduling her appointment this morning, which suddenly opened my day up quite a bit. I'm always a little sad when that happens because I love my clients, but when I choose to look on the bright side, there is always a blessing in the works. The first blessing is being able to get caught up with my writing and send the finished pages on to the next step. By then, I had a slight headache, so I thought maybe a little nap would help. The diffuser is plugged in with two oils, 'Calm and Headache Reliever.'

My worship music is playing softly in the background, and the fireplace is on. The house is exceptionally quiet. When I finally wake up and come to my senses, it is **two hours later**! My headache is gone, and I feel so refreshed! Perhaps sometimes God knows better what we need than we do. Actually, I'm pretty sure *he always does.* Sometimes I believe he takes the liberty to even rearrange our schedules. You see, I had no idea how tired I really was and needed to catch up on my sleep because remember how important rest and sleep are? What can you do to get your sleep? Can you go to bed for fifteen to twenty minutes a night earlier? Can you sneak a nap while your little ones are napping? Your work will wait, and your body and mind will thank you. Our bodies are the Lord's temple, and we need to take care of them. 1 Corinthians 6:19: "Do you not know that your bodies are the temples of the Holy Spirit who is in you?"

Prayer Declaration:
Jesus, thank you for rearranging our schedules and leading us daily. Thank you for teaching us the importance of rest and taking care of our bodies so we can be more in tune with Holy Spirit inside of us

February 10
Take the Bitter with the Sweet

Ugh! Is there anyone who enjoys a visit to the dentist? Do you believe the old saying no pain, no gain? It definitely holds true for some situations. Today was a fun visit for a change because they said it was the last one of many. My husband and I both had the Invisalign braces done. It took several years, but we would totally recommend them, and we are both happy with our straight teeth now. Going to the dentist growing up Amish was something we did only on desperate occasions, but we also had pretty good and healthy teeth, just not straight.

Seldom did they do braces back in our growing-up days, so this definitely did feel like another luxury and something I'm extra thankful to have done. The dentist reminds me of the saying my dear mother-in-law used to quote. She always said, "In life, you take the bitter with the sweet." She was an exceptional Amish lady and loved us with all her heart, even after we left their way of Amish life. Her love never wavered. It reminds me of Isaiah 49:15, "Can a mother forget her nursing child she has born?" Even though my husband was adopted into an Amish home, they loved and cared for him as if they had conceived him on their own. I cannot say enough good about his adoptive parents, but they are both in heaven now, and we miss them dearly. My husband has since met his birth mom, a chapter for another day, and his story to tell.

Prayer Declaration:
Jesus, thank you for your perfect plan of turning our pain into purpose so we don't have to suffer at times for nothing. Thank you for adoption and the beautiful thing it is.

February 11
Dreaming With God

Fridays are my favorite days of the week. The week's work is mostly done, and the whole weekend is before us. We have weekend guests coming to our Airbnb for Valentine's weekend, so I had so much fun adding extra touches of wine, chocolate, and flowers for them. Finally, putting away Christmas decorations and adorning with some pretty red Valentine's décor. Of course, candles are a must. As I work and get things ready for them, I remember when I used to only dream of owning an Airbnb and getting paid to do something I love to do, which is hosting. It truly is one of the most rewarding jobs I've ever had. Once again, I'm so grateful. Proverbs 20:4 says, "May he give you the desires of your heart and make all your plans succeed."

Does that mean all my plans have always succeeded? No, but I truly can look back and see time and time again where God has fulfilled the desires of my heart. He really does care about our dreams. In fact, this is a song I wrote about this in 2008.

Dreams
I care about your dreams; I will set you free
Together we will dream, as you draw close to me.
Chorus
I love you child, it is my desire
to touch and heal, for I love you child.
Second Verse
Your future is in my hands, I know the path ahead
Just put your hand in mine, and trust that you will be led.

Jesus whispered these words to me in a melody at a time in my life when I wondered if any of my dreams would ever come true. He truly cares. Trust him.

Prayer Declaration:
Jesus, thank you that you care about the deep desires in our heart. Thank you for healing our hearts first and showing us how to dream with you for your Kingdom purposes in your glory.

February 12
Blessed to Be a Blessing

A slow Saturday morning, is anything sweeter and more relaxing? No alarm clocks. No appointments except for one call with a team couple. It's a joy to FaceTime them with their coffee, strategize and brainstorm with them on life and business goals. One of my husband's and my favorite things to do is give away what others so freely gave us and helped us with. Whether it is in business, life, marriage, raising children, or our faith. We have been poured into and mentored along by others, so it truly is a delight to us to now do the same for others. We are blessed to be a blessing. I've also been thinking about Ephesians 3:20 recently. It's one of my favorite verses in the Bible. It goes like this: "Now to Him who is able to do immeasurably more than all that we can ask, think, or imagine, according to His power that is at work in us."

Don't you just love that verse? I don't know about you, but I can imagine a lot of things! Don't you agree? So often, we use our imagination to think of the negative things that might happen. What if, instead, we started thinking and imagining all the good things God has in store for us? God truly has done the above verse in our lives. When we look back and see all that He has done and rescued us from, we are truly grateful. What about you? What do you need today? Ask your Father in heaven. He loves you. He is for you.

Prayer Declaration:
Jesus, I asked you to bless and heal every person praying this. Do Ephesians 3:20 in their lives. Teach them how to think and imagine your thoughts and your dreams that you have for them.

February 13
Celebrating Our Children

Last night I decided to throw together an impromptu Valentine's dinner for our three children, who are still single. Daughter Lorinda came home for the weekend. She is currently still single, as well as our youngest son John and our oldest son Duane. We baked some cookies and dipped some strawberries in chocolate, set the island up with candles, red hearts, and plates, and served a festive, simple dinner. I wanted them to remember how loved they are, in spite of going through life single.

Today, I decided to go to church where our son Dennis and daughter-in-law Elise are playing on the worship team. It does my mother's heart so good to see them exercising their gifts again after taking a few years off. I'm reminded of the verse where it says, "I have no greater joy than to see my children walking in the truth, or to see them use their gifts and talents for God's glory" 3 John 1:4. It's wonderful and makes the difficult teenage years worth it all! Later that night, we watched the Super Bowl with some of the family. The team we were rooting for won. It was a joy to hear their quarterback and other players declare afterward, "God is great!" or say, "It's because of the team," giving that honor and glory to God especially warmed my heart! Do we remember to thank God and those around us when we are in the spotlight? To me, it displays humility and gives honor where honor is due.

Prayer Declaration:
Jesus, teach us how to walk in your truth, and who we are in you more and more, constantly pointing others to you, Jesus, declaring your goodness. Help us to remember also how loved we are by you, and that no partner will ever love us or fill our God shaped hole in our hearts.

February 14
Valentine's Day

Do you celebrate it? Do you hate it? I know people on both sides of the spectrum. My husband and I celebrate it now. He always brings me luxurious flowers; we love to go out to our favorite places to eat. This year we picked Olive Garden because that place has a special meaning to us. Let me tell you why. Growing up in the Amish culture, we didn't celebrate much of anything. Valentine's Day, birthdays, and even anniversaries could be very easily just another day where the husband goes off to work, and the wife cooks, cleans, and takes care of the children, just like any other day. Imagine my delight then after we became part of a church years later, where we all decided to start driving cars together: This opened up a whole new realm of freedom we had never experienced before.

It was liberating and wonderful (except for breaking our Amish families' hearts), but that was very hard. Suddenly now, we can go to places without always having to hire and pay someone to drive us around, then wait for us. One of the first places my husband and I went to was Olive Garden to celebrate our anniversary. It was such a special time. Can you think of a time when God set you free? Do you remember how it felt? Never forget what Galatians 5:1 says, "It is for freedom that Christ has set us free. Stand firm, then, and do not let yourselves be burdened again by a yoke of slavery/bondage."

Prayer Declaration:
Jesus, show us where we need to be set free. What yokes of bondage are we entangled in? Thank you for the freedom that comes from You alone. Help us and teach us to walk in your freedom and not the world's freedom.

Healing Inside and Out

Have you ever had chronic pain of any kind? If your answer is yes, you know how it can wear on you physically and emotionally, even spiritually, when you have prayed for healing. About two years ago, when everything shut down because of Covid, our gym also shut down, so after waiting for several weeks, hoping the gym would reopen, I decided to do a home workout with weights. I ended up injuring my left arm and shoulder somehow. I had so much pain and limited mobility. I couldn't even do my own hair. It took an entire year to get the mobility back, and finally, I resorted to a cortisone shot to get the pain under control. Sweet relief!

Another year later, I am still dealing with the after-effects – a painful and sore spot in my back. My chiropractor said he couldn't do anything more for me, but consistent deep-tissue massage might help. So today, I went to a massage lady, and she did a wonderful job on the trouble spots. It hurt so good! I have hope she will help me heal. Have you found the help you need? Maybe it's not physical pain, but the pain in your heart that you need help with. God is our ultimate healer, yet He also heals through people, nurses, doctors and counselors, etc. Don't wait to reach out for healing from your pain. God is willing and able to heal us and point us in the direction of healing. Jeremiah 30:17 says, "But I will restore you to health and heal your wounds,' declares the Lord." What a beautiful promise! Claim it!

Prayer Declaration:
Jesus, thank you for your healing and hope. Thank you for doctors, nurses, counselors, and all the people you use to bring divine healing. Heal us from the inside out.

February 16
A Listening Ear

Meeting new clients is always a joy. Even though we are both usually a bit nervous in the beginning, I love when that melts away as we communicate and get to know each other. Today is filled with clients, each one different, each one unique, and each one a joy. I feel so thankful that they chose me as their therapist. I truly enjoy processing people's pain and struggles with them, even more, celebrating their victories and wins. Life can be rough, and we all need a listening ear every now and then. Do you have that in your life? If you're married, it could be your spouse, but we also encourage couples to have someone else too: woman to woman and man to man.

We never want to look to or depend on our partner, to fix us or look to them for the healing that only God can bring us. Oftentimes, depending on how deep our pain and unresolved issues are, that's when a counselor can be an excellent choice, as well. I'm the first to admit that I need all the help I can get to become the best version of myself physically, mentally, and spiritually. I love Jeremiah 17:4, "Lord, if you heal me, I will be truly healed; if you save me, I will be truly saved. My praises are for you alone." I'm so thankful for all the brokenness Jesus has healed in me, often through others. I'm also grateful that he has saved me and that healing and salvation are available to all of us.

Prayer Declaration:
Jesus, thank you that you love us so much you made a way for us to be saved, healed, and delivered. Help us to receive and believe it and get help if we need it. Thank you for your perfect plan for our lives.

February 17
Life Is a Vapor

Another busy day has come and gone. A day filled with appointments and clients. When you are doing what you love, time truly does go so fast. I'm reminded of this fact again this evening. Our son and his wife dropped off the little grandsons at our house. They said the boys had been asking for us all week. Two-year-old Zion is getting the hang of potty training. He is the sweetest, and last night, as we sat there waiting in the bathroom for something to happen, he finally asked, do you have any milk, Gramma? The vitamins and the water didn't work, he declares! He often makes us laugh with his big words and vocabulary at two years old.

I sit there thinking, how is it that we are already here again? It seems like just yesterday when I was potty training our six children. It was always a bit daunting. Do you realize just how fast time goes by? How fleeting our time here on Earth is. It truly is but a vapor, as it says in James 4:14. How do you know what your life will be like tomorrow? Your life is like the morning fog. It's here a little while, and then it's gone. Some translations say mist or vapor. Are we living for this short life, or are we living for eternal life? Are we teaching our children and our grandchildren what is truly important? They are, after all, the only thing we get to take to heaven with us. Let's not miss it.

Prayer Declaration:
Jesus, help us to set our hearts on things above, to live for eternity, and not just our short span of life here on Earth. Thank you for your wisdom and strength to teach and lead the generations to come to you.

February 18
Seasons of Life

My husband and I both had a full morning of tying up loose ends before we headed out for Indiana around one in the afternoon. The roads are good, so we have smooth sailing until Chicago when we get caught in traffic a few times. Still, we get to our hotel at a nice time in order to get checked in and go for a nice relaxing dinner and evening together. Even though this is a business trip, we have learned whenever time allows us to make these trips more leisurely, to actually take the time to stop, eat, and have an early evening to connect and rest before our meeting tomorrow.

We didn't always have this luxury, though. When we were raising our six children, and they were in school and sports, we often made flying trips back home as soon as possible so as not to miss a football or basketball game, a dance recital, or piano recital, or whatever they were in at the time! There was a lot of it with six of them. We enjoyed it all and hustled a lot! This empty nesting season is quite sweet, too – so different but so rewarding. I encourage you right now, whatever season you are in, to do your best. You don't want to look back with regret and wish you would have done things differently. We get one shot at each season of life we are in. Ecc. 3:1 says, "For everything there is a season, a time for every matter under heaven." Embrace the season you are in right now, and do your best to live with no regrets. Your older self will thank you one day soon.

Prayer Declaration:
Jesus, thank you for giving us different seasons of life. Teach us to do our best in each one and enjoy it to the full, knowing it will never return again. Help us to lean in and learn all that You have for us in each one.

February 19
Seek Wisdom

It took the third try to get good coffee this morning. My husband and I are not very picky except for our coffee. We don't even like the same coffee either. We are as opposite as day and night, yet we make a good team since we have learned to respect and embrace each other's differences. We do, however, both enjoy a good cup of Starbucks. So coffee in hand, we travel to our friends' houses, and support them in a business opportunity meeting. After that's done, we celebrate our friend's 30th birthday at Red Lobster before heading back home.

As we drive, we have lots of time to reminisce about where we've been, where we want to go in life, and how to get there. Listening to self-development books on audio, reading other books, talking about how much we love being our own bosses, having the time freedom to travel, and helping our friends achieve their goals and dreams. It's a wonderful job! Maybe you love your job, or maybe you don't, or maybe you dread going to work every day. If that's the case, how could you change that? It's up to us to change the things in our life that don't bring us that abundant life. If you don't know where to start, ask God. Proverbs James 1:5 says, "If any of you lack wisdom you should ask God who gives generously to all without finding fault and it will be given to you. He is so willing to help us when we ask him."

Prayer Declaration:
Jesus, thank you for your wisdom and understanding. Help us make the changes we need in our lives. Help us to recognize patterns where we are stuck and unfulfilled in our lives and set us free. Show us your will and your way, Amen.

Hold on Pain Ends

Waking up to no alarm is always a treat. I fix my coffee and check the weather. It says it will be close to fifty degrees today. This gets me excited and fills me with hope again that spring will eventually come in Wisconsin. Yes, we will probably get lots more snow first, but days like today give us a glimpse of spring. I could even smell it. It smells like hope and reminds me of the winter seasons of my life. I've had seasons where it felt cold, dark, and lonely. I wondered if the work in my soul and the winter of my soul would ever end. Some call it the dark night of the soul. I've been there, maybe several times; I've battled rejection, depression, health issues, and loneliness. Maybe you're there currently? My friend Jane shared this acronym for hope with me one time; I never forgot it.

Hold
On
Pain
Ends.

It's true. The Bible also has a lot to say about hope. One of my favorites is 1st Peter 5:10, "The God of all hope who called you to His eternal glory in Christ after you have suffered a little while will himself restore you and make you strong, firm and steadfast." He will do it for you; whatever you are going through, don't give up hope. He will restore you. We enjoyed the balmy evening by going into our woods for a bonfire, roasted bear brats and marshmallows over the fire. Most of the children were there, and the fire and fellowship restored my heart even more.

Prayer Declaration:
Jesus, thank you for your living hope. Thank you for restoring our winter seasons with hope. Remind us that we are never alone no matter what we are going through. You are always with us.

February 21
Healing Is Available

Today I have a late lunch date scheduled with a friend in La Crosse, WI. Ever since I read her book 'Behind Blue Curtains', I have wanted to meet her. Her story is encouraging of how she overcame so much. She, too, left the Amish culture and has since become a voice for those who have been abused in any way, as she was in multiple ways. We ordered, had lunch, and talked as fast as we could, only having a few hours. There's so much to talk about; we felt an instant connection because of our backgrounds.

When raised in the Amish culture, you have so many things in common. We both have a deep desire to bring hope and healing to women. Especially those of our culture who don't have a voice. Many of them do have a story to tell. She travels and does conferences for women. I mostly work with local women, but we have the same mandate found in Isaiah 61:1, "The spirit of the sovereign Lord is on me because the Lord has anointed me to proclaim good news to the poor. He has sent me to bind up the broken hearted, to proclaim freedom for the captives and release from darkness the prisoners." What about you? Have you been used or abused physically, emotionally, or spiritually? If so, please reach out to someone. There is hope and healing available. You are not alone, bring your broken heart, your broken body to the feet of Jesus, and let Him love you to wholeness.

Prayer Declaration:
Jesus, please touch and heal every person reading this, thank you for putting them in touch with the right people to help them walk out of darkness into a light healed, whole as kindred spirits.

February 22
Keep Running

It took a while to feel my workout this morning. If you work out, you know what I mean when I talk about a runner's high or pushing through the wall. This morning it took extra-long to push through the wall to get to that zone. I felt extra tired but kept pushing through and did it. It felt so good afterward. It reminds me that if you can walk, even if you have to crawl, you must never give up. 1st Corinthians says, "if you know that in a race all the runners run, but only one wins the prize, you must run in such a way that you may be victorious."

This can be applied to our earthly race towards heaven, our final goal and destination. Philippians 3:14 says, "I press on toward the goal for which God called me heavenward in Christ Jesus. What a reward, it's waiting for us, let that motivate you today." Maybe you are tired and weary, ready to give up. I encourage you instead of giving up to lean in against Jesus instead. Let him be your strength; let go and let Him move. We cannot do things with our own strength, so today, let those burdens roll off of your shoulders and bring them to the feet of Jesus. Get rid of the heavyweight so you can run again, but whatever you do, keep pressing onward and upward until your workout is complete, and we see Jesus face to face.

Prayer Declaration:
Jesus, thank you for being strong when we are weak and ready to give up. Thank you for reminding us why we can't stop our destiny in You. Our heavenly home will be worth it all, to see You face to face.

February 23
True Unity

Yesterday was 2/22/22. I love numbers, so this is a fun fact for me. Did you know that numbers have meaning? Number two speaks of unity. According to the Bible, it's a symbol of unity; for example, we have the union between Christ and the church, the union between man and wife. Marriage in both of these examples of unity is so beautiful when they are done in the way God intended them to be done. What comes to your mind when you think of unity? Maybe this is even a trigger word for you. It can certainly be when you have been pressured to be unified or identified with things you didn't agree on.

Some churches feel that unity means everyone looking and dressing alike, believing the exact same thing. Not leaving much room for personal convictions or individuality. My husband and I were both raised in churches a lot like this. When married, two can suffer when husband and wife struggle to become like one another. In an attempt to be unified or one. What if God's way would be liberating instead? Embracing and celebrating each other's uniqueness and creativity, setting each other free to have our own convictions, and walking with Jesus. Galatians 3:28 says, "There is neither Jew nor gentile, neither slave nor free, nor is there male or female, for we are all one in Christ Jesus, that's the unity we want to be in! We are all equal to Jesus."

Prayer Declaration:
Jesus, teach us what your idea of unity looks like Jesus, we let go of control and fear and trying to make people conform to our man-made ideas of unity. Forgive us Lord, Amen.

Submission God's Way

It's monthly Bible study at my house today. The coffee is ready, the house is clean, and the ladies start trickling in with potluck dishes. A few candles are lit, and we gather around the table for a delicious meal. We always catch up on each other's lives as we eat. We refill our coffee cups and move into the living room with our bibles and journals. Everyone gets comfortable with blankets and pillows. Our sweet daughter-in-law leads us in worship. She always creates such a relaxing, comforting, Holy Spirit-filled atmosphere. We discuss what God spoke to us during worship, and then we dive into our study, which is the entire book of Ephesians. It's so good, so deep. We have lots of good discussions as well as rabbit trail discussions. Today's study includes the verse, "Wives submit to your own husbands in everything...." Ephesians 5:22- 25 also says, "Husbands love your wives just as Christ loved the church and gave himself up for her."

We discussed the topic at length. We asked the oldest woman to give her opinion. I loved her answer. She said if the husbands truly love like it says to love their wives, then the rest should be easy to do. I do think submission can be abused and misused instead of a natural thing that is birthed out of love and trust in a marriage where God truly is the center. If you are in a situation where submission is demanded and forced, then know it isn't love. Reach out for help to someone you trust.

Prayer Declaration:
Jesus, thank you for your beautiful plan for marriage, teach us how to submit and love according to your perfect plan, and rescue anyone who is abused or hurting. It's not your heart or will for us in marriage.

February 25
Generational Blessings

A topic we discussed at length in our Bible study this week was generational blessings. Our daughter-in-law led us in the 'Blessing' song by Kari Jobe. It's a powerful song that speaks about how God is for us and not against us, how He will bless not just our generation but our children and their children, generations to come. This song is based on Numbers 6:24-26, "The Lord bless you and keep you and make His face shine upon you and be gracious to you, the Lord turns his face toward you and gives you peace." Psalms 100 says, "Your faithfulness continues through all **generations**."

Wow, that just fills me with hope for our generations to come. When my husband and I went on our journey of truth that gradually and slowly led us out of the Amish culture, one question we got a lot was, what about your children? What will happen to them? My answer was always the same. It will only be God's grace that will keep and protect them. It wasn't until we started reading the Bible more and asking the Holy Spirit to show us what it means for us that I started realizing there is actually scripture to confirm my thoughts and prayers. You see, today, I have much more faith in Jesus that He will keep my children in the palm of His hand then I do in the enemy's schemes. He won't win because Jesus is way more powerful than Satan. Jesus is big enough to save the generations to come. Cry out for them now as parents and grandparents; that is our job. He is able; He is for us; He is for our children and our children's children's children!

Prayer Declaration:
Jesus, help us to flip the script in our heads and truly believe in your power and goodness, thank you for saving and protecting the generations to come, our children & children's children, we thank you that You are able, Amen.

February 26
Prioritizing Rest

Saturdays are supposed to be slower. Yet my day started pretty normal, waking up to my alarm clock. The first thing on the agenda was a three-way call with team members and my husband, who is out west snowmobiling on a father-son trip. A few times a winter, he will say the mountains are calling again. I say the beaches are calling me again. We are so completely different. My day proceeds with a new client consultation and then a regular client. I finally have time to eat, and by midafternoon, I must decide if I want to take the rest of the day off or tackle some messy cupboards or the pantry. But because I'm trying to deliberately make rest a priority, I decided to take the rest of the day off. I have felt extra tired all week. A good book and a cuddly blanket on the couch wins. I fell asleep to worship music and woke up genuinely refreshed. I managed to be pretty productive the rest of the day, also taking extra time to worship and pray. I feel rejuvenated and ready for a new week. Matthew 11:28 says, "Come to me all you who are weary and burdened and I will give you rest. Rest is best when you're tired and weary." Are you overwhelmed? Do you need rest in your body, in your soul, or maybe both? Put some worship music on, grab a blanket, cuddle up for some quiet time with a good book, or just you and Jesus; make good rest a priority.

Prayer Declaration:

Jesus, help us remember That you two rested when you were here among us. Help us to simplify our lives so we have time to rest. Teach us how to rest in You above all to let you carry our burdens that weigh us down and make us tired.

February 27
Worship in Spirit and Truth

"You are worthy of it all, you are worthy of it all, for from You are all things and to You are all things, You deserve the glory." As the worship team is singing that chorus several times, my son is building momentum on the drums. At just the right time, the voices enter, and finally, we end worship with just the voices. I felt the Holy Spirit and the whole congregation singing acapella was beautiful. The holy presence of God was so strong for a while; everything was hushed, and we just waited in God's presence. People were praying to God. Some were on their knees, and some came forward to share what God was showing or speaking to them. Isn't this how they did the church in the Bible?

1 Corinthians 14:26 says, "When you come together, *each of you can preach*, each of you has a hymn or song or word of instruction, a revelation, a tongue or interpretation, everything must be done so the church may be built up. I can't help but think back to how we did church growing up Amish; no interaction except for singing and kneeling together. A meal at the end was always special. Our services were often three to three and half hours long. We sat on benches with no backs, and yes, even the little ones were required to sit still for this long, even though they understood very little of the message, if any. I am so thankful my little grandsons get to go to the nursery during services, where they are taught on their level. Zion, three yrs. old said after we picked him up, "Can we go get Old McDonald's?" Oh, the hearts of children! They make me laugh and fill me with joy and wonder. Today ask yourself, is the church I am attending truly alive? Are you allowed to use your gifts and talents there? Is the Holy spirit welcome there?

Prayer Declaration:
"You are my God. I worship you. In my heart, I long for you, as I would long for a stream in a scorching desert. I have seen your power and your glory in the place of worship. Your love means more than life to me, and I praise you. As long as I live, I will pray to you," Psalm 63:1-4.

February 28
True Friendships

In true friendships, some of the best discussions are held over a cup of coffee. That certainly was true for me today. I drove twenty minutes into town to meet one of my dear friends. We've been friends ever since our children went to school together, and we still keep in touch. It's one of those iron sharpens iron friendships. Proverbs 27:17 says, "As iron sharpens iron so one person sharpens another." When we moved to this community twelve years ago, I longed and prayed for like-minded women to connect. My friend Ann was one answer to those prayers. Moving here was the first time we weren't associated with an Amish community, and it felt so different. I felt lonely at times, like I didn't fit in. I really struggled with living here for quite a few years. There were times I felt like God had forgotten about me. There were times I was angry at God, but I also cried out to Him at the same time.

God is always faithful, and today I clearly see why he brought us here. He also brought me several close friends to share the deepest part of my heart with, over a period of time, on His timing, not mine. Today we fill our cups with delicious lattes, talk, laugh, and cry together. We pray for each other's children; we brainstorm about what we think heaven will be like and talk about our frustrations too. I drove back home to start dinner with a full heart today. I pray you find like-minded friends who get you, cry with you, rejoice with you, and sharpen and strengthen you.

Prayer Declaration:
Jesus, I pray for every person reading this to find true biblical friends, I pray you bring your comfort to every lonely person and show them their purpose and show them their purpose and why you have planted them where they are.

Re-Evaluate vs. Giving Up

Another new month before us, a clean slate, a new beginning. Maybe we should take a look at our goals, dreams and re-evaluate what is or isn't working. Do you need to tweak your eating habits, and exercise program, to better fit your lifestyle? Please don't give up on your goals. Instead, adjust them if you need to. Maybe you need an accountability partner or a workout buddy. Moderate exercise has been a part of my lifestyle all through my adult years. I never needed to worry about extra exercise growing up on a farm. You work out morning and evening by shoveling silage, feeding cows, carrying milk to the strainer, and watering calves, pigs, and chickens. It's a lot of physical work.

After my husband and I moved off the farm, things changed. Even when my six children were small, I would wait until my husband came home from work, then I would slip away for a quick run or walk. It was always just what I needed physically and mentally. Now with my children all grown, I'm free to pursue different avenues for exercise and genuinely enjoy it. Do you? If not, start with something you do enjoy. Start with ten to fifteen minutes a day. Change usually doesn't require radical change, but small changes daily lead to success. Remember, exercise is as much for our mental health as it is for our physical health. Philippians 4:13 is a good reminder for all of us to push through. It affirms, "I can do all things through Christ who gives me strength, what a promise."

Prayer Declaration:
Jesus, thank you for our strength, teach us to see food as fuel and to lean into your strength to become the healthiest versions of ourselves, physically, emotionally and spiritually. Thank you for leading us in this, the right path for each one reading.

March 2
Cleaning the Clutter

Do you enjoy spring cleaning? I dread it every year, possibly from the never-ending cleaning. Growing up on a farm, it seemed like it never ended. But my mother knew how to clean, and she taught us well. Once a year, when we hosted church services at our houses, everything that could be cleaned was cleaned, inside and out. It was a huge task that took weeks to accomplish. Not only did we clean our own houses, but we also had a group of neighbors that we helped do the same, including any family of ours whose turn it was to host church. It was a wonderful feeling when everything was done, and guests started arriving Sunday morning.

I always did enjoy our turn of hosting church at our house. To this day, I would rather host and cook than clean. I've scaled my spring-cleaning way back now, but yesterday I genuinely enjoyed cleaning out my messy pantry and some cupboards. I adopted a friend's philosophy of storing everything possible in glass jars. It's easier to see what you have or need, plus it's a lot healthier. As I sorted, tossed, cleaned, and organized, I thought about how we need to invite God to do the same to our hearts, clean out the clutter, and purify us. Psalms 51:10 says, "Create in me a pure heart, Oh God and renew a steadfast spirit within me." Psalms 26:2 expresses, "Test me Lord and try me, examine my heart and mind."

Prayer Declaration:
Yes Lord, that is what we want, clean us up even when it gets messy. As you clean us, we invite you to examine, purify and cleanse us from all unrighteousness and clutter. We give you permission to sweep out the darkest parts of our hearts. Today we invite You in.

March 3
God's Abundant Grace

I went to bed with butterflies in my stomach last night and woke up with them again this morning because today I am going to face my fears and go to an audition for the worship team tonight. This is the same church my son and daughter-in-law play, and they have been encouraging me for a while now to follow my passion for worship and join the team. Here is why I haven't done it before.... growing up Amish, we didn't learn anything about music theory or timing, so that has always held me back in my desire to worship freely on a team. I'm very grateful that since leaving that culture, our children all had the opportunity to learn about music. They have taught me a lot about timing, even helping me practice for several hours, the song I'm singing tonight.

By six in the evening, my nerves had calmed a little. I had friends praying for me. Thank you, friends; you know who you are. I did mess up on the timing, so I didn't know what to expect, but the worship leaders both assured me they were willing to help me learn timing. They told me I have the heart of a worshiper; that's what they are looking for, not perfection.

I almost cried tears of joy that they saw my heart like God does. It was such a reminder to me how God doesn't judge us on our mess ups and mistakes, but He too sees our hearts. I feel a little bit like Paul did when he said, "My grace is sufficient for you, for my power is made perfect in weakness, therefore I will boast all the more gladly about my weaknesses so that Christ's power may rest upon me," 2nd Corinthians 12:9.

Prayer Declaration:
Jesus, thank you that your mercy and grace saves us from what we deserve, thank you for being strong in our weak places, thank you that you see our hearts before anything else, thank you Jesus.

March 4
Preparing the Way

My husband and I had time to catch up with each other this morning over coffee and reading. We try to make this a habit to stay connected. Sometimes, it's easier than other times. Our little boys came at nine o'clock this morning. It was game on! First up was Grandpa's delicious breakfast, then lots of playtime, including numerous games of hide and seek. Zion has the hang of it, but Zander always gives away where the person is hiding. It's so cute. We made protein balls and banana peanut butter smoothies before bath time.

All of this in between potty training. It is always so good to be in 'that world' for two hours or a day again. If you are in the young mom stage, please do not underestimate what you are doing. It is the most important job you will ever have. You are raising the next generation of young people, and you get one shot at it. I cannot encourage you enough to embrace it. The years go by so fast.

Finally, we are ready for our snuggles and songs. Jesus loves me, among many others. As I hear the boys sing in perfect time, hitting the songs on the beat, I'm once again in awe that they are learning this effortlessly. I'm so thankful that there are many things my children will have an opportunity to go much further in life, more than I probably ever will, but isn't that how it should be? We should prepare the way for them, as Jesus said about us. "Very truly I tell you, whoever believes in Me will do the works I have been doing and they will do even greater things than these, because I am going to the Father" John 14:12.

Prayer Declaration:
Jesus, can you help us to believe and receive this for us, our children, and generations to come. We say yes and Amen Lord.

March 5
Double Portions

My twin daughters and I met at church last night for a women's gathering. We stayed at a hotel together, Stoney Creek. We went back to church for the conference for the next several days. We ordered our coffee and picked it up at Caribou. It was delicious. I didn't get much sleep the night before. We got to enjoy wonderful worship and amazing women speakers, including some of our favorites. We laughed, cried, worshiped, and had an enjoyable lunch from Panera Bread. We took notes as fast as we could. Times like this with my daughters are so precious. They would tell you that growing up as twins was not always easy or fun. I will tell you, parenting twin daughters who were naturally as opposite as day and night wasn't always easy either.

Throw in an entire culture change, there were times we as parents had no idea what we were doing, but God, He is faithful. He again doesn't judge us according to our shortcomings. His grace and mercy are always enough. I'm reminded of the verse where it talks about God giving us a double portion. Isaiah 61:7 declares, "Instead of shame, you will receive a double portion, instead of disgrace you will rejoice in your inheritance. You will inherit a double portion in your land and everlasting joy will be yours." If you are in a difficult season right now, remember this verse and keep going, don't give up. God has certainly done this for me and our twin daughters. Today they are my best friends, I love them so much, and we have many similar interests.

Prayer Declaration:
Jesus, thank you for giving us your mercy and grace and even a double portion, thank you for strengthening anyone who is weary and discouraged. Speak to them and let them know it is worth the struggle.

March 6
Serving from Rest

Having a wonderful restful Sunday morning at home with my husband, drinking our coffee, making brunch, and watching services online. My body is begging for a stretch workout I missed earlier in the week. Christian yoga instructors, not the weird kind, as with anything, just be careful who you follow. It helps me tremendously with sore neck, shoulders, flexibility, and headaches. It's basically a fancy name for stretches. After that, my cooking mood kicks in. I put together some homemade peach ice cream, baked a pan of gluten-free fudgy brownies, and put together a big pot of chili. Now a fresh pot of coffee is needed as we have friends coming over at three. We had a wonderful time with them.

By five o'clock, the children start trickling in for the family night. We have more food, fellowship, fun, laughter, and playing with the boys. The little ones are usually the focus of our evenings together. I'm so grateful for these evenings. I'm appreciative that our family is still all together and love each other after all we've been through. I don't even know how to describe it, but it wasn't always easy with the culture change, but we grew closer as a family. By the time everyone left and the house was quiet again, my heart was full and rejuvenated even though I didn't get much rest physically today. My heart feels rested; sometimes, serving and hosting can be a form of rest. When we can do it without striving and performing. Romans 12:13 states, "Contribute to the needs of the saints and seek to show hospitality." Hosting is something I really enjoy when my energy level cooperates.

Prayer Declaration:
Jesus, show us how to serve from a place of rest, help us to remember that people will remember how we made them feel more than what they eat or how clean our houses are.

March 7
He Took Our Punishment

Another dentist appointment; something, I always dread but must be done. I drowned out the pain and sound of the piercing, high-pitched drill, put on my headphones, and turned the worship music way up. It nearly drove me over the edge lying there, wishing it was over. It took almost two hours. I thought of Jesus and how He willingly suffered much greater pain for us and bled to the point of death. Can we really grasp what He did for us? Can we grasp how high, how wide, and how deep His love for us is?

He was completely innocent, and yet He allowed himself to be nailed to a cross for the sins of the world, for you, for me. He was brutally beaten, even before the cross. 2nd Corinthians 5:21 says, "God made Him who had no sin to be sin for us, so that in Him we might become the righteousness of God." John 3:16 says, "For God so loved the world that He gave His one and only Son that whoever believes in Him should not perish but have everlasting life."

Don't you want that everlasting life, where we will live forever in heaven with Jesus? There is a song that mentions heaven and how it will surely be worth it all. I believe that with all my heart. Whatever you are going through, hold on; heaven is coming. Jesus is coming back for us. Are you ready?

Prayer Declaration:
Jesus, I cry out to you for every person to know you as their personal Savior, for your gospel to be preached to the ends of the earth, in all people groups, countries to be reached. Show us our part in helping to spread your good news.

March 8
Testimony Tuesday

Every day is a good day to remember what God has done for us. Often on Tuesdays in the ladies' group (I lead online), we share testimonies because what if we were as eager to share what is right in our lives as we are about what is wrong? Did you know it takes more energy, plus it drains your energy to be negative than it does to be positive? Let's start with you, yes, you who are reading these words right now.

I challenge you to journal or make a list of all the answered prayers and all your blessings, then choose one more thing you are extra thankful for today and share it with someone. Revelations 12:10 says, "They triumphed over him by the blood of the lamb and by the word of their testimony." You see, when we share our testimonies, it not only glorifies God, but it can also bring hope and expectancy to others because if He did it for you, He can do it for me.

One of my biggest testimonies in life is how God led us out of the Amish in a gentle way. He did it, allowing us as much time as we needed, ten years to be exact. It was not something we set out to do, but it's where our journey led us. My husband says it best, *"We were hungry for God, and it led us out; we were never looking to leave."*

"God has done exceedingly abundantly beyond what I can think or imagine" Ephesians 3:20. That's only one of my testimonies of his goodness, mercy, and grace. May we be much quicker to praise than to complain.

Prayer Dedication:
Teach us, Lord, how to be more intentional with our testimonies, give us eyes to see, hearts of gratitude for all that you have done in our lives. Thank you for setting each one of us free from our own prisons we had built for ourselves.

March 9
Times and Seasons

My husband and I are in a very good season of life right now. If you aren't, be encouraged because it will change. Seasons come and go. Some are way more difficult than others, but whether we are on the mountaintop or in the valley, our God never changes. If we can lay hold of that truth, we can endure a lot. Today was an extraordinarily fun day, starting with coffee, of course, and our connection, reading time together. I was even able to squeeze in a quick workout before our little boys came. Zion and Zander's daddy brought them over. The guys had a work meeting. My husband and four sons run our family-owned business together. Today was a communication meeting; they brought me on board for those. Next, the boys needed their snacks and snuggles. We played, listened, and danced to their children's worship songs. Worship songs out of the mouth of a child is the sweetest thing on earth.

Later in the day, my husband and I spontaneously decided to run some errands, have a date night, eat dinner at one of our favorite places, and count our blessings.

Blessings make the difficult seasons worth it all, times of isolation, sickness, and loneliness. Seasons of being home alone daily, raising six little children on a farm, while my husband worked 8-5. Slowly times and seasons changed for the better. But just like nature flourishes with both sun and rain, we need both to grow as well. Charles H. Spurgeon said this. "The seasons change and we change, but the Lord abides evermore the same and the streams of His Love are deep, as broad and as full as ever!"

Prayer Declaration:
Jesus, thank you that you are, "...the same yesterday today and forever," Hebrews 13:8. Teach us how to hold fast to you our Lord and Savior Jesus Christ in every season, rain, sickness or health whatever we are going through.

March 10
Speaking the Truth

Is it easier for you to say what others want to hear instead of the truth? I struggle with this at times, and while it can come from a pure heart, not wanting to hurt others, does it actually help them with their best interest in mind? It can be so easy to tweak, fudge and say half-truths. We may even call it a little white lie, convincing ourselves its okay. It's an easy trap to fall into, always wanting to be liked and to please everyone. Yet the Bible says, "Speak the truth in love" Ephesians 4:15. Isn't that a huge key to making sure we do it out of love? Ephesians 4:25 says, "Therefore laying aside falsehood, speak truth each one of you with his neighbor, we are members of one another."

Years ago, one of my sons had a habit of not always telling the truth when he was little. So one day, I had him look up all the Bible verses he could find online about telling the truth. It opened his eyes to what God has to say about it more than his parents telling him. I encourage you to do the same. There are a lot of verses in the Bible about speaking the truth. Search them out for yourself and may we keep our lips from lying and honor God and others with the truth, spoken in love.

Prayer Declaration:
Jesus, we come to you in repentance for not always speaking the truth. Will you teach us how to do it in love, to speak it gently and be as honoring as we can? Help us to think before we speak and ask ourselves is this the truth?

March 11
Worth the Struggle

Work, cleaning, laundry, and exercise; my list was long today, but thanks be to God, I got it all done in time. We welcomed our guests for dinner at seven in the evening. They're staying in our Airbnb this weekend and are here for couples counseling. What a privilege this is. You see, I don't believe God allows us to go through the hard seasons of life without reason. He sees what he has in mind in the big scheme of our lives; He has a plan. I would never have chosen to go through the difficult times in our own marriage. But when we can now turn around and help others from what we ourselves experienced, it makes it worth the difficult times. Marriage takes a lot of work. Hallmark and Netflix, and the world in general, portray a very twisted version of relationships; it's not real life.

We can fall into the deception of wanting it to be real and compare our marriages to movies. Marriage, in a nutshell, is serving each other, setting each other free to be your own person in the context of marriage. It's beautiful and worth it! If you are in a difficult relationship today, there is hope. There is help available. Reach out, find someone; maybe it can be an older couple you trust or look up too. I can truly say after being married for thirty years, our marriage is more fun and better than it has ever been. Yours can get better with age, too, don't settle. 1st Corinthians 13 sums it up, "Love is patient, love is kind, it does not envy, it does not boast, it is not proud, it does not dishonor others, it is not self-seeking, it is not easily angered and keeps no record of wrongs, [in everything,] ...the greatest of these is love."

Prayer Declaration:
Jesus, help us to live these verses out in our marriages, thank you for turning our pain into purpose and now allowing us to serve others.

March 12
Search for Wisdom

Burr, another cold morning, minus two degrees, goodness, how long will winter hold on? We never know here in Wisconsin. Sometimes, we will get snow until May. Isn't that how our lives feel at times? In life's climate, we wonder how long winter will last in our hearts. Maybe you have been in a season that felt like wintertime for a long while. If you are discouraged, know that spring will come, it always does. My husband and I have been through the winter seasons. We sought counseling and healing, both together and separately.

Unless you are both emotionally healthy, you will both bring baggage to your marriage. I am so proud of couples who seek help early on, or at any point, to become healthy and healed and be the best version of themselves.

We worked with a young couple recently and marveled at the good questions they asked. Those questions took us twenty years to figure them out. I am so thankful counseling and therapy are being normalized in our culture today. I know most of our struggle was simply a lack of understanding and knowledge of our previous culture. There is lots of help and guidance available today. I'm appreciative of the counselors and mentors my husband and I have had, along with the Holy Spirit, the best counselor of all. "But the Counselor the Holy Spirit whom the Father will send in my name, He will teach you all things and bring to your remembrance all that I had said to you," John 14:26.

Prayer Declaration:
Jesus, thank you for the Holy Spirit and all other counselors, teachers, mentors you have to help us. Impart us with wisdom, show us how to live free and healthy and healed. Thank you for your cleansing blood.

March 13
Rest and Rejuvenate

My husband cooked up one of his mouth-watering breakfasts for our guests and some of our children. Soon after, our guests left, and our sons left for work in another state. They're driving there today to rest up and start work tomorrow morning. They are helping one of our contractors with a large project in a warmer place. Our daughter and her friend leave around two in the afternoon. By now, a nap is a must for me. As I said before, naps are God's gift to humans, at least to me. I woke up still tired, though, and realized again how easy it is to overextend myself at times.

Sometimes I wish I needed less sleep like my husband; it would free up so much more time. I packed my bags in order to leave in the morning to be gone all week, then get ready and head off to church, where we are having special services called Hope Weekend. It's wonderful to be in the presence of God during worship and to see people get healed, saved, and baptized. I crawl into bed at ten thirty, tired yet rejuvenated. God can do that; you can be tired in your body yet alive in your spirit. Psalm 73:26 says it best, "My flesh and my heart may fail but God is the strength and my portion forever." Psalms 3:5 says, "I lay down and slept, I awoke, for the Lord sustains me." Aren't you extremely thankful that our God carries us when we are physically and emotionally tired? He is strong when we are weak.

Prayer Declaration:
Thank you, Jesus, for your perfect peace, resting in your love and strength. Teach us to not plan our lives so full that our bodies cannot keep up. Physically teach us how to continually make rest a priority. Thank you for teaching us how to find rest for our souls' body and most of all our spirits.

March 14
Rest from Our Burdens

My husband and I packed up the truck, locked up the house, and were on the road before nine o'clock. Our destination is Kansas City to meet up with some new team members for training. It's an eight-hour drive for us. It feels wonderful to sit and rest before being with people for the rest of the week. We listen to self-development books on audio. I also read out aloud. It's something my husband always enjoys. The roads were good; no snow or ice, which is a blessing. We eat on the run from our favorite truck stop then I settle in for a nap. My thoughts go to the verse, "Come to me all you who are weary, I will give you rest, take my yoke upon you and learn from me for I am gentle and humble in heart and you will find rest for your souls, for my yoke is easy and my burden is light," Matthew 11:28-30.

What heavy burdens are you carrying today? What does your soul need rest from? I invite you to take some deep breaths and release them to Jesus right now, trading him for the yoke of Jesus that is easy and light. These verses are some of my favorites in the Bible. He promises several times to give us rest in His rest, the best kind there is. Arriving at the hotel at five, we meet some of our friends at Cracker Barrel for a delicious dinner before we go to our first meeting. I feel blessed, refreshed, and ready to take on the week. Jesus is faithful, He is good, and He cares about all of our lives.

Prayer Declaration:
Jesus, thank you for your word and your promises that bring life and rest to every part of us; soul, body, spirit. Teach us to lean into your Word and your Spirit. Teach us to exchange our burdens for your yolk, learning peace and gentleness.

Soil of our Hearts

Today we enjoyed a delicious breakfast at the breakfast buffet here at our hotel. Along with coffee, it prepares us for our meetings, enabling us to listen to teachings all day. My husband and I have been in this business for twenty-five years, yet every time we bring new people and sit through the training with them, we learn something new. Today one of the speakers talked about the parable in the Bible of the sower and the seed, about how important it is to build our roots in the soil of the good and fertile ground. The parable goes something like this, Jesus expresses that if a farmer sows seed indiscriminately, some seed falls on the path or wayside with no soil; some falls on rocky ground with little soil, some on soil which contains thorns, and some on good soil.

Jesus later explains to his disciples that the seed represents the gospel, and the sower represents anyone who proclaims it in the various soils represented. People's responses to this popular story in the Bible can be found in commentary books too. Our speaker today challenged us to examine the soil of our own hearts. Let's ask ourselves right now if our hearts are hard, rocky, and tainted with bitterness, pain, and negativity. Maybe we've had too many hard knocks and disappointments. If that's the case, let's bring our hearts to Jesus and let Him make them tender and fertile again so that we, too, can grow to our full potential, yes, even 100-fold.

Prayer Declaration:
Jesus, help each one of us examine the soil of our hearts. Teach us how to be tender, fertile and receptive to you. Move through us and all you desire for us.

March 16
Preach the Gospel

This morning I'm blessed to have breakfast with one of my friends. Over coffee and breakfast, we discuss many things. One is we are both in the early stages of writing books and brainstorming. I've made so many wonderful iron-sharpens-iron friends in our business. Sometimes it feels more like a family reunion than it does like a business. Today we get to hear from the owner of the company. He almost always shares his testimony of how he and his wife got saved at one of these meetings. It never gets old to hear a multimillionaire, owner of multiple businesses, share his testimony and openly tell the whole room about making Jesus the Savior of their lives.

He is unashamed of the gospel and teaches it at our business meetings. It makes me think of Luke 9:26, "For whoever is ashamed of me and my words, of him will the son of man be ashamed." My heart longs to be bold and share the testimony of Jesus more, no matter what it looks like. Preach the gospel at all times and use words when necessary because, truly, our actions in how we treat people speak volumes. Our lives are always speaking. How sobering, what we preach versus live.

Prayer Declaration:
Jesus, will you increase our boldness to share the beautiful gospel, may our words, actions, testimonies always bring others to you. Jesus, make us vessels of which you can freely flow through to bring hope and healing wherever we go.

March 17
Abundant Life

My niece and I have part of the day to do what we want to, while our husbands have other commitments. This is a treat. She also left the Amish culture and didn't see her family very often. It's always a special time when she and I get to connect. We start our day at Caribou coffee with tasty lattes. Complete with great heart conversations, we also do a little shopping and later get some ice cream at Chick-fil-A. The weather is lovely and warm, which adds to our glorious fun. We agree this girls' day is the self-care day; we both needed it. I appreciate my two nieces, who I get to see a lot more since they, too, left the Amish.

I feel they both did it for the right reasons. They were both searching for more of life, the abundant life. The term 'abundant life' comes from John 10:10, "I come that they might have life and that they might have it more abundantly." 'Abundant life' refers to the abounding fullness of joy and strength, soul and body. Whenever the three of us are privileged to be together, it's often what our conversations consist of. How do we continue to grow in God? How do we rise above the trials in hard things? How do we take hold of all that Jesus wants us to have? From experience, it always comes back to this prayer...

Prayer Declaration:
Jesus, do not leave us to our own will, do not leave us orphans but let us be your sons and daughters. We want everything there is to experience in you. Show us how to always be led by your spirit and to be more and more sensitive to your voice. Your thoughts, ways, will for me and my family I pray in Jesus' name. Amen.

March 18
Spring Is Coming

It feels like spring has sprung while we were gone this week. When we left Monday morning, the ground was still pretty much covered in snow, with lots of ice patches. Definitely still felt like winter. Last night, just five days later, the ice was all gone, most of the snow too. How encouraging, even though I know realistically that spring probably isn't here to stay, we will enjoy this warmer beautiful weather while it lasts.

The month of March is my least favorite, partially because it's so unpredictable, especially here in Wisconsin. It's not uncommon for it to snow, rain, sleet, and have sunshine all on the same day. It starts thawing, and we deal with mud, water puddles, and all that goes with it, but on the other side of March, April awaits. May is truly spring here; even though we've had snow in May, we never know for sure when spring will arrive.

Isn't it a lot like our lives? We know until the cold becomes less in our hearts, we begin to thaw once again, becoming completely healed by the gentle warm spring rains and the delightful sunshine. Let it rain, Lord! Nature has different seasons, and so do we. Genesis 8:22 says, "As long as the earth endures, seed time and harvest, cold and heat, summer and winter, day and night will never cease." This is God's design for His world and ours. You may have had a harsh winter in life, but spring has sprung, and your blessing is near.

Prayer Declaration:
Jesus, thank you that you are always the same no matter what season of life we are in, let our roots grow deep in the difficult times, teach us how to trust you and lean on you all the time.

March 19
Do Not Fear

Did you know that fear and worry are sisters? At least, it's what I heard in an audiobook. It makes so much sense. We are afraid of what could happen, so we worry about *what if.* Instead of dread, we can use our imagination for good. It would be a good way to keep fear away. It starts with taking every thought captive. Paul said it best in 2 Corinthians 10:5, "We take captive every thought to make it obedient to Christ." Memorize this, and use it next time your mind and thoughts start becoming negative or fear-based. Repeat it mentally and verbally.

Joyce Myers, one of my heroes, often says we have to talk to ourselves and talk back to the adversary.

When the enemy comes to deceive and condemn us, the Bible says 365 times not to be afraid. That's enough for one every day of the year. Jesus must have known how prone we would be to fear and worry. What burden do you need to lay down today and overcome with God's truth? As mothers, we probably worry the most about our precious children and grandchildren. Will they turn out okay? Will they love Jesus with all their heart, soul, and mind? Will they find godly compatible partners? One thought that always brings me deep peace is knowing that God loves them even more than I do. They are His first, and he has a divine design for them.

Prayer Declaration
Jesus, today we surrender our worry and fear and exchange it for trust and faith. Teach us how to take every thought captive and rise above the negative condemning voice of our enemy. We overcome in Jesus' name.

March 20
Jesus Prepares a Place

John 14:1-3 says, "Let not your heart be troubled, neither let them be afraid, in my father's house are many rooms and if I go and prepare a place for you, I will come back and take you to be with me so that you also may be where I am." I can hardly wait, what about you? Do you long for our heavenly home some days, no more cares, worries, heartache, pain, disappointment, or death? Just this past week, a neighbor and family friend was laid to rest. He lost a long battle with cancer; well, actually, he gained, and we lost. He was saved; we can know where he is. With this, a season of losses started. In March 2017, I lost my father. We lost our beloved Judy; she was the wife of the president of our company. She was one of the sweetest, classiest, most humble yet powerful women I have ever known.

She called me when my father passed away of a heart attack, cried and prayed with me: Imparting kind, beautiful things to me, yet in two short months, she was gone too. In two separate incidents, former Amish family friends were murdered. Nonetheless, in light of all our grief, will we not lose our hearts? In light of sorrow, we do not let our hearts be or stay troubled because of what's coming. Dear friends, we hold on to the hope of eternity. As our pastor says, *this life is only a short camping trip compared to what's coming; hallelujah!*

Prayer Declaration
Jesus, thank you for heaven and what you are preparing for us, teach us how to live above these earthly heartaches and disappointments. Let us look to you and what is to come. The best is yet to come, eternity with you.

March 21
Adoption Is a Gift

Monday is often a wonderful catch-up day for me. I love to get the Airbnb clean and off the list for the week. I'm the queen of lists; it motivates me, and it's so fun to see things crossed off. If you haven't, try it sometime, you can thank me later. This came from my mom. As I remember, she would always have her list of things to do. She was one of the hardest-working women I know. Today's to-do list includes sending flowers to my sister-in-law; she's quite special to us.

My husband has since met his two biological sisters, but I want to talk about his adopted sister today to honor her birthday. She and my husband were both adopted into an Amish family when they were tiny babies, only days old. His sister left the Amish culture ten years before we did; in some ways, she prepared the way for us. She has a big heart and would do anything for anyone. We're so blessed to have her in our lives. We think adoption is a beautiful thing. It just shows again that family isn't always flesh and blood. After all, we are all adopted into the family of God. Ephesians 1:5 says, "In love, he predestined us to be adopted as his sons and daughters through Jesus Christ in accordance with his pleasure and will."

Prayer Declaration:
Jesus, thank you for letting my husband and adopted sister find a wonderful family so I could meet them. Thank you that you guide and direct our steps. You have good plans for us from the time we are conceived

March 22
Let Me Be Content in You, Lord

Guess what day it is? Its Bible study group. We decided to meet at my friend's house and make a bunch of homemade donuts before we did our study. It was such a fun time and reminded me of the past, baking with mom and sisters, and precious memories. We laughed, talked, and made donuts until lunchtime. Of course, we ate way too many. We all got to take some home. Our study today was Philippians, and it was good. Paul wrote to encourage the church even while in prison. It amazes me. Would we do that? I was convicted at this moment.

Wouldn't it have been so much easier for him to feel sorry for himself and ask *why me* God? Instead he goes on to say in Philippians 4:11-13, "I have learned to be content in whatever the circumstances, I know what it is to be in need and I know what it is to have plenty, I have learned the secret of being content in any and every situation, whether well fed or hungry, whether living in plenty or in want. I can do all things through Christ who gives me strength." I don't know about you, but these verses convict, inspire and fill me with hope. Paul proves to us that it is possible to live content in spite of our circumstances. He went through a lot. What if we spoke positive declarations over our lives and praised God in spite of our pain or lacking? I imagine we could be filled with joy just as Paul was.

Prayer Declaration:
Jesus, thank you for your written word in the many examples we have to live our lives. We can live to your fullest will. You increase our joy, our faith and our hope today. Whatever we are facing right now, we can do all things through you.

March 23
Using Self Control

Matthew 26:41 "...the spirit is willing but the flesh is weak." Jesus said this to his disciples at night. They were in the garden of Gethsemane, and while He agonizingly prayed before He was crucified, the disciples kept dozing off. It's also our story. Our hearts might be in the right place; the spirit desires to do the will of our heavenly father. It costs us, yet we can be so weak in our flesh our earthly bodies get tired and overwhelmed; Jesus persevered. He was obedient even till death. We will praise Him through all eternity for His great sacrifice and price. He paid for all who were willing to believe and receive Him.

My flesh definitely felt tired when I woke up this morning. Maybe it was the overdose of gluten yesterday. Fresh donuts, one of my biggest weaknesses, I caved, so today I paid the price for indulging. Sometimes we create our own issues when we lack self-control. Personally, I am working on my life to let no food or drink control me. It's like we tell our children our stuff becomes a sin when we let it control us instead of us being in control. What vice do you indulge in, maybe you have yours all under control, but maybe you don't. Proverbs 25:28 says, "A man or woman without self-control is like a city broken into and left without walls."

Prayer Declaration:
Jesus, will you strengthen our spirits and help us to walk in victory? Thank you for teaching us how to use moderation and self-control instead of being slaves to our flesh.

March 24
Restore Relationships

Today is another special day. I get to go home to spend it with my Amish sisters and my mom. This is always a treat and well worth the five hours round trip. My husband left for a snowmobiling trip around three in the morning. After he left, I lay awake for a long time, wasting precious sleep. I was thinking about the coming day in anticipation. All too soon, my alarm went off, and I made my coffee to go, plus a cup for a friend. She was here for the night. We chatted as we gathered things together. The car is packed, and I'm taking a pan of lasagna for lunch to share. The trip seems short, between calls, music, and podcasts. I arrive at eleven fifteen. I'm welcomed by everyone, including two of my nieces and their little ones. With lots of good food and coffee, we laugh and talk (sometimes all at the same time). It's fun, rich, and chaotic.

How did I specifically restore my Amish family's relationship? I simply asked what it would take. I marvel at these wonderful days and do not take them for granted. We reached a compromise. I could be me, and they could be them. I didn't try to change them; they didn't try to change me. When I'm on their turf, I willingly wear a dress and put up my hair, lightly covering it. It's easy to equally honor one another for love and respect. We have a great relationship. Didn't Paul also say similar things in the Bible when he talks about shaving his hair before going to Rome? Thank goodness I wasn't going to Rome.

Prayer Declaration:
Jesus, thank you for my restored relationship with my mom and sisters, only you can heal and restore hearts and relationships. I pray for every person reading this. Do it for them, show each one their part. Allow us to restore relationships.

March 25
Letting Go and Letting God

I had to leave my sister's house early yesterday in order to be back at our church in the evening. One of our twin daughters was singing for the first time on the worship team. She has a beautiful anointed voice. As she sang, my heart filled with gratitude and praise. I was back in time to attend worship night. It made for a short day; I did lots of driving but worth it. The Holy Spirit was there, and as my daughter described it in song, it was glorious, yes, it was a baby girl, and I'm so proud of you. I drove many miles today, and I had a lot of time to ponder and think back, remembering what Jesus has done in our lives. I reflected on some of the hardest days of my life when we were separated from my extended family.

I missed my mom and sisters tremendously. When we moved the first time, we moved away from both our families to another community. Sometimes it was very lonely and hard. I shed tears, telling God, I cannot do this without you. I must have more of you above all else. Our God is faithful; gradually and gently, He leads us. Tenderly, he brought new friends, new experiences in Him, new opportunities, and helped us start a church, which was a wonderful experience. Through pain, there was also progress. Letting go and letting God have his way with us was significant. We moved out West for eight years. During that time, I saw even less of my family but again made a new family in the spirit. Luke 18:29 declares, "Everyone who has left houses or brothers or sisters or father or mother or children or lands for my namesake will receive one hundredfold and inherit eternal life."

Prayer Declaration:
Thank you, Jesus, for this powerful promise. Thank you for teaching us how to follow you no matter the cost.

Calendar Space

Today was a wonderful, quiet, slow, peaceful day; one of those rare days when I was home alone. No appointments, no commitments, and no place I need to go. I took a deep breath. It felt amazing. I could feel the stress of the previous busy week starting to melt away. I woke up with no alarm. What a treat to sleep in. I lingered over my coffee, reading for a long time before doing my workout routine. Isaiah 30:15 says, "In repentance and trust is your salvation, in quietness and trust is your strength but you would have none of it." I felt the worth of these words. The stillness and the quiet slow-paced day restored my strength and my confidence. With Jesus, I can do all the things, and at the same time, I repented for once again saying yes to putting too many things on my schedule.

I almost collapsed under it all. My husband has been telling me to slow down. I'm ready to listen to him. My caring mom said it the other day; *you have too much going on; you weren't yourself the other day. Are you OK?* When we continually say yes to more than we have grace for, it will catch up with us, and we will struggle to do anything well because we are pulled in too many directions at once. Do you listen to those closest to you when they tell you what they see? Why is that difficult to do today? I am starting over, saying yes to more white space and margin on my calendar, yes to more time with my husband and those who truly matter to me.

Prayer Declaration:
Jesus, thank you for your sweet peace and conviction. Teach us how to choose our 'yes' carefully and never at the expense of our families. Forgive us for coming under the pressure of being human doings instead of human beings. help us to know balance.

March 27
Dare to Dream Again

It's cold again this morning. Sixteen degrees is what my car said on the way to church. We also had snow and high winds the last several days, but it's March; anything can happen weather-wise. It doesn't take me by surprise anymore. Church was amazing today, with wonderful worship and message. I soaked it all in and am eagerly anticipating my turn on the worship team. I'm thankful one of the questions our pastor asked us today was: *Can we believe God for more?* Getting back on the worship team after twelve years was something I didn't have the faith to pray for. One of my greatest longings was tucked down in the corner of my heart somewhere.

I couldn't see how God could possibly make it happen. Dare to dream again, no matter how menial. I do believe it was something God asked me to lay down for a season because I was finding my identity leading worship more than just being a worshiper. It's what I learned to do in the past twelve years, worship to an audience of one. I am learning to worship through chords on my guitar, bringing great joy and meaning to my personal worship times with Jesus. Occasionally, I will lead my ladies' Bible study when my daughter-in-law can't. Hebrews 11:16 says, "God rewards those who seek and serve him, He rewards the faith of those who passionately seek him." What is it that you long for? Can you lay it at the feet of Jesus and just seek him above anything else?

Prayer Declaration:
Jesus, help us to always worship you for who you are. Jesus, help us to always worship you for who you are, much more than what you can do for us. Teach us how to find our identity, not by actions but by abiding in you first and foremost. Amen.

March 28
Giving Ourselves Grace

Ok, it's another new week, a fresh Monday. You probably heard all the names for Mondays, mundane Monday, blues Monday, and manic Monday. Believe me; I felt all those and more. Mondays used to be the most overwhelming day of the whole week, except for Saturdays. There's so much I could have and should have done differently. If only I knew what I now know. The first thing would have been to ask for help. Why on earth did that seem weak? With six little ones, the laundry piles were mini mountains. Getting all of that done with an old-fashioned Maytag wringer washer was no easy task. There was no dryer either, clothespins and clotheslines outside to dry; yes, even in winter. Unless you were lucky enough to have a warm basement, the original stairmaster, constantly running up and downstairs to check on the children, nursing one or two.

You guessed it, by the time I was done, I was exhausted. The second thing I wish I had known is that depression is normal when your body or hormones are out of balance. After giving birth to twin daughters, I silently struggled with postpartum depression for quite some time, then felt guilty for being depressed. After all, here I had these two beautiful baby girls I wanted. It was a dark time in my life, but once again, Jesus rescued me and set my feet on a solid rock. One of my favorite passages of scripture is Psalms 40:2, "He lifted me out of the slimy pit, out of the mud and mire, He set my feet on a rock and gave me a solid firm place to stand."

Prayer Declaration:
Jesus, for the rest of my life I will praise you for what you have done. Bless and guide anyone who is feeling overwhelmed, sad or depressed and lead them into your life everlasting. Allow me to show grace to myself.

March 29
A Dream is Birthed

This will be a short week here at home. We are getting ready to travel to Erie, PA, to attend our first event of the year, where we promote Africa and raise funds to drill wells, something we started in 2008. We started our nonprofit organization; it's called "Simple Faith Ministries." Running a nonprofit isn't easy and has stretched me to my limits often. Again, when you have a dream, you do whatever it takes. This dream started in 2017 when our twin daughters, sixteen at the time, went to Mozambique, Africa, for the first time. This particular part of Africa had been in my heart for years, long before we had the means to travel. One ticket alone is over $5,000. For my daughters and I, we needed to come up with $15,000, and we did.

Through some fundraising, we were able to go with a group traveling there; we knew only the leaders. It was a trip we will never forget. We stayed on the base, right across from the beautiful Indian Ocean. The loveliness yet utter poverty was beyond anything we could ever experience. We all had emotional meltdowns. The children were starving not only for food but also for love and attention. We were constantly surrounded by need. Seeing lack wrecked our hearts in a good way. We helped serve one meal a day to thousands of children. My thoughts would go to the verse, "Truly I tell you, whatever you did for one of the least of these brothers and sisters and children, you did it for me." Beautiful red-letter writings of Jesus, in his own words, Matthew 25:40.

Prayer Declaration:
Jesus, thank you for letting us experience your brokenness. Will you break our hearts for what breaks yours? Open our eyes to see the need, lack and hunger around us and outside our world.

March 30
Birthing Pains

Just as we have childbirth pains, it can be similar to birthing a dream. It can be intense, uncomfortable, and downright painful. It's what happened to me after we came back from Africa for the first time. I couldn't function and continue with life as we knew it. The number one question that haunted me was, *how can we live like we do here in America when we know about the situation in Africa?*

We, of course, bountifully serve our own world, but those precious little faces kept flashing before my eyes. I saw their small bloated bellies because of starvation. The rest of their bodies were skin and bones. I remember all the young mamas with babies on their backs, some as young as thirteen or fourteen, having been violated, it's rampant, and the government refuses birth control. Young girls would often have to walk a whole day to get water for their families from a contaminated water hole.

They would sometimes sleep there and walk back with water buckets on their heads. Their hands were heavy with hard work, but even worse, they were susceptible to men taking advantage. This alone breaks my heart. My husband and I will never be the same again. He decided to go back with me the following year, in 2018. He was wrecked by what he saw. Together we launched "Simple Faith Ministries," and it has not been easy. Jeremiah 22:23 speaks of birth pains, "You who dwell in Lebanon, [for us it's Wisconsin], nestled in the Cedars, how will you grow, how you will groan when pangs come upon you pain like a woman in childbirth?"

Prayer Declaration:
Jesus, thank you for these growing birth pains to provide fresh water in Africa, and anything outside our world. Thank you for showing each of us what you want us to do and where to make a difference. Birth a dream in each one of us, make us uncomfortable or whatever it takes. Let us say, here am I, send me Lord.

March 31
Here Am I

We woke up to the beautiful waters of the Bayfront at Lake Erie, such a beautiful place our friends picked to host their annual seminar. My husband and I are extremely grateful they have chosen to partner with us in our ministry every year. They allow a slot to briefly speak about what we do in Africa, and they do an auction to raise funds to drill wells for the villages in Mozambique, Africa. Once again, we feel so humbled, thankful, and blessed as thousands of dollars are being raised, every penny for this cause. This is what a community looks like. This is what it looks like to be a part of something so much bigger than us.

This is what it looks like when God breathes on your dreams to make a difference when you are willing to say here am I. Lord, send me. Do you know what that is for you? I totally encourage you to ask Jesus and dream, even if you don't know how. Dreams could possibly happen when you don't know how. Jesus is not looking for the most talented people; He needs teachable people. He is looking for willing hearts. This same community in Africa also desperately needs people to support their food programs. My husband and I do some of that, too, but there are still many famished children. Right now, ask Jesus, *where do you want me?* Isaiah 6:8 says, "Then I heard the voice of the Lord saying, whom shall I send and who will go for us and I said here am I, send me, yes Lord send me," [again and again].

Prayer Declaration:
Jesus, teach us to hear and obey your voice on where it is or what it is you have for each one of us to. Where do you want us to invest our time, money, or resources to make a difference?

April 1
Every Dream Has a Flipside

Yesterday's event was full of fun and very inspiring. As we learn from different speakers and panels on different subjects. We ended the evening hanging out with some of our team members, enjoying superb food and great conversations together. So, this morning we slept a little later and again soaked in the beauty of Lake Erie and drove around it a bit before getting our coffee and starting the trip back home.

We drove through some snow and sleet, but it's toasty and cozy in the car as we talk, catch up, read, stop for a late lunch, and listen to audio. At one point, I get into the back seat to stretch out my back and take a nap. Have you ever had chronic pain in your body anywhere? If you say yes, then you know how it can wear you out. Ever since I had a frozen shoulder a few years ago, I have had a spot in my left shoulder blade area that will flare up pretty consistently. It is the worst when sitting for long.

Car rides are not my favorite thing. Today we have eleven hours to go. Ironically, my husband and I do travel a lot. It comes with the business and lifestyle we have chosen. We have this saying, though, we constantly remind each other of. Every dream has a flipside; whether it's chronic pain or traveling many miles and sleeping in lots of hotel rooms, it's still worth it. We just want to get to the end of our lives and hear Jesus say, "Well done thou good and faithful servants" Matthew 25:21 21.

Prayer Declaration:
Jesus, thank you that your grace is always enough to carry each one of us through pain and whatever we might face as we journey towards heaven and our final destination.

April 2
Like Father, Like Grandson

We woke up to snow this morning again. No joke, if it was yesterday morning, we would say April fools! I must admit it looks beautiful, those big lazy floating flakes lazily resting on the ground. Before we know it, it's raining. Then the sun shines, which makes a beautiful rainbow in the sky. It feels wonderful to linger over our morning coffee, watching the weather and recapping our week. I ran into town for groceries and a birthday present for a little grandson who turned two yesterday. We weren't home, so we Face-Timed him. As I go through pictures from his birth to two years, the memories come flooding back. How on earth is he already two?

I'm reminded again of how fast time goes. It seems like yesterday, our son and daughter-in-law brought him home from the hospital and named him Zander Isaiah. How I love his strong name and this little boy. He was more Grandpa's baby than Grandma's, and as he grew, I began to see why. They are natured a lot alike and bonded easily. It's been so fun to watch. They are both hilarious, determined, sweet, and salty. Zander will growl like a lion and try to scare Grandpa and vice versa. Just like his grandpa, Zander will do what it takes to get where he wants to be. They are quite a team. Psalms 103:17 says, "But from everlasting to everlasting, the Lord's love is with those who fear Him and His righteousness with their children's children."

Prayer Declaration:
Jesus, thank you for your promise to our children, thank you for giving us precious grandchildren to love. Help us to teach them, honor and glorify you.

April 3
Children and Grandchildren

Our daughter came home to visit last night. What a treat; she is a very busy young woman in college. Not only does she go to school full-time as a senior in nursing school, but she also works as a CNA at Gunderson Hospital in La Crosse. She started her clinical internship at Mayo Clinic. Having her home for brunch and devotions with us is a treat, even when she has a good bit of homework to do by five. The rest of the family starts gathering for dinner to celebrate Zander's birthday. Pizza, relish tray, ice cream, cupcakes, and gifts, Zander is delighted with it all. We go outside to play with his new trike, then inside again to play with his other gifts.

Zion, almost four, understands well it's not his birthday quite yet. The boys do so well in sharing. I'm amazed their parents have taught them so well in this and also the importance of good manners. It's wonderful to have the whole family together again for family night. As empty nesters, these evenings are very special to us. Our families are the only thing we get to take to heaven with us. We get one chance at raising them for God's purpose, in his glory. I love Proverbs 22:6, "Start children off on the way they should go and even when they are old, they will not turn from it." What a promise. When they are young, the age of our grandchildren is the time to start teaching them about Jesus. They are just like little sponges and absorb things quickly. Make sure it's good things.

Prayer Declaration:
Jesus, thank you for your plan for children, family and grandchildren. What a blessing, show us the way to their hearts and to continually teach them and point them to you, especially by our example.

Unconditional Love

I woke up in a funk this morning. We just had a great family night and a wonderful, fruitful week. What is wrong with me? I asked myself, feeling guilty for feeling this way. Maybe it's cabin fever, wishing, longing, waiting for winter to end. Perhaps the gnawing pain in my back, knowing I have a dentist appointment today—something I dread every time. Today was no different. As the needle sunk deep into my gum tissue, I flinched and tried to be brave. Later a friend came over for dinner, though, and we brainstormed about fundraising and finding sponsors for our cause.

We talked about our victories and our current struggles. She's that kind of a good, safe friend. By the time she left, I felt better. I was still emotional. It reminded me of what I often tell others in life. *We will have highs and lows, and sometimes, we won't even know exactly why we are feeling low.* We look for things to blame, just like I did this morning. These days I am very thankful for two things, a husband who sticks by me through thick and thin and a God who loves me unconditionally. He loves us as much on our worst days as on our best. Isn't that so comforting? Romans 8:39 says it best, "Neither height nor depth nor anything else in all creation will be able to separate us from the love of God that is in Christ Jesus our Lord."

Prayer Declaration:
Jesus, thank you for your precious promise for never withdrawing your love from us. Help us to remember when we and the ones around us are the most unlovable, that's when we need your love the most.

April 5
Saving Grace

"It is by grace you have been saved through faith and this is not from yourselves, it is the gift of God not by works so that no one can boast" Ephesians 2:8-9. Thank you, Jesus, for your grace and mercy. Without it, we would be toast, burnt toast. Aren't you thankful for God's infinite love, grace, and mercy? For many years I didn't really understand it. I'm still trying to grasp it fully. For many years, I struggled with guilt, shame, and condemnation. Many times, after my children were in bed at night, I would lay there and relive my mistakes and shortcomings and condemn myself. I was also terrified of dying because even though I knew Jesus, I didn't yet believe in His grace, mercy, and forgiveness. It was quite a journey, but today my understanding of this verse is much greater and brings me peace.

As long as we are human beings on this earth, we will need large doses of grace, mercy, and forgiveness. In the physical or natural sense, it's much easier to give myself a break when I need it, like today.

It was a self-care day, a massage for my hurting back, then home to literally rest and take care of myself until it was time to make dinner. Is there a place where you need or long for more grace? Where is it, and what could you do to start practicing that in your life? It's only when we start seeing ourselves through the eyes of who He says we are, worthy of His love, as His sons and daughters.

Prayer Declaration:
I pray everyone reading this has been saved by grace. Jesus continued to teach all of us the richness, the blessing and freedom that is packed into these wonderful verses. Thank you for your saving grace. Amen.

April 6
Feel Reveal and Heal

More snow, more rain, and more pain are definitely coming out of the winter season. It feels dreary and endless this morning, but I know this, too, shall pass. I push through the aching and do a light, mostly stretching workout. It hurts so good. My mood still matches the weather, and that's okay. I'm learning to sit in and feel my emotions. What are they trying to tell or show me? Did you know we must feel before we can heal? We can't heal what we don't reveal. Isn't it so much easier to hide our true feelings, stuff our emotions and tell our hearts to shape up or even shut up? Believe me, I did all the above for many years, never knowing how to express my true self, and even if I had, I would be afraid of hurting someone's feelings.

It all worked just fine until I reached menopause, then I started unraveling. I'm pretty sure every stuffed emotion came out over the next ten years. It wasn't always pretty. To this day, I still have a mentor/counselor, on my journey to healing and wholeness. I cannot encourage you enough to do the same. Be true to yourself and who God is calling you to be. Don't try to walk in shoes that don't fit just to make others happy. Say what you mean and mean what you say, or as the Bible says, "Let your yes be yes and your no be no" Matthew 5:37. In other words, speak your truth in love and stand firm in it.

Prayer Declaration:
Jesus, I pray for each one of us to be healed, healthy and whole physically, emotionally and spiritually. Show us what steps to take to walk in our true authentic self. Help us be the person you want us to be for your honor and glory alone.

April 7
More Than Traditions

This morning it's snowing again, which makes it a cozy, relaxing day for our monthly Bible study. Like normal, the ladies trickle in, bringing scrumptious food. My daughter-in-law can't make it, so I lead worship. I prepared our study, taking us through the entire book of Colossians today. We marvel at Paul's faithfulness even while still in prison. He preached, taught, and prayed; he had a true burden for the church and lost souls. We discussed this quite a bit and asked ourselves, who are we telling the good news of Jesus to? Do we have a heart for those who don't know Jesus? Colossians 2:7 was also brought up, as many of us remember having been admonished when we left the Amish. The theme scripture reads, "Rooted and built in him, strengthened in the faith as you were taught and overflowing with thankfulness."

We were brought up to believe we cannot leave the culture that we were born into partially because of this scripture sentence, "As you were taught," many still believe this today. However, the next verse, eight, says, "See to it that no one takes you captive through hollow and deceptive philosophy which depends on human tradition and the basic principles of this world rather than on Christ." As we read on, the next verse sets us free [See to it that no one takes you captive], so that's the rest of the story, so to speak. I do appreciate many things about my Amish background, but I'm personally not sure where you will find more human traditions than among my former beliefs. This was again a reminder to me to read the whole Bible and not just take one verse out of context.

Prayer Declaration:
Jesus, thank you again for your freedom and help all of us to put our faith and trust in you, in more than traditions or the principles of this world. Salvation comes from you and you alone, we praise you and we worship you, we thank you forever.

April 8
A New Thing

"See I am doing a new thing, now it springs up, do you not perceive it. I'm making your way in the wilderness and streams in the wasteland." Isaiah 43:19. This verse was in our message at church today. It was also one of the songs we sang on the worship team. This verse touched a place deep inside my heart because it truly feels like God continues to do new things in my life, especially today. As I sang on the worship team after laying that down for many years, it felt redemptive, wonderful, right, and truly like the beginning of a new thing for me. I'm grateful and also thankful God gave me the grace to be obedient and to not do that until He chose to bring that back into my life.

You see, just because something is a good thing or God thing, it doesn't always mean it's the right thing or the right time for us. My mentor taught me to go with grace and peace to determine God's will and heart for me. It has been helpful so many times. What new thing is God doing in your life right now, or maybe he is asking you to let go of something old, to take some time off, to sit in His presence? Perhaps you need time to get healthy and healed. Honestly, that has been a big part of my last twelve years is all of the above. I don't regret it at all. Rest assured, if something is right for you or meant to be good, He will restore it for you at the right time. You can trust Him with your hopes, dreams, and desires.

Prayer Declaration:
Thank you, Jesus, for the new thing you are doing in each of our lives. Thank you for pruning and trimming us where we need it for the best growth possible for us thank you that you are always looking out for the best for us pruning our lives

April 9
Intentional Living

Next week is travel week again. My husband and I will be back in Kansas City for most of the week. Over our morning coffee, we plan our day and decide to cut down our work today because tomorrow will be at church, and then we will have the little grandsons in the afternoon, and our daughter will come home. Precious time is coming up; never a dull moment when our little boys are around. They keep us on our toes and keep us young. We have things we both need to wrap up today, office work, odd jobs, phone calls, etc.

The sun is finally out, nice and warm, so I spend some time outside basking in it. It feels so absolutely wonderful after the long cold winter. Later in the day, we went out for dinner and date night, intentionally taking time to connect with each other as we will not get much private time the next week. Being intentional with our time, money, relationships, and the things we focus on can have huge benefits for our lives. We can be pulled to and fro, in every direction, frittering, giving our time and attention to things that don't matter, or we can practice being intentional and have a much better quality of life. We can be much more present and rested for the most important things in our lives. Ephesians 5:15 says, "Really look carefully then how you walk not as unwise but as wise making the best use of the time because the days are evil therefore do not be foolish but understand what the will of the Lord is."

Prayer Declaration:
Jesus thank you for teaching each one of us to be intentional with things in our lives that truly matter, thank you for your wisdom and knowing what's most important, not just for today but for all eternity. Help us to choose carefully with hearts for your Kingdom, renewing our minds.

April 10
Pruning and Trimming

Speaking of pruning and trimming, we can read about this in John 15:1-2, "I am the true vine and my Father is the vinedresser, every branch in me that does not bear fruit, He takes away and every branch that does bear fruit, He prunes, that it may bear more fruit." Did you get that? Even those parts of our lives that are bearing fruit, He prunes so we can be even more faithful. What if we could keep this in the forefront of our memory when hard times come when we are tested to our limits? Could it be that we are being pruned in places that are bearing no fruit?

God wants us to bear much more fruit. One area for myself was fear of men; that was a big one for me. It's part of my nature to serve and please people, which, again, when taken out of context, isn't always a good thing. That is one of the areas God saw this girl is going to need some help. It was brutal, yet gentle, sometimes quite painful and rewarding.

My journey took ten years, to be exact, of leaving my Amish culture in spite of being misunderstood by family, friends, and former communities. Knowing we were hurting our families, I truly felt at times like the disciples when Jesus asked them to leave it all and come follow Him. He was pruning me to listen for His voice, His leading, and to look to Him for affirmation and guidance and not give up. He has since healed our family relationships which I'm enormously grateful for.

Prayer Declaration:
Jesus, give us grace and strength to go where you call us, to submit to your pruning, to look to you, for you are true and we are only the branches.

April 11
Give Thanks in all Things.

More snow this morning and, thank God, less pain. My mood is much better in spite of the ongoing winter outside. I'm tempted to start leaving the Christmas decorations out year-round. Seriously though, I'm so thankful to be inside working where it's nice and warm. My back feels much better since the deep tissue massage and several rounds of icing it.

Today is a wonderful day for catching up on all the things, laundry, paying bills, and office work for our nonprofit. Those can be a real pain and a lot of work, yet it's always worth it. Studies show we don't nearly use the full capacity of our brains, but I dare say this, I activated parts of my brain I didn't know I had. I'm really longing to come to a place, though, where even things like pain or being stretched beyond my comfort zone and limits won't affect emotions.

Thessalonians 5:16-18 says this, "Rejoice, always, pray continually and give thanks in all circumstances, for this is God's will for you in Christ Jesus." I confess I'm not there yet. It's easy when everything is going 'well and good,' but when the hard days come, it's not easy. It doesn't mean we have to be thankful for the problems. However, we are encouraged to thank our way through them. How much easier is it to complain, grumble and lament? Try praise, gratitude, and joy.

Prayer Declaration:
Jesus, help us all when we are going through trying circumstances. Lord, remind us of these verses. Teach us how to walk these verses out and make these our mandate in all things. Lead us, teach us, and guide us, Lord.

April 12
Continue to Learn

We woke up on the 9th floor of the Hilton in Kansas City, not a bad view in spite of the rain, actually. I'm thankful it's raining because it makes it easier to be inside sitting in meetings all day. Thankfully this hotel has a Starbucks; that's how we start our day. Even though we sat through parts of these seminars many times over, I'm always amazed at how I learn something new every time or hear something in a different way. This helps me realize how much we can continually learn if we have a teachable mindset. We probably all have been around people who seem to know it all or have everything figured out. It can be hard to even engage in a great conversation with people who have that mindset. In our humanity, we will always be able to learn and grow until the day we leave this earth, maybe even constantly evaluating what we do know and if it's still true for us.

Does it still apply? Do we still need this old belief system, or is it time to get rid of it? The Bible speaks about renewing our minds in Romans 12:2, "Do not be conformed to this world but be transformed by the renewal of your mind that by testing you may discern what is the will of God, what is good and acceptable and perfect will." Don't you just love this? I love the words *transformed* and *renewal*. This has been our journey for the past twenty-plus years after we started our search for the whole truth about salvation, Jesus, and life in general. One thing I know, Jesus is faithful to reveal Himself to the degree that we are willing to seek Him with all of our hearts and minds.

Prayer Declaration:
Jesus, thank you for giving our minds the capacity to continually grow and transform, thank you that you are faithful to renew us to the degree that we are willing to pursue you. We want even more Jesus so we never stop seeking out the truth.

April 13
Trusting God

"Trust in the Lord with all your heart and lean not on your own understanding, in all your ways submit, acknowledge Him and He will direct your path," Proverbs 3:5-6. I remember this season of my life when these verses became so real to me. I actually had to let go of my own understanding and start leaning into God's path for me; it was scary and exhilarating at the same time.

I clearly remember being on my knees one day and telling God I will do anything you want me to except leave my Amish family. Could it be He saw that's where my biggest trust issue was? Letting go of my understanding and trust in Him completely.

Even though we had already moved many miles away from our families, 100 to be exact, in our former marital years, we were still somewhat accepted into their circles, invited to family functions, etc. However, it started changing more and more, and eventually, we weren't accepted anymore. Though no one formally excommunicated us from the church, it was an unspoken thing. We are not invited to family gatherings, weddings, holidays, etc. While this was painful and lonely, on the one hand, it also helped me to lean not on my own understanding and trust God more than ever before in my life. It also helped me so much to not hold it against my family because I remembered how we were taught and raised, so I understood why. Just like God promised, He continued to be faithful in directing our paths into more than I could think or imagine. I trust God more than ever.

Prayer Declaration:
Jesus, thank you that you always know what's best for us and for our future, thank you so much for your faithfulness in leading us into your paths of righteousness, for each one of us, even when it's hard, teach us to lean into your understanding.

April 14
Sons and Daughters, not Slaves

No meetings this morning, so I was able to get some extra sleep. The older I get, the more I realize how important self-care is. Joyce Meyer, one of my heroes, speaks about the importance of this, too, and how she didn't always take care of herself in her younger years. It caught up with her in her later years. I am only fifty, but I can already identify with some of that. In fact, I clearly remember being so tired at times, to the point of tears, especially when our six children were small. Instead of taking naps when they did, that is when I would often quickly sit at the sewing machine and sew pieces of clothing as fast as I possibly could.

I sewed all our clothes for many years, pants, shirts, guys' jackets, dresses, aprons, capes, and girls' coverings. Again I could totally have asked for help, but sewing was something that I actually kind of enjoyed, except for the thick coats; I never did master that very well. Then there were always chores at the end of the day. Getting the kiddos bundled up and out of the house was good for them but no easy task. Our days were filled to the brim with hard work, and I'm thankful we learned those principles. It makes me even more thankful for the lifestyle we get to live now, but it's still very easy for me to do more than I can or should.

My husband constantly reminds and helps me with that, which I'm extremely grateful for. To remember my worth doesn't come from what I do but from who I am is reassuring. Galatians 4:7 says, "So you are no longer a slave but God's child and since you are his child; God has made you also an heir."

Prayer Declaration:
Jesus thank you for helping us know where our worth comes from, in you alone. Teach us how to live as sons and daughters, as your heirs instead of slaves. Teach us how to live holy, vigilant and be concerned about the things that truly matter.

April 15
Good Friday

Today is a very sobering day to me, the day we honor, in remembrance of Jesus going to the cross for the sins of the world. Though He was completely innocent, without sin, with an illegal trial, He took our place and became our punishment so we could go free and have eternal life in heaven forever. 1 Peter 2:24 says, "He himself bore our sins in His body on the cross so that we might die to sin and live in righteousness, for by His wounds we are healed."

Friends, do we truly grasp what He did for us? He left his home in heaven and came down to earth for us, for you and me. My friend, if you haven't yet, ask Him into your heart to be your Lord and Savior. This is empowering. I urge you to do so today. It's easier with God's help than trying to change on your own.

Our little grandson, almost four, asked Jesus into his heart last week one day. This melts Grandma's heart. Imagine how much more Jesus rejoices every time His sacrifice is acknowledged. Once again, His perfect will is that no one is lost and that all will inherit eternal life through salvation. My thoughts go to his mother Mary, who watched him suffer and be brutally killed. His disciples who followed Him faithfully; did they not think this was the end and probably had so many questions. Yet Jesus had a plan beyond any human understanding. He knew it was Friday, but he also knew that Sunday was coming. He was willing to go through the horrendous process for you, me, and humanity. Choose him today.

Prayer Declaration:
Jesus for the rest of our days and all eternity, we thank, worship and praise you for making a way for us. Thank you for the blood you shed for the sins of the whole world, thank you for the price you paid for us.

April 16
Sunday Is Coming!

Saturday, in the middle of Friday and Sunday, there are many things I wonder about. My heart hurts when I think of what Mary, the mother of Jesus, went through. Did she know He would rise again? It does say in one place she took a lot of things in her heart and pondered them. Let's look at Luke 2:19, which says, "But Mary treasured all these things and pondered them in her heart."

One of those times was after the wise men came to worship Him and brought Him gifts. Another time was when they found Jesus sitting with the elders at the synagogue at only twelve and, of course, the miraculous way she became pregnant after an angel appeared to her. With all that, seeing her son beaten almost beyond recognition, falsely accused, and finally hung on the cross to die, it had to be excruciating for her, awfully unjust, dreadfully unfair, but God had a plan, and yet I imagine back then, the *in-between* day was a long sad difficult day for all of Jesus followers.

It looked like evil won. If you want a vivid picture of what that day looked like, there is a movie called *The Passion*. I will never forget the first time we watched it; it moved me deeply. I was not only profoundly stirred by the anguish and pain Jesus suffered but also by the humility He displayed through it all. Jesus could have defended himself; He could have gotten down off that cross. He could have done so many things, but many times He uttered not a word, no response to their jeering and mockery. My dear friends, we can learn from this man, Jesus, who humbled Himself unto death for us. May His sacrifice not be in vain. Let's share what he has done.

Prayer Declaration:
Jesus my Lord and Savior, we cannot ever repay you for what you did for us but we can accept your precious gift of salvation and live our lives for your honor and glory for the rest of our days.

April 17
Easter Sunday, He Is Rise

He's risen indeed. Today feels consequently joyous in light of the past few days. How wonderful it is to pause and remember the sufferings that Jesus went through for us, knowing of the resurrection on the third day. It's the ultimate story of redemption. There are many scriptures telling this beautiful story. Read it for yourself in Matthew 28:1-6.

Our family celebrated Jesus yesterday by going to church. It was an incredible time of worshiping together with many others. Later that evening, we gathered around our long dining room table, all thirteen of us, as well as some dear friends. We had a simple dinner of soup, bread, condiments, and wine. My husband led the whole family in the Easter story from the Last Supper with the disciples to the resurrection morning.

We ended the meal with communion together and reminiscing on these verses, Mark 14:22, "While they were eating, Jesus took the bread, gave thanks and broke it and gave it to his disciples and broke it saying, take, eat, this is my body," [my husband took the whole loaf and broke it in half, we all took some, the little grandsons too]. "This is my blood of the covenant, which is poured out for many, He said to them, do this in remembrance of Me," Mark 14:24. Again, we all partake, wine, grape juice for the children, my heart is filled to the brim for what Jesus has done and also for this rich, wonderful sacred time with family. All around the table, we shared this beautiful intimate tradition of ours.

Prayer Declaration:
Jesus, thank you doesn't seem enough for what you have done, help us to show you our gratitude for the rest of our lives. Thank you for the cross, the resurrection, for family and fellowship, we praise you, Amen.

April 18
Jesus Is Gentle

As the rain comes down this morning, it's a good time to slow down and reflect. What is it about a good rain shower that is delightfully relaxing? It almost feels like permission to linger a little longer with my coffee and quiet time. My thoughts cannot help but go to Jesus and the disciples this morning. What are they talking about this morning?

We know one of them doubted. We can read about Thomas in John 20:24-29. I love how Jesus invites Thomas to put his fingers into the nail prints of his hands. Only then did he believe and cry out, My Lord and my God! Jesus asks him, have you believed because you have seen Me? Blessed are those who have not seen and yet have believed!" What do you think you and I would have done? Would we have believed? It's easy to think we would have, having been His disciple and hearing Jesus tell of what's going to happen.

Before we judge Thomas, let's think of times we, too, have doubted and just simply refused to believe someone's good news or someone's testimony unless we had evidence. Hearing it from people we knew and trusted wasn't enough. Maybe we were being stubborn, or perhaps we had been hurt by believing before, or we were lacking faith. Especially after a weekend like the disciples just had, I can't even imagine all the emotions and questions they must've had. I love how Jesus dealt gently with Thomas when he was struggling to believe. This same Jesus has this same grace for us!

Prayer Declaration:
Jesus thank you that you are incredibly long-suffering with us. Thank you for being gentle and kind with us, particularly in our times of weakness and unbelief. Help us to believe even when we do not see, or understand things in full. Teach us to trust Jesus in people.

April 19
Nature and Friendships

On this chilly, snowy morning, I'm quickly catching up on things needing done before I head off for a mini vacation. I wish it was somewhere warm, but at least it's two hours further south on the Mississippi River with one of my friends for a few days of rest and fellowship. We reserved this cute little B&B.

Rest and friendships are vitally important for balanced healthy lives. I'm quite excited for this getaway. I wrap up all my loose ends, pack the car and head out. It's a beautiful drive. It's cold and dreary, but Wisconsin has some pretty scenic areas, and I soak it all in on my two-plus hours drive. Worship music is my companion, and by the time I arrive at three thirty, I already feel somewhat rejuvenated. Next, I unpack my bags and get some fresh coffee brewing. This little cottage is adorable, complete with a fireplace, so fun and cozy.

The view from the living room window is beautiful, water, a boat landing, ducks, and pelicans. Later at night, we saw a huge barge coming in with bright lights and a stunning sunset over the water. My soul comes alive in beauty and nature, and I'm thankful God made it all for us to enjoy. Job 12:7-10 says, "But ask the animals and they will teach you, or the birds in the sky and they will tell you, or speak to the earth and it will teach you or let the fish in the sea, which of these does not know that the hand of the Lord has done this, in his hand is the life of every creature and the breath of all mankind."

Prayer Declaration:
Jesus thank you for your beauty in nature you have created for us to enjoy. May we always stop to appreciate all that you have given us so freely, thank you for friendships, rest and nature.

April 20
Lifetime Friendships

Falling asleep last night took a while, till midnight, to be exact. The bed here in the cottage is quite hard. Trains rumble past in the night, not too far from here. At times they'd vibrate, and the whole house shook, plus there was a strange sound I still haven't figured out. Still, a few hours of sleep is still better than none. My friend and I have a light breakfast along with nonstop conversations.

Do you have that friend you can always pick up right where you left off? You may not have talked for a long time, yet this friend is that kind of friend. We have known each other ever since she was a little girl. In fact, we lived as neighbors when we were both still Amish, so there is never a lack of conversation. She and her two sisters would often come to our house when they were growing up.

After we were married and lived next door to them, I appreciated their help. Anytime they would come over to play with the boys, they would also help me with my never-ending workload. One of the three sisters, the middle one, ended up marrying my brother. It's quite special to me. She is the best sister-in-law a girl could ever have.

These three girls have always had a special place in my heart for reasons that are not my story to tell, but I do love how God brings these special people and friendships into our lives that sometimes last a lifetime. Proverbs 17:17 speaks about these types of friendship, "A friend loves at all times and a brother, [or in this case sisters], are born for a time of adversity." The four of us have been friends through the thick and thin of life and definitely our share of adversities.

Prayer Declaration:
Jesus thank you for friendships that last a lifetime. Thank you that the hard times drew us together instead of splitting us apart. I pray for each person to find good long-lasting friendships in their lives.

April 21
Protect Your Sleep

Have you ever had a bad dream or a nightmare? If you did, then you know the awful feeling of wanting to run or speak, and yet you absolutely can't. Or you desperately want to know what it means, but when you ask God, you hear nothing. I went to bed early last night after a delicious dinner with my friend at a restaurant called The Barn. They're a unique and special place. However, I literally could not sleep till hours later in spite of feeling exhausted. When I finally did fall asleep, I woke up shaking and crying out. It felt like a nightmare because it was so real. It felt like someone had come into my room and was standing beside my bed, it seemed like they had evil intentions, but try as I might, I couldn't speak, couldn't move until I woke up.

Needless to say, sleep really eluded me for a long time after that. As I lay, I pondered, prayed, and rebuked what felt like an evil or a [Biblical reference] 'dumb spirit,' meaning you can't talk and maybe deaf too.

I told my friend the next morning, and we kind of laughed about it, but at the time, it was not funny at all.

I do, however, believe that dreams often can mean something, or it might be a way of our subconscious telling us something. Perhaps it can even be a warning that God allows us to have. The good news is, we can take authority over those and declare it will not happen to me or my loved ones in the name of Jesus. We pray for these things. James 4:7 says, "Submit yourself, [your dreams included], therefore to God, resist the devil, [his evil intentions], and he will flee from you." Psalms 4:8 says, "In peace I will both lie down and sleep, for you alone O Lord, make dwell in safety." There are many comforting and powerful verses for our dreams and sleep times.

Prayer Declaration:
Jesus thank you that you will protect us and teach us to dwell on your promises, in your truth, especially before bedtime.

April 22
God's Best

Waking up in my own bed this morning with my own pillow and my husband. Sometimes blessings in life are so easily taken for granted until we don't have them for a few nights. We went to bed early. I slept twice as well as I did the last two nights. When I was younger, missing sleep was something that wasn't such a big deal, but once you're over fifty, things change. After packing up the cottage yesterday, we had one more coffee and lunch together. My friend and I both headed in opposite directions toward home. My drive was again beautiful and scenic along the Mississippi, the mighty Mississippi that I love.

I stopped at my daughter Lorinda's house. We had a good time in her cozy quaint place. I fell asleep until my next appointment, a facial. If you have never had one, I would encourage you to try one; they are heavenly. Once again, I fell asleep!

I drove another hour home through the rain and had a very relaxing evening with my husband. With hot cups of tea, I fill him in on my mini vacation. He tells me about what happened here at home. My friend and I reminisced a lot about the days gone by and the things we experienced. Coming from the same background, we know each other so well and had many of the same struggles coming out of the Amish culture. As I settled into my chair last night with my cup of tea, the rain falling outside and my husband beside me, my thoughts go to this verse in Psalm 16:6, "The boundary lines have fallen for me in pleasant places, surely I have a delightful inheritance." Yes, I do thank you, Jesus, for all my wonderful blessings, in my rich Godly inheritance. I will forever be grateful to my parents for that and, most of all, to You, Jesus.

Prayer Declaration:
I praise you Jesus for your goodness, your mercy and my inheritance as your daughter.

Let Him Carry You

So how are things going in your life right now? Are you in a season of smooth sailing, on the mountaintop, or are you in the valley and life feels hard and unfair? I told one of my clients this the other day. It's actually in the hard times that we grow. Only if we lean into it and learn what we can from the tough times we become better and not bitter. I pray you choose to become better because bitterness can eat us from the inside out.

My devotional this morning said, "In the middle of the pain you didn't cause, the reality is, you didn't know what was coming in your life, but it can still be beautiful," Lysa Keurst. She speaks from experience and has some excellent books on how to overcome heartbreak and disappointment. Perhaps you are just in over your head with work and struggling with the everyday grind of life. There is help for that too.

Isaiah 40:29 says, "He gives strength to the weary and increases the power of the weak." Isn't that encouraging? This hasn't been the best week for me either, dealing with different issues and things, like health and office work, and feeling overwhelmed. Once again, I found God's grace is always sufficient, and again He says, "For my strength is made perfect in weakness" 2 Corinthians 12:9. We don't have to be strong every minute of every day. Let's remember to lean into God's strength and let Him carry us through the hard times. Whatever you are feeling or facing today, pause and give it to God. He has the best plans and answers for us.

Prayer Declaration:
Jesus, teach us how to surrender quicker, teach us how to invite you into our pain. Speak to us, thank you for being strong where we are so weak. Thank you that your grace truly is sufficient.

April 24
Memories of Dad

Today is exciting for a few reasons. One, the weather is warmer. Two, working with my husband, who agreed to work on a project with me that had been waiting for a long time, mostly because we needed nice weather to do it. We start our day with an early brunch, so we don't have to stop for lunch. We work hard until five thirty and get the job mostly done. What a wonderful feeling of relief. Three, one of my favorite things to do as a couple is to work on outside projects, whether landscaping, gardening, or mowing the lawn. It has always brought me so much joy to do it with my husband. We do make a great team. I'm usually the dreamer; he brings them to life and often adds great tips I didn't think of.

He chuckled at me as I pulled on my gloves. He never wears any. My answer is always the same, "I learned this from my dad," and I did. Growing up in the middle of nine siblings, I don't have a ton of memories of doing things with my dad. I have four brothers and four sisters. I was the middle child, but I do remember cleaning up outside with him. Dad's farm was meticulous, and he always said to us, *'butzet uch'! Which means* 'cleanup'. He loved a good fire. We would burn trash and stray branches, clean out the fence rows, or fix fences. No matter what we were cleaning, we almost always had a fire going. I loved it!

I, to this day, love a good fire! My husband could tell you stories. I may have needed the fire department a time or two. My dad always wore gloves. I'm grateful for all he taught me as a little Amish girl. His legacy lives on even though he is gone. I long to the best of my ability, to live out Deuteronomy 5:16, "Honor your father and mother that your days may be long in the land the Lord your God is giving you."

Prayer Declaration:
Jesus thank you for Godly parents who taught me so much and most importantly about having a relationship with you. May every parent, son and daughter's relationship be restored because of You.

April 25
Pursue Relationships

My dad is one of my heroes. One of the strongest men I know, having prevailed over different obstacles in his lifetime, he overcame several addictions in his time here on Earth as well as battled diabetes in his later years, and finally, heart failure. Yet he hardly ever complained. He was a man of few words, seldom, if ever, judging anyone. He showed me how to live life in a lot of ways. I will always treasure the relationship we had, especially in his last five years here on Earth.

I want to plead with those of you who have left the Amish as we did. Don't be too proud to dress a certain way if that's what it takes to go home to visit your Amish parents. This is one way you can honor them. I hear so many say they haven't seen their family in years because they won't accept them or let them come home unless they dress a certain way. If you can't dress a certain way for a few hours to honor someone, you might not be as free as you think. It's my humble opinion.

I reached out to my parents after moving back here to Wisconsin. I asked them what it would take to have a relationship with them. They requested I dress plain. It's not impossible, friends, and well worth the salvaged relationships. Let's remember we are the ones who left their culture for reasons they may never understand. Maybe it really is up to us to pursue relationships, no matter what culture any one of us is in today.

If we have strained or broken relationships, let's look at ourselves first and ask what we can do to make things better. Love always wins. Relationships are worth it, especially with our families. In Matthew 15:4, "We hear it again, honor your father, mother and anyone who curses their father or mother is to be put to death." The Bible quoting this was a firm return to respecting parents as many had abandoned doing: Not death to the body but to our pride.

Prayer Declaration:
Jesus teaches true honor and humility especially to our parents, to treat them as we want our children to treat us. I pray for restored relationships in every family, starting with us, Lord.

April 26
Hope and Promises

Today I had a rough start. My back pain flared up again, as well as a nagging headache; they often go hand in hand. Guess what? We are getting more snow and rain this morning. I let the weather and the pain get to me and end up having a silly argument with my husband, which puts me in an even worse frame of mind. He gives me the space I need, some time to myself, and tells me to just do what I need today to feel better. So to the couch, I head with my ice pack and oils in the diffuser for the headache. I fell soundly asleep and slept for several hours; waking up, I feel entirely better now. Now would be a good time to call my husband and apologize for my bad attitude.

He, of course, graciously forgives me, and gently reminds me that the weather shouldn't dictate our attitudes. I know this, but some days my humanness is so human. Do you ever have those days? If so, how do you cope? I found a nap usually works wonders, especially if there is pain and fatigue involved. Yes, I long for the day I will be able to rise above it all, whether it's a tiff with my husband, physical pain, or endless winter.

Romans 5:1-4, "Says therefore since we have been justified through faith we have peace with God through our Lord Jesus Christ. Whom we had gained access by faith into His grace. In which we now stand, we rejoice in the hope of the glory of God. Not only so but we also rejoice in our sufferings because we know suffering produces perseverance, character and character hope, and hope does not disappoint us because God has poured out His love into our hearts by the Holy Spirit whom He has given us." Hold on to hope; it doesn't disappoint.

Prayer Declaration:
Jesus, when hard times come, teach us to meditate on verses like these, to hold on to all we have in you, to count our blessings and not let our trials completely break us, fill us with your restoring peace, joy and hope every morning.

April 27
Choose Your Attitude

Today I feel silly that I allowed yesterday's weather to dictate my mood, even for a short period of time. My disclaimer is: even my doctor says my menopausal body needs more Vitamin D. I feel significantly better in the sun, but still no excuse.

There is this saying that is meaningful, and it goes something like this, *how we respond to what happens to us, is almost always more important than what happens to us.* It seems like a mouthful, but the point is we can't always control what happens to us, but we can always choose how we respond. Our attitude is a choice, and that's good news. It's incredibly difficult at times. It's easy to have a good attitude when everything goes right, life is good, and we are not facing any giants in our lives. Those are the days we feel we can conquer the world, and having a good attitude is easy. But what about those other days, the days we struggle with chronic pain or a diagnosis from the doctor or whatever it is?

Perhaps a wayward child, a person in your life, an argument with your husband, or something silly can make us feel misunderstood or overwhelmed. If life seems to be too much, are we still required to have a good attitude? It really is our choice, but we would do well to live out Ephesians 4:31-32, "Let all bitterness and wrath, anger and clamor and evil speaking be put away from you with all malice and be tenderhearted forgiving one another even as God for Christ's sake has forgiven you."

Prayer Declaration:
Jesus, it is only through your grace and power we can live in victory above our circumstances, help us, teach us how to use our worries as steppingstones, that we may choose our words and attitudes carefully in every season. Jesus, we want to walk pure and blameless to represent You to the world around us.

April 28
Travel Light

Do you enjoy packing your bags for a trip? If you do, I need all your tips and secrets. I used to completely not enjoy it and even dread it, but I've learned the more I do it, the easier it gets and the less I stress. I'm also learning to pack lighter. Do we really need to take forty outfits for a few days? An exaggeration, but you get the point, right? This time we only brought carry-ons for a whole weekend, which feels like progress.

This can also apply to our journey/ trip through life. If we do that hard thing over and over, it will eventually become easier for us. It's the same as if we drag less with us. What kind of baggage do we carry? What type of luggage are we hauling that we don't need? It may be emotional wounds, pain that hinders our progress, perhaps physical pain, excess weight or financial debt, too much stuff, or too much clutter.

What could you get rid of today that would help you travel lighter on your journey? Do you need to forgive someone and get that weight of unforgiveness off your shoulders? Whether you are carrying physical, emotional, or spiritual baggage today, please know there is help available. Counselors, therapists, nutritionists, doctors, and above all, the Holy Spirit and God's Word. They are available, and we must make that choice. Change is up to us; no one can do the work for us. We can choose and partner with the right people to help us. Hebrews 12:1 says it well, "Therefore since we are surrounded by such a great cloud, let us throw off everything that hinders us and the sins that so easily entangles us and let us run with perseverance the race marked out for us."

Prayer Declaration:
Yes, Lord, this is our heart's cry, teach us how to walk light, free, unencumbered from the world, from any addictions and baggage that hold us back.

April 29
Thank Ask Praise

My husband and I are currently sitting on the runway in Denver, CO, waiting for takeoff. We will be spending the weekend with friends and team members in Montrose, CO. An early morning flight required two cups of coffee to get through all that goes with flying. The actual flight is enjoyable and almost always lulls me right to sleep. The long lines, getting through security, and lack of space are not so fun.

As a little girl growing up Amish, I remember how excited we would get on the rare occasions we would see an airplane fly overhead high in the sky. We would always excitedly tell each other. Another wonderful memory is when our whole family had *fun days* in the summer. My mom was very good about planning those days and making them happen. Now they are among some of my favorite childhood memories. We would go to local parks for picnics and sometimes travel to a zoo, but my favorite of all was the several times we went to an airport and watched the planes take off. This was way before 9/11, so they even let us come inside the airport. It was fascinating to watch, and at that time in my life, I never dreamed that one day I would get to fly in those big birds.

Take a moment today to count your blessings, maybe even make a list of the ways God has surprised you in your life. What unexpected blessings and gifts has he given you? We do well when we remember what God has done and ask him, *God, what else do you have for my life?* Remembering, thanking, praising, and asking is a powerful combination to move God's heart.

Prayer Declaration:
"Let all that I am praise the Lord. May I never forget the good things you did for me," Psalms 103:2. *Yes and Amen Lord! One thousand thank you proclamations will never be enough for what you have done. You are a good, good Father. You have good plans for our lives when we let you lead us.*

April 30
Water is Life

We arrived here in beautiful Colorado yesterday afternoon in time to help our friends and team members set up for their event today. We ended the evening with great food and fellowship. This morning we all gathered along with many others for wonderful food, learning, growing, and raising enough money to drill another well.

Our dream would be for every village in Africa to have their own well. Water is Life is our logo for Africa. The villages that don't have wells are subject to contaminated water holes. The villagers' children who do have water are usually more able to go to school if their parents can afford it. My husband says it best, he says for them, water is the gateway to the gospel. Water makes so many things possible for them. It accurately describes the gospel as we are able to meet people's needs in a physical way. It will often leave them more open to spirituality. Our Father cares about them.

Have you ever been thirsty for a few hours? For me, it's difficult, yet we can so easily take our fresh, good water for granted. My daughters and I had the privilege of being present when one of the wells in Africa was dedicated. The pure joy of rejoicing and worshiping around a new well that night was something I will never forget. This was a special, holy moment. Heidi and Roland have helped so many in Africa drink the 'living water' as well. John 4:14 speaks of Living Water; Jesus said, "But whoever drinks of the water that I shall give him shall never thirst but the water that I shall give him shall be in him a well of water springing up into eternal life."

Prayer Declaration:
Jesus, we thank you for the living water that never runs dry. Lead us to continually share that water with people daily. Thank you for helping us make a difference in the natural as well.

May 1
Jesus, the Master Pilot

This is the day that the Lord has made; let us rejoice and be glad in it. It's a beautiful spring morning. I'm hoping to get outside and enjoy it later today. Currently, though, we are high in the sky, flying home from beautiful Colorado. Their endless sunshine and the pristine snow-capped mountains make this one of my favorite places to visit. There's something about the mountains that brings peace and tranquility to my soul, especially when they are snow-capped against a blue-sky backdrop. There is also something very soothing about flying that literally lulls me to sleep. It isn't uncommon for me to sleep through whole flights. My husband will attest to this, it's peaceful, and often, so my blanket is always a must. Soft movement and sounds of air make perfect sleeping conditions. However, our flight from Denver to Montrose on Friday was quite the opposite.

Never have I experienced such high turbulence for such a length of time. It was quite scary, to the point where some were screaming and almost crying. I, too, was quite uncomfortable and scared. I closed my eyes tightly, hung on to my husband's arm, and prayed to my master pilot. I knew that He was in control ultimately, and He would take care of us just as He promised numerous times throughout His word.

When we give Him full control of our life's plan, so to speak, we truly have nothing to fear because He always has the best plan in mind for us. Psalms 91 is a huge comfort to me. The first time we ever flew in a jet was not long after 9/11. I was praying, telling God about my fear, and I heard him say read Psalms 91. It has become an anchor for my life.

Prayer Declaration:
Jesus, thank you for your protection and your guidance in the turbulent times of our lives. Teach us to trust you unconditionally and to remember you always see our whole lives and not just one event.

May 2
In-Law Relationships

One of our lovely daughters-in-law has her 27th birthday today. She is the epitome of beauty inside and out; not only is she the best wife for our son but also an amazing mama to our two grandsons. Our son met her at a music and arts camp. They fell in love and got married five years ago this month. She is a wonderful addition to our family, a true description of "Not letting adornment be merely outward but adorning the hidden person of her heart with the imperishable beauty of a gentle, quiet spirit which in God's sight is very precious" 1 Peter 3:3-4.

Have you ever met a person who just exudes warmth and acceptance to everyone she meets? Who never judges anyone or says anything negative but is quick to always point out the positives. It's not because she has had life handed to her on a silver platter. She has a wild story, having been given up for adoption as a baby and then adopted by a loving Christian family. At this point in her life, she has a thriving relationship with both her biological parents and her adoptive parents. She has a wonderful redemptive story to tell.

It makes me sad when I hear of difficult in-law situations. Perhaps it's become so much the norm that people just expect that? What can you do to pursue relationships with your in-laws today? You can have a beautiful and blessed relationship! Put in the effort; it is well worth it.

Prayer Declaration:
Jesus, I ask for favor and blessing on every person. I ask for favor and blessing on every in-law relationship today, heal and restore what is broken and show us what we can do.

May 3
Spring and Spiritual Cleaning

Blessed and delightful sunshine this afternoon. Sitting in it for a few minutes, soaking it up, healing permeated throughout my body and soul. I feel like this is the longest, coolest spring we've had in a while, which will make us appreciate the warmth even more, when it comes to life. In nature, we have so many common themes, even spring cleaning or any cleaning for that matter. It's similar to purging our thoughts, hearts, and minds. My favorite way to deep clean is to put on some worship music and sing along. It's not my favorite task by far, but once I've started, it's very satisfying again.

With any hard thing in our lives, like a new eating plan or workout regimen, isn't it so rewarding once you get started and see the difference you are making? What are you facing right now that looks big or overwhelming? Get started. Once you are in a rhythm, momentum builds and gets easier. If you hit a wall, take a break but don't quit and don't give up, and you will see wonderful results. Seeing my sparkling clean kitchen and living room windows is worth every bit of effort it took to do it all. While we clean, we can take that time to worship or pray, asking God to cleanse our inside. One of my favorite prayers from scripture is, "Create a clean heart in me O God, and renew a right spirit within me," Psalms 51:10.

Prayer Declaration:
Jesus, do that in all of us, teach us how to be clean vessels for you to dwell in, give us strength and courage to tackle the overwhelming tasks and habits in our lives, renew a right spirit in us daily.

May 4
Peace and Trouble

John 16:33 says, "I have told you these things so that in Me you may have peace in this world, you will have trouble but take heart I have overcome the world." What if we could remember this whenever we are going through hard times? Remember that Jesus has already overcome anything. He says we may have peace. Give me a dose of that already! Most times, when we think of trouble, we tend to think of huge obstacles, perhaps death, sickness, rejection, or all kinds of things, but what about the little things that want to pull us down on a daily basis? Today I hustled around to meet a new client appointment. It's finally so beautiful and sunny outside I am itching to get outside. However, I'm wrestling with brain fog, headache, back pain, and guests wanting to stop by and need beds tonight. We have more guests coming this weekend, which I'm grateful for in spite of the way I'm currently feeling.

I humble myself, ask for prayer, and am completely honest with a few trusted friends. Hours later, my spirits have lifted, the headache is gone without pain pills, and my doctor has a new plan for me to try. I even get to finish a big project we've been working on outside. I feel my friend's prayers; I know this peace God speaks about. He helped me rise above my troubles today. He also helped me practice what I preach by and make boundaries and say no to the guests wanting beds tonight. It's okay to say no sometimes. We don't have to serve beyond what we are able to at times. Physically and emotionally.

Prayer Declaration:
Jesus, thank you for your peace, help us to rise above our troubles just as you taught us to, bless and touch every person in whatever area of struggle they are facing right now, Amen.

May 5
Run to Him

My devotional had this verse in it. I had already been pondering it in my heart. Luke 11:39 says, "Then the Lord said to him now then you Pharisees clean the outside of the cup and dish but inside you are full of greed and wickedness." Spring cleaning makes me think about these things. I was reaching some dirty hard-to-get corners in the laundry room and the main bathroom, thinking, isn't it a lot like us humans? Sometimes we put out our clean and most polished together moments for others to see, whether it's on social media or in person. But what about those ugly, dirty, tucked-away corners of our hearts? What if we invite God into those areas and give him permission to heal us, clean us up, and bring those parts of our hearts back to life?

This is exactly what I did last night. After a rough day, I surrendered and invited God into the mess with me. I confessed to him, Jesus, I don't know why I keep going through this same struggle over and over. What do you want me to learn, and why do I feel so hopeless and broken in this area? Instead of hiding, the next step is calling my counselor and being real and vulnerable with her.

Dear friends, nothing is too messy for Jesus. There is no condemnation from Him, so let us remember to run to Him and not from Him. When he illuminates our issues, our dirty heart corners, he is the master cleaner and healer. He can make us like new!

Prayer Declaration:
Jesus, help us to run to you and let you let you reach those hidden places. Jesus, we invite you in, you are welcome to bring your cleansing and healing power.

May 6
Pursue Healing

Where there is trauma in your life, there will be triggers. The trauma area is often out of our control, but the triggers are ours to deal with. Pursue healing with me, my friend; what is it for you? What triggers you? One of my triggers is when I feel I'm being taken advantage of. When I'm being taken for granted and expected to do things even when I don't have the physical energy or the will to do what is being asked of me. I'm also still coming out of the toxic traits of wanting to please everyone all the time. I find myself in over my head quite frequently. Saying no is one of my hardest words. I believe our strong points are also often our weak points; that is why we need others to help us to see what we can't see, to gently point out our blind spots. Do we allow this? Do we have those trusted people in our lives?

Proverbs 11:14 speaks of this, "Where no counsel is, the people fall but in the multitude of counselors there is safety." I don't have a multitude of counselors, but I have a few, and they are working with me on getting completely free. Do you frequently say yes when your heart is screaming no?

Please stop and check your heart. It could come from a place of people-pleasing over God motivated. Don't hear me wrong. We should lay our lives down for one another, but not at the expense of our own health and destiny. The   Boundaries book has some excellent biblical advice on saying no and prioritizing what God is asking of you first and foremost.

Prayer Declaration:
Jesus, help each one of us recognize where we are triggered and why, I pray for counselors and trusted people to help each one of us to be brave enough to go after complete healing.

True Hospitality

Today my husband and I started out with coffee, connection, and devotion time. Next, we host a call with one of the couples we mentor. Before we are done, a few more of our friends and team members arrive, weary and worn after traveling all night. We serve them a hot breakfast. One of my favorite Saturday clients arrives. It's always a rich and rewarding time with her.

Somewhere along the line, our daughter Lorinda comes home. She and I take the time to soak up some beautiful sun and catch up with each other. She and her dad watched the Bucks basketball game while I prepared food for our evening guests. My niece and her little family arrived late in the afternoon, and we had a sweet time together. It's a day and evening of food, fellowship, and hospitality.

Romans 12:13 says, "Contribute to the needs of the saints and seek to show hospitality," or Hebrews 13:2 "Do not neglect to show hospitality to strangers for thereby some have entertained angels unawares." Wow, wouldn't you like to entertain angels today? It's an easy free, flowing day of hospitality for me because I've learned a few things about hosting people. They will always remember how you make them feel. My floors and windows were not cleaned today, and guess what? No one cared. What mattered was the rich conversation that happened over homemade ice cream and grilled chicken. I recently read this; true hospitality is when people leave your home feeling better about themselves than they do about you; amazing, I want that, Jesus.

Prayer Declaration:
Teach us the true meaning and gift of hospitality your way, help us to remember it's all about You and not about us. Help us to bless, encourage and give up our time, energy, and resources for our guests.

May 8
Mother's Day

It's one of my favorite days of the year; my day starts early with a 6:00 AM shower. I get ready, grab my coffee, and head to church. I'm blessed and delighted to be on the worship team for Mother's Day. My Mom and I have a heartfelt chat on the way to church. We discuss how it's easy to dwell on all the ways we fell short as mothers, but if we did the best, we knew how it's all God requires of us. My mom is one of my heroes. Her life was not all roses and butterflies, but at almost 80 years old, she is one of the strongest, healthiest people I know. She also taught me the importance of having a relationship with Jesus and praying to Him in my own words.

Thank you, Mom. I saw her on her knees beside her bed many times and also reading her Bible. I specifically remember her fasting for a couple of days for me in my rebellious teenage years, and I recall feeling convicted. Again, thanks, Mom! Most of the family meets me at church, and afterwards we go eat at one of my favorite places.

We decided to go golfing, my first time on a big course; so much fun being out in the sun with my family. They showered me with gifts and flowers, and the girls gave me a beautiful dress. My heart was full by the end of the day. My children's love reminds me a lot of God's love. They love me unconditionally. There are so many things I would do over as a mom whose children are now grown. Yet they love, bless and honor me beyond what I deserve, as Jesus does for all of us. My biggest desire for my children as a mother is to see them walking in the fullness of all that god has called them to. Proverbs 31:28 "Her children rise up and call her blessed, her husband also and he praises her." I certainly felt celebrated by my children and husband today. I pray this for all Mothers tonight!

Prayer Declaration:
Jesus, I am blessed among women, thank you that in spite of all my imperfections and shortcomings, my family still lavishes love on me, I am undone.

Mystery of Healing

After a full fun and wonderful weekend, today is a perfect day to take a break and go get a massage. My back pain is to the point where I can hardly even take a deep breath. While I wait for my divine healing, I keep pursuing healing in the natural with things like deep tissue massages and good supplements. Do you ever wonder why some ailments get healed and others don't? It remains a mystery to me. When Jesus healed people when He was here on earth, seldom did He do it the same way twice.

Sometimes He only spoke the word, and people picked up their beds and walked. Another time he used mud and spit, and yet another time, a man was told to dip in the Jordan River seven times. Do you think Jesus used a variety of ways so that we can never make it into a formula? Jesus sent out his 12 disciples with these instructions in Matthew 10:8, "Heal the sick, raise the dead, cleanse those who have leprosy, drive out demons, freely you have received freely give."

In my own life, I'm so thankful for the healing I have received physically and emotionally, whether through disciples of Jesus or doctors and therapists. I truly believe, just like in the Bible times, your healing can come in different ways. If you need healing today, don't be afraid to ask Jesus. He is the master healer, and He loves to partner with His people to bring divine healing and hope to every hurting or broken part of his sons and daughters.

Prayer Declaration:
Thank you, Jesus, for your plan not only to save us but to make us healed and whole. Show and teach us how to partner with You and bring healing to others through Your power with the Holy Spirit, Amen.

May 10
Birds and Us

What a beautiful balmy spring morning. Orioles, hummingbirds, and wrens are back. The little wren's song is bigger than its body and never ceases to amaze me, the same with the tiny hummingbird and how they hang there sipping the sugar water; their tiny wings are just whirring. They completely fascinate me. How do they survive on sugar water? It doesn't seem very nutritious now, does it? Isn't it so kind of God to make all these unique little and big birds for us to watch and enjoy? The little wren sings loudly multiple times a day, the oriole has a unique song, and the hummingbirds fight and chase each other away from the feeder. Doesn't it sound like humans in some ways?

What the Bible has to say about the birds is very encouraging to me. "Look at the birds of the air, they do not sow or reap or store away in barns and yet your heavenly Father feeds them, are you not much more valuable than they are?" Matthew 6:26.

Let that sink in for a second. There's also this poem I learned years ago that goes something like this, "Said the Robin to the Sparrow, I should really like to know why these anxious human beings rush about and worry so. Said the Sparrow to the Robin, "friend I think that it must be that they have no heavenly Father, such as cares for you and me," by Elizabeth Sheeney. So, what can you and I learn from the birds of the air? A lot, I think. We are more valuable to our heavenly Father than the birds; let's trust Him to take care of our needs, too. He is able and willing sometimes; we just have to allow Him to.

Prayer Declaration:
God, thank you for your provision and care, help us to remember to look to you and not our own strength, in our own ways, to let go and let you be a father to us.

May 11
Relationships vs Rules

One of my nephews left the Amish culture about a year ago. He came to our house last night for dessert. He was on his way back from spending the winter on a ranch in Arizona. He is a cowboy at heart and loves horses, roping, riding, and all that goes with it. We talked late last night and again for several hours over breakfast this morning. My husband and I processed with him and helped him find the answers within himself. He has a heart of gold. His one desire is to please God and be at the center of his will. At one point, he exclaimed, *being in a church with no rules is actually harder than having rules.*

Yes, son, you're absolutely right because that puts the responsibility right back on us. We answer to God directly; we must search out the answers and rules in the Bible for ourselves instead of man-made rules. These rules vary so much from one community to the next, depending on what men made them and what community you live in.

My nephew's journey reminds me so much of our own journey. He, too, is hungry for God and all that is to be experienced in Him, but he's not always sure where God is to be found. Especially outside of his structured culture, where our relationship with God depends so much on our performance. God always desires relationships over rules. In fact, Isaiah 64:6 says, "All of us have become like one who is unclean and all our righteous acts are like filthy rags, we all shrivel up like a leaf and like the wind our sins sweep us away." We never want to live in willful sin, but we underestimate God's mercy and free gift of salvation. His grace is enough. We are saved through Grace.

Prayer Declaration:
Jesus, thank you for rescuing us out of our sinful states and making us clean through what You suffered on the cross, show us Your heart of mercy and love, teach us to focus on relationship with You Lord which means more than rules. Amen.

May 12
Summer Has Come

It's been in the upper 80s all week. We went from an endless cold spring to summer almost overnight. My cold sun-starved soul is soaking it up with delight. This is my type of weather. Why, then, do I live in a state where it feels like winter for so many more months per year than it does summer? I will have to ask God about that when I get to heaven, but for now, I will try my best to bloom where I am planted. One of my distant dreams is to have a beach house somewhere warm and spend part of our winters there. However, my husband thrives on cold, snow, and snowmobiling. He doesn't do well with the heat at all, so that may never happen. He had a heat stroke baling hay back on the farm in our Amish days. He has never been able to do the heat very well ever since. We compromise and find ways to get both of our needs met. He encourages me to go somewhere warm several times a winter to get my 'sun fix.'

These beautiful summer days make me think of the verse in the Song of Solomon, "For behold the winter is past, the rain is over and gone, the flowers appear on the earth and the time of singing has come, the voice of the turtle dove is heard in our land."

As I sit here on my patio with a second cup of coffee, listening to the birds singing and the wind chimes, seeing the green grass and the trees budding out, my soul rejoices. So, let's remember no matter how long the winter is, summer will come. In the spiritual sense, too, if you are in a dark and difficult place, take heart; this too will melt into something warm and beautiful soon. Hold on to hope.

Prayer Declaration:
Jesus, thank you for all four seasons. Teach us how to embrace, learn and even grow from our cold dark, hard seasons. Help us to find hope in You and look beyond our circumstances.

Roots of Revival

Repotting, rearranging, and moving my house plants around take up a good portion of my morning. Some have outgrown their pots, and some didn't make it over the long winter. It's so satisfying to trim them up and find the best summer places, then soak them with fresh fertilizer water. I read recently that we are no different than house plants, minus the emotions, meaning there are a lot of similarities. When you think about it, we need sun and water, and sometimes we outgrow our current pots, so to speak. Yes, God needs to trim off our unproductive leaves, too, so we can grow taller, fuller, and stronger. Everywhere I look these days, I see green and growth.

My desire is for that new life and growth to carry over into our spiritual life. Every day, every season, and every year, I pray we would grow bigger, deeper spiritually, more mature, and more settled, but never satisfied. Jeremiah 17:88 says it best, "They will be a like a tree planted by the water that sends out its roots by the stream, it does not fear when heat comes. Its leaves are always green, it has no worries in a year of drought and never fails to bear fruit."

Tonight at church, we sang about revival, God doing a new thing, and raising a Hallelujah in the middle of the mystery. We live in a world that's gone a little off the rails, confused about so many things. I, too, pray for revival. It starts with us encountering Jesus and His Presence.

Prayer Declaration:
I pray that Jesus would encounter each one of us and wake up the deepest darkest places in our hearts. Bring new life, new hope and new growth that will result in revival over the earth. Jesus, start with me. Come and do a new thing in each one of us, teach us how to grow deep roots in you that will never run dry.

May 14
Look to Jesus

It's a beautiful, sunny, and very busy day. My daughter Lorinda came home last night, so we had coffee and connection time on the back patio. Since she is currently single so she comes home more often, which makes Mama's heart happy. She helps me not take myself so seriously and does crazy things like hiding behind our bedroom door, jumping out, and scaring the living daylights out of me. Or singing at the top of her lungs to music, using a broomstick for the mic. She keeps me young and makes me laugh. Isn't that our kids in general, though? Lorinda also writes amazing songs but sings them for only Jesus and me. I'm okay with that and feel quite privileged.

One of our sons needs help with moving to their own property today. They are moving 15 minutes closer to us and on the same road as one of our other sons. Which is so fun; they will live only a mile apart.

We bring home the little boys, our grandsons, for a few hours, play and catch up with them. We hadn't seen them for three weeks, and it's absolutely wonderful to be with them again.

They play with Grandpa while I get ready for church; we eat ice cream cones before we leave. Listening to their favorite little worship songs all the way to church, little Zander sings along word for word, and he melts Grandma's heart. Zion settles in for a nap. I checked them into their rooms at church and slipped into the sanctuary for worship. One of our sons and daughters-in-law are on the worship team tonight.

Worship is anointed and amazing, then I slip out of the service and hurry home to pack my bags for an early morning flight. This is my blessed life; this is my family; this is why family is so worth all you go through to raise them up for Him. You can do this, parents. Look at Him alone; He alone has the answers.

Prayer Declaration:
For this reason, I kneel before the Father from whom every family in heaven and on Earth derives its name. Thank you for your Son Jesus, His plan for family, the only thing we get to bring to heaven with us. Thank you for giving us wisdom, courage and strength to raise them for You.

May 15
Friends for Life

Our family is able to do things now we never could have done with our horse and buggy. Like this morning, we left our house around 5:00 AM and made it to Portland, OR, in time for a 4:00 PM wedding. These are the things we will probably never take for granted, the conveniences of flying, technology, and many more things. We arrive in plenty of time, rent a car and check into our hotel early, to rest and get ready. Rain showers are off and on in this part of Oregon, with a lush and almost tropical feeling.

The drive out to the wedding is winding and dazzling, the ceremony is beautiful and heartfelt, and the fellowship with longtime friends is wonderful. This particular family became some of our closest friends, like family. For eight years, we did life with them, when we lived out West, on a journey of freedom together. To this day, they are some of our best friends.

Don't you just love how God puts the right people in your lives for the right seasons of life when you need them? If you do have those close friends around you currently, don't take them for granted. These types of rich friendships often last a lifetime. We are always able to pick up right where we left off, be real and vulnerable and laugh a lot too. There's always good food too! Mast family, if you are reading this, you will always have a special place in our hearts, you believed in us in a time when we ourselves didn't, and that was a huge gift to us. Thank you for all you've been to us. Thank you for your friendships, even now, all these years later. "We thank God for you and mention you in our prayers" 1st Thessalonians 1:2.

Prayer Declaration:
Jesus, today I thank you specifically for deep friendships, for progress from horse and buggy to airplanes. Bring the right people for advancement to each one of us, in the precise, right seasons Jesus, Amen.

May 16
Roots and Home

Sitting at the airport in beautiful Portland, Oregon. Sipping on an extra hot cinnamon sorghum latte; so delicious, just what I need for the flight. Normally sleep is my favorite thing to do on flights, but today I should catch up on reading, writing, and editing. After a whirlwind weekend, thinking of going home fills me with joy. I love home and what my husband and I have built from the ground up, not just homes and land but the roots we put down with our family and grandchildren.

I rejoice in this feeling of belonging and security. There were plenty of times when we were finding our way out of the Amish culture that didn't feel like this. Sometimes it felt like we were all alone in the world and we didn't belong anywhere. It can be a lonely, confusing feeling, which is why we shouldn't go by our feelings only because we never were actually alone. It just felt like it sometimes.

God was always right there with us every step of the way. He loves to teach us to put our trust in Him alone, and to truly follow Him instead of people, places, and things. Deuteronomy 31:6 says, "Be strong and courageous, do not be afraid or terrified because of them, for the Lord your God goes with you. He will never leave you nor forsake you," This is our testimony. I'm so thankful for what God has led us to and how He has blessed us. If things in your life right now are unsettled and it doesn't all make sense, just stay close to Jesus, hang on to the hem of His garments, and He will lead you. He is trustworthy even when we are not.

Prayer Declaration:
Jesus, thank you for your faithfulness, teach us to trust You even when the road gets rough and hard at times, to trust you when all around us feels unstable and lonely, You will lead us home.

May 17
Psalms of David

When all around, my soul gives way, He then is all my hope and stay. That's a little of what my life feels like this morning. Like it's pressing in on every side. I just want to go back to bed and pull the covers over my head and let the world go on without me for a while. Instead, I do get up, push through my workout and my morning routine, get showered, dressed, and ready to drive the 2.5 hours to my doctor's appointment in Madison. She has been one of my saving graces in this menopause season. She is caring and compassionate, very wise and knowledgeable. If I'm ever able to help other women when they get to this stage in their lives, I would be more than happy to. Everything I've learned has been through my own experience and research for the past 10-ish years.

These days I can identify so much with David in the Psalms. I just love how real and honest he was with God. One day he was praising God and seemed to be on top of things. In the next day or chapter, he was deeply discouraged and crying out to God for all the things. David, I feel you, me too. In Psalm 61:1-2, we can read some of his prayers, "Hear my cry oh God, listen to my prayer from the ends of the earth, I call to you, I call as my heart grows faint, lead me to the rock that is higher than I," verse 5-6, "Find rest, all my soul in God alone, my hope comes from Him, He alone is my rock and my salvation my fortress, I will not be shaken."

There are so many heartfelt and beautiful Psalms. Read them for yourself if you need encouragement or even to know how to pray or praise, the Psalms are all this in one. There are multiple ways to communicate with God through Psalms.

Prayer Declaration:
Jesus, thank you for being a rock that will never move, that You are unshakable when all around us is shaking. Teach us how to cling to You in our dark and discouraging times. Amen.

May 18
Prioritize My Time

Things look brighter, better, and more hopeful today. Again, I'm drawn to the Psalms, "Praise be to the Lord, for he has heard my cry for mercy, the Lord is my strength and my shield, my heart trusts in Him and I am helped. My heart leaps for joy and I will give thanks to Him in song," Psalms 28:6-7. Yes, Lord, thank you for your help and mercy. When You allow us to go through difficult things, it is not to hurt us but to grow us and sanctify us. Pruning is never fun but so fruitful. The long drive to the doctor yesterday provided the time to have some much-needed and difficult conversations between my husband and me. It brought clarity and understanding to both of us. Why do we avoid the hard conversations in life?

Why are we so afraid of the real, raw, and messy parts of people's lives, especially in our own lives? Being open and honest with ourselves and others is the purest form of relationship.

Some of the difficult lessons I'm still learning are how to make boundaries with people. How to prioritize my time so those closest to my heart don't only get the scraps of time that's left of my tired self? My husband and my doctor are both concerned about my constant fatigue and headaches, but thank God we all have a plan moving forward. I'm so grateful for people in my life who care about me and my health and help me take steps toward healing.

Another friend just dropped me a few sweet encouraging text messages tonight, filling my heart with gratitude. This thing of taking care of myself first seems to be a hard test for me to pass, but with God's grace and help, I will. You can, too, start self-care now while you are still young instead of taking pain pills and thinking you are indestructible like I used to. It catches up with us.

Prayer Declaration:
Jesus, thank you for healing me and helping all of us to prioritize our time and our health to steward it in a way that is pleasing to you.

May 19
More Decluttering

I woke up knowing I must get rid of some clutter in my life. I know it's the Holy Spirit when it comes to me clearly in the morning like this. The first thing that comes to mind is to delete Instagram, so I did. At first, I just moved the button to the back part of my phone, but I knew that's not what the Holy Spirit really said. That would have been partial obedience. Finally, I deleted the entire thing off my phone. Does that mean Instagram is wrong? By no means, but for me, it drew me in and sucked precious time away. I didn't post much but I love to scroll and see what everyone else is doing.

Precious time; I don't have time to waste. One of my healing strategies is to prioritize my time better. My daughter Luanne greatly encouraged me in this when she recently deleted several social media apps. We are both doing this to be more productive with our time. To be more in the moment of our current lives. To be truly present in every moment, and extra present in the lives of my children, my husband, and my precious little grandsons.

Turning 50 and knowing my life here is very well halfway over has made me reevaluate my life and ponder what truly is important. I'm working on some other areas, too, making boundaries, and learning how to communicate my needs in a healthy way instead of expecting people just to know what I need when I need it.

How about you, do you have those days too? Do you ever feel overwhelmed or in your head? What would it look like for you to get rid of some things you don't need? It's completely between you and Jesus, but I promise you will feel lighter and freer. Ecclesiastes 3:6 says, "A time to seek and a time to lose, a time to keep and a time to cast away," let's release the unnecessary together and cast away from us the things we don't need.

Prayer Declaration:
Jesus, thank you that you continue to cleanse and purge us from all the things that don't serve us in different seasons of our lives. Teach us to sort through, throw away or keep, as You give us wisdom, thank you, Jesus.

May 20
Choose Obedience

I could've totally moved that Instagram app to the back of my phone and used my willpower and only checked it on special occasions or once a week. I would have been able to do that, but that would only have been partial obedience. Partial obedience will never bring the same blessing. Full obedience does. Do you know the well-known story of Ananias and Sapphira in the Bible? Acts 5:1-11 tells this frightful and sobering story. You can read it for yourself.

The moral of the story is that they didn't tell the whole truth again, an act of only partially doing what they knew they should do. Where they went wrong was when they agreed to lie about what they got for their piece of land. They both paid for their lies with their lives. Wow, what a consequence for not telling the truth.

Whether it's a half-truth, partial obedience, or whatever it is we are not being open and upfront with it, it may very well have consequences for us too. God forgives us when we sin, but we often still need to clean up the messes we made. Romans 3:23 says, "For all have sinned and fallen short of the glory of God." We all need forgiveness and grace every day, don't we? None of us is perfect, and as long as we are on this earth, we will be tempted to do wrong. Every time we say no to sin and temptation, the easier it will become to do so, and the stronger we will become in our walk with Jesus. So, what is it today that He is asking you to turn away from? Maybe he's asking you to give something up, too; it could be a grudge you've been holding onto, it could be unforgiveness, it could be social media. What *thing* do you choose obedience over pleasure? Ask Him and listen for His answer.

Prayer Declaration:
Jesus, speak to each one of us. Show what's in our hearts that isn't benefiting us anymore or causing harm to our bodies and soul, reveal any hidden sins to us, God.

May 21
Redemption Story

Our second son Dennis and his beautiful wife, Elise, are celebrating their five-year anniversary today. How an Amish boy met Vegas Girl is a wonderful story to tell. This much I know, it hasn't always been easy for them, coming from two completely different backgrounds, but they have done so well in navigating the ups and downs of marriage. We are so proud of them and the life they are building together, including bringing two beautiful baby boys into our family.

The little boys are the sunshine in our lives. In fact, we get to enjoy them all weekend while their parents are away to celebrate. They had a beautiful, simple wedding right here on our property. My husband married them. Even though the weather didn't cooperate very well, it was perfect otherwise. It was cool and misty. They had a touching ceremony with both her adopted parents and her biological parents present and participating. The evening ended with fireworks. Maybe someday, my son and wife will write their story. It's a wonderful redemption story between families.

This is our God. He is a God of redemption. He is the one who can take the ashes of our lives and make beauty out of them. He is the one who takes all the parts of our lives and turns them into good if we trust Him, if we love Him, if we let Him. As long as you and I keep holding on to our broken pieces, Jesus cannot put them back together. It takes letting go, surrender, and vulnerability. Maybe right now, you are in a situation that you don't think could end well; try God. Give him a fair chance and see what he will do with your life. Redemption offers us a reset.

Titus 2:11-14, "Jesus Christ, who gave himself for us to redeem us from all wickedness, and to purify for Himself a people that are his very own, eager to do what is good."

Prayer Declaration:
Jesus, thank you that you already paid the ultimate price of redemption for us on the cross. Teach us to open our hands and give every piece of our lives to you.

May 22
Perfect Love

It was a beautiful day, and I needed this time to rest. After chasing after our little boys for several days, I have so much renewed respect for young parents. It's a reminder to not be so hard on myself in all the ways I failed back when I had six little ones. Right now, the little grandsons are two and four years old and so much fun. I marvel at their different personalities. I also marvel at how in tune their parents are with the boys and their emotions. They take the time to talk through things with the boys, and they respond well to this kind of parenting.

Yes, I do wish we could do lots of things differently with our now-grown children. Again like, as my mom and I discussed recently, we all did the best we knew at the time. We must trust God's grace to cover our mistakes. It could look like apologizing to our children. If our children tell us of their pain or struggles they endured, let's listen.

My husband and I have done some of that. We have pursued healing as a family at different times. Control-based parenting might work while our children are young, but as they grow older, they may resent it and us. It is very important for them to have a voice. Giving them the freedom to practice making good decisions while they are still young. Another regret I have is parenting with fear. There are healthier ways to parent other than fear and control-based. Do you want to raise robots or thriving young adults, able to think and make decisions for themselves? "Boundaries for Children," by Doctor Henry Cloud, is a wonderful resource to start with.

Remember, perfect love, casts out fear. 1 John 4:18 says, "There is no fear in love. But perfect love drives out fear because fear has to do with punishment. The one who fears is not made perfect in love."

Prayer Declaration:
Jesus, forgive us for the times we parented out of our fear or control. Cast out fear far from all of us. Fill every parent with your wisdom, love and understanding. Teach us how to grow in wisdom and revelation, on how to parent in every age and stage of our children's lives!

May 23
Glory to Glory

"I believe what you start, you complete. I believe that You'll never stop taking me from glory to glory." This song came across my Spotify this morning on my run; it spoke deeply to me today. What God started in you, in me, in our children, whoever or whatever it is, He will complete it. Paul writes about this in Philippines 1:6, "Be confident of this, that He who began a good work in you will carry it on to completion until the day of Jesus Christ." Isn't this an amazing promise? It was what I needed to hear this morning. I hope it's encouraging for you too. There are definitely some unfinished and unresolved areas in my life. If we are honest, we all have some. None of us have arrived; we never will until Jesus takes us home. We do have the privilege of being taken from glory to glory while still down here on this Earth; don't you want that?

I certainly do. I'm not exactly sure what that all looks like, but maybe it means every time we pass a test in life or learn from the trial or hard things we've gone through, we get to come up a little higher. We become a little more like our Abba Father. Through Jesus, a little bit more of his glory shines in and through us! Remember this the next time you are tempted to ask why; instead, ask what? Lord, what do you want me to learn from this? Trials are meant to grow us, not destroy us. Jesus, start with me. I need this message as much as anyone.

Prayer Declaration:
Jesus, thank you for your good plan. Take us higher in You, finish all that you started with us and our loved ones. Teach us to ask what instead of why. Help us to trust your sovereign plan for our lives.

May 24
But God...

As the rain pours down this morning, somehow, it's comforting. Daughter Lorinda and I had a slow morning with coffee and reading our Bibles together, processing the grief of a dear friend and young mother who died way too young in our minds. We light candles and the fireplace, put some soft music on, and just sit in what we are feeling. This beautiful person had an impact on many children and teenage lives when they would go to music camp in Nashville every summer. Her death leaves us a little shaken. We grieve with her young husband and newborn son.

These are the times it's hard to ask what instead of why, when our minds just want to make sense of tragedies like these. Like I said to my children about early or what seems like *untimely* deaths, maybe it's not God's perfect will, but for some reason He allows it.

This brings me to Isaiah 55:8-9, "For my thoughts are not your thoughts, neither are your ways my ways. All the heavens are higher than the earth. So are my ways higher than your ways, and my thoughts higher than your thoughts." I read somewhere recently if we worshiped a God, we could figure out what kind of a God He would really be? I believe there will always be mystery in who He is entirely. One thing we do know is He is good, and He is God. No matter what we go through here on Earth, loss of loved ones, pain, sickness, sadness, betrayal, rejection, the list goes on (*but God...* those two words many have preached and written about for years). God has eternity waiting for us; this we know. This we can look forward to with hope. So once again, we turn our teary eyes back to him: Our only hope.

Prayer Declaration:
Jesus, comfort broken hearts today. Teach all of us to turn to You in our pain and not away from You, because You are our only hope for all eternity.

May 25
Yeast in Our Lives

Cloudy, cold days usually find me in my kitchen. Baking is a form of therapy for me. Creating something from scratch with my hands is a very satisfying feeling. Daughter Lorinda makes us mouthwatering lattes while I make a perfect rhubarb torte. Next, we stir together some cinnamon roll dough and let it rise while we go run some errands. We grab some groceries, check out a greenhouse and stop in to see how son Dennis and his wife are doing. They are also dealing with the death of our dear friend from Nashville. They served together as missionaries with this couple in Nashville for several years. We talk, process, and play with the little boys, who are delighted whenever we stop by. When we get back home, the rolled dough is spilling out over the bowl onto the counter.

Time to punch it down and roll it out. Lorinda's friend from college is not coming until later tonight, and she wants to roll them out with us. So, I set the dough outside where it's cool to slow it down. Still, it keeps rising. This yeast is working very well. It made me think of Galatians 5:9, "A little yeast works through the whole bunch of dough." In this case, this is a good thing, but sometimes the yeast in our lives can be good or bad.

Let's make sure that what we allow to work through our whole soul, body, and spirit is indeed a good thing, things that will feed our spirit rather than kill it. Let's make sure the yeast we allow in our lives measures up with the fruit of the spirit, love, joy, peace, kindness, gentleness, and self-control. Let that work its way throughout our life.

Prayer Declaration:
Jesus, teach us to be careful what we allow into our hearts and mind. Cleanse us from any unrighteousness and evil, make us pure like You are. Help us to live out the fruits of the Spirit in our lives with Your help.

May 26
Humble Beginnings

Another cool and cloudy day. A perfect day for Bible study, complete with candles, a fireplace, good food, and lots of coffee. Daughter Lorinda and I lead worship. It's a treat to have her home to lead us on the piano. She's very gifted. We have two new ladies joining us today, which makes my heart so happy. Having finally found my tribe of ladies is an answered prayer for me. Remember how lonely I was after moving here 11 years ago? Whenever I complained to God, He had the same answer. Start something.

It took me several years to listen, but I finally gathered four other women who were also looking for a deeper connection. We started meeting in the loft of a coffee shop; it was anything but cozy. It was a place set up like a library, musty and tight quarters. We did that for several years with just a handful of us. After we built our new home and I had the space, we decided to meet here at my house. This group has now tripled in size and continues to grow.

The ladies that come all have similar backgrounds from either Mennonite or Amish. I will always have a heart for my culture of women. My basic mission is to help women understand our worth in Jesus and how much He loves us because out of that flows everything else. Knowing how much our daddy God loves us.

It took me many years to grasp that His love is unconditional. Now I'm passionate about passing that love on to others. Today, I'm grateful for those early days in the coffee shop attic. I learned a lot from two older women during that time. Zechariah 4:10 says it well, "Do not despise the day of small beginnings, for the Lord rejoices to see..."

Prayer Declaration:
Jesus, thank you for small and humble beginnings. Teach us to be obedient to what You ask us. Thank you for continuing to bring the people you want us to surround ourselves with. Teach us to know Your voice and our worth as women in You! (Men too)

May 27
Alive in Christ

No longer I who lives, but Christ in me, for I've been born again, my heart is free. The hope of heaven before me, the cross behind. Hallelujah, you brought me back to life.

What a wonderful song, one of my favorites, because it's also my testimony, and I hope it is yours too. I clearly remember when Jesus rescued me from the life of sin I was living. At the time, I didn't have a language for what was happening in my life, but I do know it was when I became born again. After being very sick with the measles for several weeks, not being able to eat, sleep or even rest, I was at the end of myself. Death would have looked kind of welcome, except I knew I wasn't ready. That's when my life began to change.

If this is what it took to bring me to Jesus, I'm grateful that He allowed me to go through that awful time. Galatians 2:20 says, "I have been crucified with Christ and I no longer live, but Christ lives in me." The life I now live in the body, I live by faith, in the son of God, who loved me and gave Himself for me. The darkest times in our lives can turn out to have blessings come out of them.

What is it for you that you are currently going through? Simply ask God to turn it into something for His glory. As you surrender your life and everything in it, He can make things brand new, better than they've ever been before. The most important question of all is, have you said yes to Jesus? Let Him rescue you too! You will not regret it
.

Prayer Declaration:
Jesus, thank you for rescuing me from my sin, shame, selfishness and simply myself. Will you please pursue every one of my family, friends and everyone reading these words? We all long and need to be saved and rescued, redeemed and set free!

May 28
Rhythms of Grace

Life has been a bit chaotic, in a mostly good way, lately. Having two college-aged girls living with us again for a few weeks has been fun and, at times, a bit hectic. Their boundless energy to do things and their fully demanding schedules are inspiring to me. How do they balance it all? There is something about that youthful energy that I miss. Today everyone has plans, and I do too. I choose to stay home alone, hear myself think, breathe, and rest. First, I putter around the house and make sure everything is in place. I load the dishwasher and some laundry and play around with my plants outside.

The slow rhythm of my day helps me relax and prepare for the rest of the weekend. I run to the grocery store for some food, and finally, I take a shower and relax. It feels good to have a slower, reflecting day.

Earlier this week, we hit a deer head-on and totaled my beautiful new birthday car. It was rather scary with our little grandsons riding with us at the time. The impact popped out all the airbags, and I'm still sporting a good-sized tender bruise from one of the airbags. Otherwise, we were all perfectly fine except for being a bit shaken.

Gratitude filled my heart and mind as I realized how lucky we were. My car can be replaced, and I'm so thankful we are all safe. "I will praise you, O Lord, with all my heart I will tell of your wonders. I will be glad and rejoice in You. I will sing praises to Your name most high," Psalms 9: 1-2. Psalms is one of my favorite books in the Bible; full of praise, thanksgiving, prayer, and lament.

Prayer Declaration:
Jesus, thank you for slower rhythms of grace and reflection. At times we need them in our lives. Thank you also that you sent our guardian angels before us, behind us and around us to keep us safe from harm.

May 29
Healing Our Pain

At church today, the pastor talked about how we deal with our pain. We all have pain in our lives; we all deal with it differently. Jesus wants to heal our pain, yet so often, instead of running to him, we run from Him. We try to numb ourselves in various different ways, but we feel even worse afterwards. Those things only medicate us for a brief time, and then our pain is sharper than it was before. What is it that you are feeling today? Do you feel depression, loneliness, or the lies someone spoke over you a long time ago? Maybe you still believe those lies all these years later. Or maybe instead of emotional pain, you have physical pain. The pain of recovery can be worse than the actual wound. Healing is often a process, and it can be painful, but it's worth it. We don't have to stay or live in our pain forever; take it to Jesus. First of all, ask Him if there is someone you could let into your hurt and help you walk out of it. To walk free and healed is a taste of Heaven. "Out of my distress, I called on the Lord. "The Lord answered me and set me free," Psalms 118:5.

We had a wonderful family evening later tonight. Most of the children came home for dinner, including my nephew, Wes. As we ate, laughed, talked, and played outside in the beautiful evening sunlight, my heart filled with gratitude once again. Our journey as a family has not been pain-free by any means, yet here we are. We all have pursued healing at different points in our lives. Nights like this, I can see the fruits of that. It's a bonus to be able to help nieces and nephews who are finding their way too.

Prayer Declaration:
Jesus, thank you for healing and hope. Thank you for being the ultimate healer. Teach us all how to recognize and find the healing we long for, to go to you for rest and not numb our pain any longer. Heal us, Jesus.

May 30
Memorial Day

Here in America, we celebrate today as a holiday. I wonder if sometimes we miss the point, though, because freedom is never really free, is it? Someone paid a price for our freedom. Jesus, first of all, paid the price on the cross for us. He paid with His own blood so we can go free without punishment. Likewise, all the men and women who serve our country are risking their lives, and many have given their lives so we can stay a free country. Those are the ones we are honoring today with this holiday.

This is always a more sobering holiday for me. When our Jon Boy was in high school, he played trumpet in the band. On Memorial Day, they would play at the graveyard services and then another service at a church to honor the fallen. When Jon and his friends would play taps, it would give me chills, such a fitting sound; I can't quite describe it. It was the perfect sound for the occasion. Galatians 5:13 is a good verse about our freedom, "You, my brothers, and sisters, were called to be free, but do not use your freedom to indulge in the flesh, rather serve one another humbly and love."

If we all would practice that verse, our world would be a better place. Growing up, my culture didn't and still doesn't observe Memorial Day. They are non-resistant and don't believe in war or fighting for our country, but what if no one ever would? Would we still be a free country? The Old Testament is full of war stories and the constant fight for freedom. This is one of their convictions, and they have the right to choose that because, thank God, America is still a free country!

Prayer Declaration:
Jesus, we thank you for the blood that was shed for our freedom. Jesus, You paid a debt we could never repay. Jesus, heal our land and let us stay a free country. Teach each one of us our duty and bless all the families of the fallen.

May 31
Letting Go

Our youngest son, Jon Boy, moved out tonight. He and his friend are renting a duplex 15 minutes from us. I'm so proud of him on the one hand, and on the other, I will miss him. I know this is the next step for him to live independently before he decides to settle down and maybe get married someday. Is there something about letting go of your youngest, your baby, or is it just me? It's exciting, hard, emotional, and exciting again when I see it through his and his friend's eyes. Looking on the bright side, it's only 15 minutes away versus over an hour, like where our twin daughters are.

This verse is my prayer for the boys as they spread their wings, fly and live on their own. "Let your eyes look straight ahead. Fix your gaze directly before you. Give careful thought to the path for your feet and be steadfast in all your ways. Do not turn to the right or to the left. Keep your feet from evil," Proverbs 4:25-27. Jon has always been levelheaded and mature for his age, a hard worker with a cheerful whistling disposition and a positive outlook in life. He will be just fine on his own. My mother's heart is letting go, little by little, as many mothers have before me.

Gods got our babies. He loves them even more than we do. We can trust that He will continue to lead, guide, and protect them. He'll grow them into all he wants them to be; that's my prayer.

Prayer Declaration:
Jesus, bless and protect our sons and daughters as they start lives and homes on their own. Teach them to always be true to their conscience and to You. Help us Mamas to let go and let You reign because You are able and trustworthy.

June 1
Perseverance Pays Off

A quick run this morning, writing, reading, and some office work, before we head off to help one of our twin daughters move today. She and her friend, who has been here with us for 1 ½ weeks, finally got to move into their apartment today. Their excitement is contagious! They both moved out of an old cheaper rental, so this apartment is definitely an upgrade. It's enjoyable to help them unpack and get settled in. It looks spacious with a nice big living room window, the perfect place for their plants. My daughter inherited my love for plants, and we both have carted them with us over the years wherever we find ourselves living.

Job 8:7 says, "Your beginnings will seem humble, so prosperous will your future be." These girls truly started out with humble beginnings. Our daughter's first place she rented with her sister and one or two others was dingy, dark, crowded, and all they could afford as a freshman in college. My husband and I support our kids going to college if that's what they choose. We have an agreement with them that we pay for their schooling, and they pay for their rent, food, vehicle, gas, phones, and anything else. This has worked very well for us and them, and we are proud of how hard they have worked and how they have skimped and saved to make ends meet. Only occasionally did they need to borrow a little bit for food or rent.

When we work hard for what we have, we are so much more appreciative of it. It's such a joy to see our daughter enter a paid internship as a nurse this summer and finally be able to afford a nicer apartment. What are you working towards today? You can do it! Don't give up! Keep persevering, and you will be rewarded.

Prayer Declaration:
Jesus, teach us to persevere through the hard and the lean times, through our humble beginnings. "Give us wisdom, strength and endurance, for in due time we will reap if we faint not" Galatians 6:9 -10.

June 2
Standing Steadfast

Guess what, today our other twin daughter Luanne is moving! Why three of our children all needed to move in the same week eludes me, but we jump in and help where we can. Daughter Luanne and her husband moved from a condo in Onalaska to a bigger house in a very nice, family-friendly neighborhood. It's maybe only 10 minutes closer to us; I'll take that. I'm amazed at their maturity level at 22 years old. They both work full-time, and this is the second home they have owned. Luanne knew early in her teenage years that she wanted to get married to the right guy and eventually be a stay-at-home Mom. Her husband is perfect for her, and to see them thriving together is so rewarding for us.

As I may have mentioned before, life wasn't always easy for Luanne. She always knew what she wanted and when she wanted it. She always stood up for what she believed in and wasn't afraid to speak up. She wasn't just another white girl, but very much held her ground and belief in any subject. We are so proud of her and the life she is building for herself, including an associate degree in social services as well as one of the lead teachers at an early childcare facility and a leader at a church youth group on Wednesday nights.

James 1:12 says, "Blessed is the man who remains steadfast under trial, for when he has stood the test, he will receive the crown of life which God has promised to those who love him." Are you being tested and tried in some way? Is it because of your faith, or is it some other trial that is hard and painful right now? If so, claim the above verse for yourself. You will receive your crown of life; it will be worth any and everything we go through while here on Earth. Be encouraged! This time here is but a glimpse of what all eternity will be.

Prayer Declaration:
Jesus, encourage each one of us in what we are contending for. Help us to be steadfast under our tests and to speak up for You, but most of all live for You and be an example of You.

June 3
Generations of Blessings

Running errands, mowing the lawn, and having a normal day feel good and relaxing. Knowing that our four youngest are settled into their new homes is a good feeling. Three of them bought their own places, and two are still renting. Our oldest son Duane lives here on our property in an apartment. Sometimes I just marvel that God blessed us with six amazing children.

The older we get, the more I see the blessing and how they, as our next generation, are following in our footsteps in a lot of ways. It's sobering, wonderful, scary, and beautiful all at the same time. There is a story in Judges 2:10 that talks about a generation that was gathered unto their fathers, "And there arose another generation after them who knew not of the Lord. Or even of the works which he had done for Israel." How does this happen? After all the miracles that happened for the Israelites, there is a generation that knows nothing of this. It's unbelievable.

I remember the first time I read this story in the Old Testament and how this stood out to me. How important is it, then, to pass on God's stories to our children? The miracles we, too, have seen and what God's done in our lives to kindle and ignite their faith. The power of a testimony is huge.

The above story can motivate us to not let that happen in our families. Read the whole story for yourself sometime. It also motivates me to pray not only for our six children but for the generations to come. There is a beautiful heart-touching song by Kari Jobe and Elevation Worship called 'The Blessing'. Listen to it, worship along, and most of all, dads and moms, let's pass on God's goodness and the salvation story to the generations in our lineage.

Prayer Declaration:
Jesus, may we feel the importance of this and speak of your goodness, your miracles, and most of all your forgiveness of our sins and your plan of salvation. Jesus, we ask you for your wisdom to help us do this. Give us your courage, strength and boldness, every single day!

June 4
Different Personalities

Our little grandboys came early this evening. Our children are attending the celebration of the life of their friend and mentor in Nashville this weekend. The oldest grandson is delighted to be here and is all smiles. The youngest one clings to Mama and doesn't want to stay. But in no time, he, too, is happy and playing. I marvel at the difference between the 2 boys. It always makes me wish I had been more aware of the unique differences in my children when they were this age. I wish we would have been more sensitive to their individual personalities. It's so easy to treat children as if they were all made from the same cookie cutter, so to speak. When in fact, our children are all so very unique and different. What works for one child may not work for another.

Partnering with the Holy Spirit is the best way to parent. Ask Him to reveal to you the needs of each child. We spent the majority of the day and evening outside because it was such a beautiful day. As the four-year-old and I snip off tea to dry, I answer what seems like a million questions. The two-year-old now loves to ask why behind almost everything I say; it's cute and comical and sometimes leaves me without answers. The two-year-old keeps asking for Mommy and Daddy throughout the day. The four-year-old tells me he wants to stay with us for 20 years; yes, I laughed out loud. The 2-year-old randomly bursts out singing 'Thank you, Jesus,' during the day, and the four-year-old keeps asking questions, as well as trying out his latest new words. When we were trying to light a fire, and it didn't want to light, he asked me, "What's wrong with the fire? Is it miserable?" I laughed again!

Children truly are one of the best blessings God could have ever chosen to give us. Tonight, my heart is full, and my body is exhausted. Psalms 127:3 says, "Behold, children are a heritage from the Lord, the fruit of the womb a reward."

Prayer Declaration:
Thank you, Jesus, for this reward of precious children. Bless every womb and make it fruitful for those who long for children. Jesus, help us to lead these little ones to you. May we ever be a good example for them and never a stumbling block!

June 5
Connection or Correction

"Whoever spares the rod hates his son, but he who loves him is diligent to discipline him," Proverbs 13:24. We were raised, and we raised our children by this verse. It is the Amish culture's way, for sure. While I do think there is a time when discipline may be necessary, I also think it can be way overused, especially since the rod can cause more pain than gain. Sure, we can make our children comply, but what about connecting with their heart and their emotional needs?

I read this interesting article where it described the rod as nothing more than a shepherd's rod gently nudging, pulling the little lambs back from the edge of the cliff and dangerous places. It resonated in my heart. Yes, children do need discipline and direction and guidance, but I would caution against overusing physical discipline, perhaps only as a last resort for outright rebellion or disobedience. Look at the child's heart behind the refusal. Learn from the little ones to ask a lot of 'why' questions.

Why does my child feel this way? Why are they acting out? Maybe your child is just begging for your attention, even any attention. My heart aches for the many children who aren't allowed to express themselves. Our two-year-old grandson spent about 10 minutes face down on the floor yesterday morning and again woke up in the middle of the night very upset because Mommy and Daddy weren't there. How else is a 2-year-old supposed to express his emotions and sadness? It's okay to let them cry and show that they are upset. How will they be able to process emotional pain as adults if we aren't a safe place for them to learn that now? Let's lay down the rod and our many rules and look for connection and relationship with our children while they are still young and their hearts are tender and pliable.

Prayer Declaration:
Oh, Jesus, give us your wisdom and your revelation about what true discipline looks like. Jesus, I cry out for the many children who are not allowed to express their feelings and emotions, especially for any children being abused, physically, emotionally and spiritually. Will you please rescue them?

June 6
Champion the Children

Mark 9:42, "If anyone causes one of these little ones to stumble, believe in me, it is better for them if a large millstone were hung around their neck, and they were thrown into the sea." If there is a heavy millstone hung around your neck, you would probably drown, right? So, who are these little ones that we do not want to cause to stumble? Some Bible verses and other versions say the deepest part of the sea.

Why is it that we take some verses in the Bible so literally, like the one about using the rod on our children, and yet we might skim over verses like this verse that says, "Fathers, do not provoke your children to anger lest they become discouraged," Ephesians 6:4, says it this way, "Fathers do not provoke your children to anger by the way you treat them." Rather, bring them up with the discipline and instruction that comes from the Lord. What about these verses? Do we take these verses equally seriously? What do these verses mean for us today?

I do believe the verse in Mark is also talking about young new believers. How important is it to champion them in their newly found faith? Just because we feel something isn't wrong for us doesn't mean we should do it if it could cause us to stumble or offend them. I also like to think it is talking about literal little children who have such pure faith in God. Our four-year-old grandson already tells us of dreams he has and the things he sees. Jesus is so real to him, and he even believes God heals dead birds. Parents and grandparents, let us not provoke these little ones and their sweet, precious trust in Jesus. Instead, let's champion their tiny pure, undefiled hearts by following these verses outlined for us in the Bible.

Prayer Declaration:
Jesus, help us. I cry out to you for these little ones that we would only ever discipline from a pure heart. Always out of love, never out of anger. Forgive us and help us.

June 7
Mystery Mingled With Hope

Life has been exceptionally busy, more than usual. A blur, actually, of moving four of our six children, having two girls live with us for a week and a half, babysitting our grandsons four days and nights, my new birthday car getting totaled by a deer, and driving to Milwaukee to pick up another one. I'm also feeling a bit under the weather physically, which has a way of making everything else seem bigger than it is. My doctor told me that even the 'good stress' in our lives can be too much at times. I'm also still grieving with my children, who lost a friend and mentor in dear Courtney, as well as another of my friends who lost her partner to cancer just this week.

Life just doesn't make sense at times, but then again, is it supposed to? As long as we are here on this earth, I'm convinced there will always be a measure of mystery, just like it says in 1st Corinthians 13:12, "For now we see through a glass darkly, but then face to face. Now I know in part, but then I shall know, even as I am known."

In other words, we will know eventually. When we see our Jesus face to face, it will all make sense. We will understand it all. All the pain, heartache, and disappointments, the mystery, will melt away the moment we see him. As my husband and I sat gazing at a magnificent sunset last night, reconnecting after a difficult, hectic last week, I drank it all in, the beauty, the healing, the hope, and realized this is only a glimpse of what heaven and eternity will be like. Friends, we must press on. Heaven will most surely be worth it all.

Prayer Declaration:
Jesus, thank you for being our strength when we have none left. Thank you for carrying us just like the footprints in the sand. Fill each heart with hope today. Come and heal us from the inside out.

June 8
Heaven Is Waiting

So, in light of how all of our lives tend to go at times, there is a verse that's such a beautiful promise. It goes like this. "He, Jesus, will wipe every tear from their eyes. There will be no more death or moaning or crying or pain. For the order of things has passed away," Revelations 21: 4. Hallelujah! Can you imagine this with me for a minute? Really think about it. Consider what you yourself are currently facing or going through. The above verse is your promise to hold on to.

If you have made Jesus your Lord and Savior, you and I get to live in eternal bliss forever and ever. No more tedious jobs or office work or all the things we do every day that we don't necessarily enjoy but it's a part of our life. But most of all, no pain, no sorrow, no suffering, no tears, no rejection, no sadness. Heaven is worth it all.

I remember my Mom would write that verse in sympathy cards she sent out. She would write encouraging letters and almost always include that verse. Once again, she was shaping and teaching my young girl's heart. Her life wasn't always easy, but she knew how to encourage herself and others in the Lord. We, too, can do that, friend.

These promises are "...for all of us who believe," Romans 10:9 makes it so clear and simple. I remember pondering over this verse with Dad, who has now gone to heaven. If you declare with your mouth Jesus is Lord and believe in your heart that God raised Him from the dead, you will be saved. We talked about how it's really that simple. Will you believe it today?

Prayer Declaration:
Jesus, today we cry out for all the souls who don't yet know you. Jesus, send the right people and Holy Spirit to them to rescue and save them from sin and themselves. Bring them to you, Jesus.

June 9
Blessing of Daughters

My husband and I drove an hour to help our daughters today. They both moved recently and now need help putting things on their walls, etc. My husband is very good at that, in fact, he put up every piece in our new house. My daughters and I are so grateful for his expert skills. He pays attention to detail. Our daughter Luanne also decides she wants to plant flowers in a charming rock garden in her cute little backyard, so off we go to Home Depot and fill a cart. She has quite a different taste in colors than I do, but I'm so thankful she has inherited my love for flowers and being outdoors in nature. We finally select quite a variety, pay and load up the car. We agree we will need more caffeine to plant all these yet, so we swing by Starbucks and get our favorite ice-cold green teas. What a great pick-me-up. We remove the small rocks, dig the holes, plant, water, and replace the stones.

It's hard but rewarding work. We finish just as my husband finishes hanging things in the house, and Luanne's husband gets home from work. We throw a pizza in the oven and, make a stir fry, enjoy a meal together before we start back home. My body is tired, but my heart is happy. I love seeing my daughters bloom and blossom, now keeping homes of their own and doing such a good job.

It especially brings me joy seeing them carry on our faith, my love for all things outdoors, healthy eating, and staying active. Tonight, my heart feels thankful, and I'm thinking of an adage, a daughter is God's way of saying I thought you could use a lifelong friend. "Virtue is the strength and power of the daughters of God, may our daughters be like graceful pillars carved to beautify a place," Psalms 144:12.

Prayer Declaration:
Jesus, thank you for virtuous beautiful daughters, who carry on our family legacy. Bless all your daughters everywhere tonight!

June 10
Breathe on Us, Lord

"On the day I called, you answered me, my strength of soul you increase," Psalms 138:3. Today was one of those days for me. The tiredness of my body, soul, and mind wanted to overtake me. My day started early and ended late. Our annual fundraiser for Africa and our team event is coming up fast. We host it right here on our property. It is a lot of fun and a great deal of work. It's a family and a team effort. I kept breathing prayers for strength and endurance as I accomplished my goals for today. Such a good feeling to get it all done. I showered and got ready to go out with friends for the evening. They pick us up in their new Ford Bronco with the top down.

It's a pleasant warm 80-degree evening, the wind whipping our faces and hair, heading towards one of our favorite Mexican places. We ordered chips and queso with all the trimmings. We connect and catch up on each other's lives. When we get back, we sit on the front porch, and watch the sunset. It looks like there are giant angel wings in the sky.

It is just beautiful and peaceful. Psalms 146:6 says, "He is the maker of heaven and Earth, the sea and everything in them. He remains faithful forever." Do you take the time to sit and soak up things our maker made for us to enjoy? Nature can bring so much calm to our souls if we take the time to notice and be out in it. The sight of fresh green grass against a blue sky with a flaming orange, red, pink, yellow, and orange sunset never gets old for me; it fills me with awe. Sitting by the ocean or gazing at snow-capped mountains has the same effect on me. What is it for you? Take the time to find what fills you with awe and wonder and know that this is God's doing.

Prayer Declaration:
Thank you, Jesus, for giving us so much beauty to enjoy and thank you for giving us strength when we are weak and weary. Thank you for your blessings. May we never lose our own wonder.

June 11
Sabbath Day of Rest

Sipping on a second cup of coffee as the rain keeps pouring down outside, I have a million things on my "To Do List." For now, I sit, write, and listen to the rain. It's soothing to hear and see it coming down and soaking into the thirsty Earth. I'm also feeling gratitude for all the outside jobs my husband, and I accomplished this past week, so let it rain today. Aren't Saturdays supposed to be slower anyway? At home, growing up, our Saturdays were super busy with chores, cleaning, baking, and then chores again. Next would be baths for everyone. I clearly remember taking a bath in a big round steel tub behind the wood stove in the living room in my younger days. We hung up a sheet for privacy. I'll never forget those Saturday nights, the feeling of everything being squeaky clean and spotless, including all of us kids. Often fresh, warm bread out of the oven was what we had for supper.

Everything was now ready for Sunday. It was a good feeling. The Amish culture keeps Sunday as work free as possible for them. This is based on Exodus 20:8-11, "Remember the Sabbath day by keeping it holy. Six days you shall labor and do all your work, but the seventh is a Sabbath to the Lord your God. On it you shall not do any work, for in six days the Lord made the heavens and Earth. But He rested on the seventh day. Therefore, the Lord blessed the Sabbath and made it holy."

We would all do well to continue this practice. It's another thing I'm extremely grateful we were taught; we practice the Sabbath for the most part. If even Jesus rested on the seventh day, who are we to think we don't need to? If you work seven days a week, could you find one Sabbath day for yourself? Maybe it's not even so much about a certain day as it is about making sure we take one day. Your body, mind, and, most of all, your spirit need and deserve to rest and reset.

Prayer Declaration:
Jesus, teach us to honor You, the Sabbath, and ourselves by taking a day of rest. Help us to understand the importance of this practice. Give us a revelation on the meaning of Sabbath. We can rest any day in you.

June 12
Blessing of Sons

Today was an extra special worship set because my son Dennis and I got to be on it together. He was on the drums, and I was singing. As I drove to church early this morning for practice, my heart couldn't help but sing praises to God. He has done so much. He has brought us so far, and now He is restoring something near and dear to my heart.

Worshiping with my son and daughters occasionally reminds me again of how God cares for those deep desires in our hearts and how thankful and faithful He is to fulfill them at the right time in our lives. Worship was wonderful today, and had moments of God's tangible presence. What is sweeter than that?

Yesterday was also our third son Lavon and Camille's 2nd year anniversary. They are true soul mates and love doing a lot of the same things. They were high school sweethearts and got married in the heart of the pandemic in 2020. They were forced to make a decision of downscaling their wedding to basically family or postpone it. They chose to go ahead with their family and had a beautiful, small, intimate wedding, quite perfect in my opinion. After the ceremony, we gathered around the outstretched dining room table we had decorated earlier in the day, complete with an ice cream cake and beautiful blooming peonies from our own flower garden.

They took all of the pandemic craziness and planned a wedding in the middle of it so well. They are such a stable couple who complement each other very well. They recently bought their first home and moved into it. We are so proud of them and the life they are building together. Proverbs speak a lot about sons. Proverbs 10:1 says, "A wise son brings joy to his father, but a foolish son grief to his mother."

Prayer Declaration:
Thank you for giving us wise sons, Jesus. May all the sons and daughters reading this continue to seek your wise counsel all the days of their lives.

June 13
Soul Body Spirit

Awake my soul and sing. Sing his praise aloud. Sing his praise aloud. This song keeps going through my mind. We sang it yesterday at church, and now it's stuck in my head; that's a good thing. My soul is awake this morning, but my body is struggling. When my alarm went off, I was still sound asleep and wondered why it was going off on the weekend. Finally, I was awake enough to realize it was not the weekend but Monday morning, a rainy, dreary one at that. The perfect day to take a couple of naps, and I do. It's one of those days where I just don't feel good.

I'm learning to listen to my body instead of just pushing through and always push it to perform no matter how I feel. Did you know that even though our bodies are weak and sick at times, it doesn't have to affect our spirit? Unless there is pain, then it becomes a challenge for me to keep my spirits up.

Reading through the Psalms or listening to worship music is always comforting to me. Psalms 57:8-9 goes with the song I mentioned earlier, "Wake up my heart and wake up O lyre and harp. I will wake the dawn with my song. I will thank you, Lord among all the people. I will sing your praises among the nations." Do you play an instrument? Would you like to? Pick one up today and learn a few chords. It is challenging, exciting, and a wonderful way to express your worship of God. If you are struggling with any type of pain or sickness, you have my empathy. Give yourself so much grace and rest when you need it. Be kind to your body, God has given you. You do not have to move mountains every day.

Prayer Declaration:
Jesus, thank you that we are fearfully and wonderfully made. Teach us to worship even on the days we don't feel good physically, especially strengthen our hearts and spirits.

June 14
In Season and Out of Season

Our faithful family dog, Buddy, died last night. We should have seen it coming, and we did to some extent, yet we were not prepared for this and so quickly. He had been sick with Lyme's disease, off and on, for several years now. We made him as comfortable as possible, sat with him and, said our goodbyes to him, then let him go. It was hard, but it was a dog and not a human with a soul. Still, it invoked lots of emotions in all of us. My husband and I reminisced about how we salvaged him from the dog pound and tried to give him a good life. We also talked about the mystery of death and how the breath just stops.

Ecclesiastes 3:1-2 speaks about time, "A time to be born and a time to die." It is part of the natural progression of life in both animals and humans. As humans, we don't need to know when we will die; we just need to know that we are always ready. 2 Timothy 4:2 speaks about "...being ready in season and out of season." I am not exactly sure what that means, but for us, it could mean living each day as blameless as possible.

If we have made Jesus our Lord and Savior, His Grace will be enough for us. One day our hearts, too, will stop beating, and eternity will begin somewhere. Seeing our dog die so quickly was a reminder for my husband and I how quickly things can change and to not take things for granted. Even though he was only a dog, we can still learn from this.

Prayer Declaration:
Jesus, may we be ready at all times, for when You call us home, or when the trumpet sounds, You will take us home with You that way. Teach us how to be ready in season and out of season, whatever that means exactly.

June 15
Pondering Heaven

We woke up to a freshly rain-washed world once again. Everything looks extra lush and green this morning. The sun is beginning to peek through. The strawberries and early garden goodies are finally ready here in Wisconsin. I am excited to take our little grandsons and go pick some strawberries soon. I'm sitting here this morning, listening to the stillness, feeling the peacefulness, hearing the happy songs of the birds, and seeing the trees whispering gently in the warm breeze. My heart feels so much peace.

A song starts running through my mind. "How beautiful heaven must be." This was one of my father-in-law's favorite songs. When he was sick and dying, our family gathered around him to sing over and with him, and when we sang this song, he helped sing as much as he possibly could. It was a holy moment and made this song even more special.

Do you ever wonder what heaven will be like? I know some people say it doesn't matter; it really doesn't. Isn't it fun, though, to dream, wonder and ponder on what we will get to experience, such as streets of gold? Seriously, imagine the beauty of that alone. I have some gold-colored specks in my kitchen countertops, and those few are so gorgeous. Can you imagine entire streets of gold? What about singing with the angels around the throne forever? How's that for glorious? Revelations 75:15-17 speaks of heaven, "Therefore, they are before the throne of God, and serve him day and night in His temple, and He sits on the throne and will shelter them with His presence..." You can read it or use your own imagination.

Prayer Declaration:
Lord, this I know; Heaven truly will be worth everything we ever faced on our time here on Earth. I am encouraged, you're coming back for us!

June 16
God Still Heals

Lab work scheduled at my doctor today, ugh. I wonder if I will ever get to the point where I don't need them. I hate needles, except for maybe the kind that can actually sew something, the type I used to use for many years, sewing most of the clothes we wore. Those were a totally different kind, and yet somehow, I managed to put one of those through my finger once. Ouch is right. Is there any wonder I have needle trauma? I'm kidding. I remember that day clearly. I can't remember exactly what I was sewing. Probably a pair of pants for my husband. I always struggled a bit more making those, and they still never fit perfectly. It was so frustrating at times. Anyway, this particular day, I was home alone, even though, at the time, we lived on the same property as my husband's parents; no one else was home that day.

We were newly married and didn't have any children yet. Here I was happily sewing along with my trusty, treadle pedal Bernina sewing machine when suddenly my finger got too close to the needle. It stung like crazy and went through the flesh of one of my fingers. It went through the side of my finger and broke off. I was horrified and couldn't bring myself to pull it out, so I walked the half mile to the sawmill where my husband was working. I closed my eyes tightly as he took a set of pliers and removed the needle. Ouch, it hurt so much. I trudged back home and probably resumed my sewing. I don't remember.

Do you have physical or emotional pain you have to deal with occasionally or constantly? If you do, I pray you find relief. Here is a verse for you, too. "But as for you, afflicted in any pain, may your salvation protect me, oh God..." Psalms 69:29-31.

Prayer Declaration:
Jesus, thank you that your protection and salvation helps us rise above any physical or emotional pain we will ever go through. Our soul and spirit will always be safe in you. Heal us.

June 17
Safe Confidants

I felt such tangible peace all of this week, even with our big events coming up next weekend. It's an absolutely wonderful feeling to feel this peace and to feel organized, even when there is still so much to do. I will thank Jesus for that and whoever is praying for me. Thank you. I feel it, and I have some wonderful prayer warriors in my life. Do you have that in your life? I wish and pray for you to have that blessing. I'll be honest; there were times in my life I didn't have that because of my own pride and fear.

It is important to have people who are trustworthy. People who will not judge you no matter what you share with them. Maybe I had more fear than pride, fear of betrayal of my confidence. Because yes, that has happened to me, and I dare say it has happened to you too. That is painful, isn't it? A very small degree of betrayal is sufficient to cause the death of trust. Proverbs 25:9-10 speaks about this. "Instead, take up the matter with your neighbor and don't betray another person's confidence. Otherwise, anyone who hears you will make you ashamed and your bad reputation will never leave you."

So, it really is a big deal if we have been disloyal. Let's ask God's forgiveness. Let's become a safe place for people, especially those who trust us with their deepest needs. Yes, Jesus is the first person we should go to, but sometimes we need an earthly being as well. We need individuals who are safe. We need each other. Today I'm feeling extra grateful for my humans.

Prayer Declaration:
Jesus, I pray that You help us all find at least a few people we can trust with our deepest secrets, our deepest needs. Teach us how to be a safe place for each other, today more than ever.

June 18
Become Childlike

One of my prayer warriors' friends also has two children who are little prayer warriors. Why not? Who better to pray than innocent children? They always believe in and want the best for people. In Psalms 8:2, Jesus said, "Out of the mouths of babes and nursing infants, you have ordained strength. Because of your enemies, you may silence the enemy and the avenger." My family has been the recipient of some of the above children's prayers, and I'm so grateful and count it as a great privilege.

The purity and simplicity of their prayer are powerful. Is it any wonder the Bible says to become like a child? Not meaning childish but childlike. When was the last time we adults walked up to someone and hugged and apologized right after a fight or argument? Am I the only one who needs space first to cool off and calm down?

What if, like children, we would quickly humble ourselves and forgive each other? I wonder if our prayers would even be more effective. We had our little grandsons today. They are always a joy. This is the last weekend they will be two and three, so close together and such good little friends. Where one is, the other one will be found. Even though they are natured very differently, they stick together, and Zion does so well in looking out for his little "brudder Zonder," as he calls him. Being grandparents is such a gift from God, and I will be forever grateful for innocent children everywhere. God protect them all!

Prayer Declaration:
Jesus, bless and touch all the little ones everywhere. Help us as parents and grandparents to raise them up as mighty warriors for You. Thank you for this privilege and honor!

June 19
Father's Day

My own dear Father has been gone for five years now, and my Father-in-law for two years. Time truly marches on, and now we are the next generation. It's sobering at times. Are we doing what we should to be a Godly example for the next generation? In a world that feels a little crazy sometimes, it's easy to worry and wonder, but God is still on the throne. We can rest in him. Psalms 103:13 says, "As a father has compassion on his children, so the Lord has compassion on those who fear him." We celebrated the Father of our children today, my amazing husband.

As I mentioned, coming out of the Amish way wasn't always easy, and there were times, as parents, we had no clue how to navigate. Those were the times my husband led us fearlessly and tirelessly. While I'm sure he felt fear and uncertainty at times, he pushed through and kept going anyway.

Today, the children honored him with a beautiful, heartfelt, tear-jerking video of the things they appreciated about him. His mom and I, too, added our appreciation. Strong, kind, caring, Godly, giving, hardworking, a man of integrity and his word. He laid a strong foundation for us as a family; those are some of the things that were said. He fought for our freedom as a family, something we are also grateful for. Through blood, sweat, tears, and lots of opposition, he had compassion for us, much like Jesus has for us, His children. Honor The Father of your home and children today. They do so much.

Prayer Declaration:
Jesus, thank you for being our Father and for strong Godly fathers. The world needs them more than ever. Encourage, bless and touch every father on Earth today. Help them to know you, their Heavenly Father, first of all, out of that flows everything else.

June 20
Our Descendants

Our second son, Dennis Lynn, turns 28 today. His firstborn and our first grandson has his 4th birthday today. These two are so much alike. I think it's fitting for them to share a birthday. They both have tender hearts. They both love Jesus. They mutually care for others and love gifts. We celebrated the two over the weekend. Dennis yesterday on Father's Day, which was only fitting as he is also a wonderful Father. It's a joy to see him parent his sons with so much patience and wisdom.

I love the fact that our children now get to choose how they want to parent their children. They do not have to make the same mistakes we made with them, but much more can start from a healthier place; we hope and pray.

Parenting isn't easy, and those babies don't come with a manual except the Bible. Zion, four, is so thoughtful and mature for his age. He is a proud big brother. He loves to introduce Zander as his brother Zonder. It's adorable. His vocabulary is ever-increasing, which is a real delight. He keeps saying he wants to be 10. He has said this so many times I can't help wondering what God has for his little life that is 10 years old. I've told him so many times he is a good boy and a good brother and smart and on and on.

We believe in speaking life and not death over them. Saturday, we were having a little picnic on the back deck to celebrate him, and he closed the sliding screen door all by himself. I heard him say to himself, "I'm a smart boy." Yes, you are Zion. God made you smart, and he has wonderful plans for you. Whatever we tell them at this tender young age, they believe. Speak gently and carefully!

Prayer Declaration:
Jesus, thank you for your gift of sons and grandsons. Your plan for generations is incredible and wonderful. Teach us how to carry your name and your legacy for all the generations to come. The Lord is good, His unfailing love continues forever. Isaiah 66:22, "For as the new heavens and new Earth which I will make shall remain before me, says the Lord, so shall your descendants and your name shall remain."

June 21
Keep Going and Growing

I'm learning how to play golf these days. Finally, at 51 years old. I had played mini golf before and never cared for it much. However, out on the big golf course with the sun, the wind, the carts, the family altogether, I say yes to that. The first time was on Mother's Day. My intent was only to ride along and be outside with the family. Alas, I got hooked, and now I'm trying to learn the technique and everything. Why? Because it's something our kids love to do. At first, they got their dad started, and now me.

I've learned that I can either stay in my comfort zone and be left behind in the family fun or I can step out and learn new things in this empty nesting season. Another example was learning how to ski. Such hard work, but also worth it. But then, aren't most things worth having like that? It takes endurance and commitment. It's wonderful if you have people who inspire and challenge you to keep growing and learning new things. You can too. The sky's the limit. When was the last time you pushed yourself to do something new or hard? Whether learning a new skill or going through a hard time in our personal lives, 2nd Chronicles 15:7 is a good verse to remember, "But As for you, be strong and do not give up, for your work will be rewarded. I have experienced the truth of this verse many times and I dare say you have too. So, let's keep going physically and spiritually.

Prayer Declaration:
Jesus, thank you for the endless opportunities we get to experience. Help us to never get complacent, or too comfortable. But teach us to keep growing and learning every day, in every season of our lives. Amen.

June 22
Lineages and Legacies

Families, sons, daughters, grandsons, granddaughters, moms, dads, grandpas, grandmas. Legacies, lineages, and generations. It's all on my mind these days, near and dear to my heart. It's a wonderful, precious, and special thing God planned for us, one we all get to be a part of. I never gave it that much thought when we were younger, but like I said before, turning 50 and having grandchildren makes it all more real, somehow, the importance of leaving a Godly legacy.

Are we declaring God's goodness to the next generations? Do we speak of the miracles he has done for us? Psalm 71:18 describes my heart these days. "Even when I am old and gray, do not forsake me, God, until I declare your power to the next generation, your might, to all who are to come."

If you have children who don't seem to be walking with Jesus, don't give up, and never underestimate your powers as a praying mother. It can be a difficult thing to pray through and keep believing in them. I think it can be normal for young adults to go through a season of finding their own faith in God. They may have been saved at a young age, and only when they are a bit older does it become more real to them. Often, they come out stronger in their faith on the other side of their search or struggles, press in, and keep the faith for them. Above all, let's remember they are watching us! Do our lives portray something they want? More is caught than taught; let's live a life worth leaving a legacy for the next generations.

Prayer Declaration:
Jesus, we need you more than ever today to raise the next generation, the only thing we can take to heaven with us. Jesus, I pray that You will be known in the generations to come, your power, your glory, your might. Amen.

June 23
Humiliating Mistakes

"Kind words are like honey, sweet to the soul and healthy for the body," Proverbs 16:24. I experienced this from multiple people yesterday, even after doing something so stupid. Remember how we replaced my new car totaled by a deer? Now this new (to me) car is also in the shop. The reason is that I literally ran into a post in a parking lot so hard that the airbags once again popped out and bruised me in several places. Again, my arm is swollen and very sore, my leg has a cut, my chest hurts, and my neck needed to be iced last night.

My husband was already inside the store where we were buying all the groceries for our event this weekend. I called him, and he came out immediately. The car horns started going off and wouldn't stop, drawing still more attention to my dilemma. Of course, now people started gathering around me, asking if I was okay.

One sweet little lady gave me a hug and assured me that Jesus would make everything better. Another complete stranger laid on his back under my car to try and find the horn disconnect. I was so embarrassed, and yet I felt so loved by complete strangers. My oldest son Duane came and towed my car home. My husband held me as I cried and then helped me shop for all the groceries because we still needed them for our big event coming up.

When we got home, my other sons were encouraging and told me of similar things they did and hugged me. My husband very kindly told me it's just life, to let it go. He jokingly said maybe I need to go back to driving a horse and buggy. I said yes, I could drive any wild horse back in the day, but these cars keep kicking my butt. Everyone knows Mom keeps her guardian angels very busy. The love and compassion I experienced today reminded me of Jesus. He doesn't condemn us for our mistakes but has grace and mercy for us.

Prayer Declaration:
Thank you, Jesus, for kind and caring people around us. Teach me what I need to learn from this accident today. Help us to remember to be kind and compassionate to others when they too need to know it's okay to make mistakes. God Forgives us and we need to forgive ourselves and others also!

June 24
Guardian Angels

Habakkuk 3:18, "I will rejoice in the Lord. I will be joyful in the God of my salvation," is exactly how I felt this morning. Though my body is a bit bruised and sore, I am again without a car. My spirit is alive and well. I'm grateful this morning for how Jesus protected me yesterday. I could have run into another car or, worse, yet another person. Instead, it was just a stupid yellow post! We figured it must have been in my blind spot. My husband helped me realize all these things yesterday. He is one of the kindest, most encouraging people I know. He champions me in everything I do and believes in me no matter what dumb mistakes I make. He's a lot like Jesus. Now, lest you think I really should go back to driving horse and buggy, I have a disclaimer, or at least a few incidents of very scary horse and buggy episodes as well.

The first time was with one of my brothers. I'm not sure what happened, but we were on the way to church, and all of a sudden, we were going down a hill way too fast, headed into the ditch, and dumped over the buggy on its side. I do believe the deep snow cushioned us a bit that day. Others came along and helped us get up; we went on to church. No one was hurt. Another time it was evening, and we were on our way home on a Sunday evening, just newly married. Our horse spooked over a dog that ran out on the road, and again, we ended up in the ditch, tipped over on the side. It was very scary in the dark. My husband hurt his arm pretty well that time. There are more wild horse stories, but for now, let's just say my guardian angels were at work even back then. Can you think of specific times of God's protection? If so, stop to thank and praise Him right now.

Prayer Declaration:
Thank you, Jesus, for guardian angels. Thank you for your mercy and protection. Help us to remember to praise You and give You the thanks you so deserve.

June 25
Community of People

The morning dawns cloudy and cool. A wonderful reprieve from yesterday's relentless heat. We get a little bit of rain, which we need, and it's wonderful. Our team starts to gather at 10 AM, and we start things off with home-cooked food. Next, we hear from numerous team members, testimonies, inspiring speeches, door prizes, auctioning off a pheasant hunt with all proceeds going to water in Africa. We fellowship all afternoon and enjoy another home-cooked meal. One of our contractors is very talented on the grill, so he made grilled chicken for everyone.

Ernest and I are surrounded by amazing people to do life with. When our team of contractors gathers with their families, it's so special. We only gather here once a year as we are scattered across the US. My husband and I are humbled and blessed to have these families travel hundreds of miles to be with us for a few days every year. This event is always the highlight of our summer. Those who must be home on Sunday begin to trickle home after the evening meal. Later in the evening, someone starts a campfire in the fire ring, and the rest of us pull chairs around it and fellowship. Eventually, the rain chases us inside, where we continue to share stories and our hearts until late into the evening. We crawl into bed exhausted, but our hearts are full and appreciative. A lot of our contractors are also people who, like us, left our Amish communities. It's always extra special to gather and do community life for several days. It's probably the one thing we all miss from our Amish days is having that ready-made community.

Prayer Declaration:
Jesus, thank you for our community of people. Teach us to really stop and remember how blessed we are. If there are people without this kind of fellowship and blessing, help them find it. We are not meant to walk alone, but in fellowship with other people.

June 26
Give Back

"Rejoice in the Lord always. And again, I say rejoice!" Yes, and Amen. There is a lot to praise Him for, especially from the past several days. Our annual fundraiser event was on Friday night then our team event yesterday. My husband got up early this morning, like always, and put the breakfast casserole in the oven, which allows me to sleep just a wee bit longer. I hear him talking with someone early in the living room and again later outside with someone at the fire pit. I stayed snuggled in my bed a while longer, counting my blessings for having a house and property to share with others yet still having my own privacy. It truly is a dream come true! When God provided these 100 acres for us, I would walk around it praying. I promised him we would use it to serve others.

God has been faithful in providing more than enough for us. What has He given you that you can share with others? Maybe it's not land or houses, it doesn't have to be, but you do have gifts and talents or some blessings that God gave you? Really think about it. As you step out and share it, it will only multiply and grow.

"…Freely you have received, so now freely give." This is the last part of Matthew 10:8. So many people feel like they don't have any special gift or aren't particularly talented in anything. Personally, I don't believe that is true. Sometimes we just need someone to encourage us in our gifts and talents and help us discover and develop them. I encourage you to look at your own life and see if you can determine what your gifts and talents are that you can use to bless others. Maybe even ask someone else what they see in you. I would love to help you discover your gifts!

Prayer Declaration:
Jesus, thank you, thank you! Teach each one of us to see what You see in us. Help us to be faithful with what you have entrusted to each one of us. Teach us to use it for your honor and glory.

June 27
Gifts and Talents

The first prophetic words I ever got from someone were when we went to Switzerland years ago. We were on our journey to freedom. We went with the church group we were a part of at the time. It was a trip to remember. At one point, they had a team of people prophecy over us. One of my words of prophecy and encouragement was that I have a gift of hospitality. They envisioned a picture of me serving cake to people. Would I have ever recognized that if they wouldn't acknowledge it in me way back then? I've heard it many times since, and it always encourages me. I do love to host, especially when my body can keep up with my heart. My husband and I both enjoy it.

This morning we have a few minutes alone to breathe, connect, and enjoy our coffee together before we start our day. His mom will be back around 2 PM today; a huge treat to have her with us for the weekend. By 6 tonight, we have steak on the grill and are gathered around the table again with our friends from the Carolinas and a few local friends, along with a few of our children. My husband's steaks are the best in the Midwest. Another evening around the table with good food, fellowship, and friends is so satisfying.

It's typical for us to host this way. Most times, it is something that comes naturally and easily for us. So again, what is it for you? I dare say you are more gifted than you think because why would God give us gifts and talents that would cause us to struggle or be hard for us? James 1:17 says, "Every good gift and every perfect gift is from above, coming down from the Father of lights." Start thanking Jesus for your gifts, talents, and blessings today, and watch them multiply.

Prayer Declaration:
Jesus, thank you for what you have put inside each one of us. Teach us how to develop and grow in these, bless your people with what you have entrusted to us.

June 28
Team Effort

"Encourage one another and build each other up, just as in fact you are doing," 1 Thessalonians 5:11. What if we would all practice this verse? Do you have people like that in your life at all? Can I encourage you to find some? Whenever we gather our team together, a lot of this happens. We love seeing profound, positive friendships develop and people speaking life over each other. Deep down, we all long for and need that. Maybe you can be that for someone else.

This year we had two ladies who worked for the same ministry we have all partnered with in Africa come to our event. This meant the world to us that they would travel from California and North Carolina to be with us, to encourage and speak life to us. They also explained to everyone what water in Africa means to the people there. Something we take for granted every day can literally be the difference between life and death in Africa.

Putting together these events takes weeks of work for our family, but the help, encouragement, and feedback from the African people make it worth all the effort. Plus, there is this saying, "Anything worth having is uphill." Does anything in your life feel like it's currently uphill? Seek out mentors who will encourage you. You can do this. Life was never meant to be an easy ride, just coasting along. Dare to row against the current at times. Dare to pursue your dreams. Surround yourself with people who bring the good out of you and run your race. I believe in you.

Prayer Declaration:
Jesus, thank you again for the good people on our team and in our lives. Teach us how to be that for others and then multiply it back to us. Give us courage that comes from surrounding ourselves with good, positive and sound people.

June 29
Amish Roots

"For, as in one body, we have many members and the members do not all have the same function." Romans 12:4 is so very true. We all have a different part to play in the big picture of life. I saw this so clearly over the weekend as we gathered together early Friday morning to prepare food and lots of other things for the evening fundraiser.

Everyone pitched in. These are the times that remind me of living in the Amish community. We came together, and the work would vanish under many willing hands. The B&B was buzzing today with one woman in charge of the pies. She is extremely good at baking pies, producing 45 pies in record time. My sister-in-law took charge of the potato salad and, under her direction and skill, turned 50 pounds of raw potatoes into appetizing homemade potato salad. Another good friend took charge of the shop and set up all the auction items perfectly. Her gifts of organizing, managing the money, and auction, kept things flowing smoothly. My two nieces took care of the food table all night, along with their husbands. Another friend and her 4 daughters served pie and ice cream all night. Other good friends grilled all the meat for the evening. The band came all the way from Nashville and sang their hearts out. The fireworks people gave us a spectacular show. Still, other neighbors, friends, and strangers donated amazing items for the auction. Several different, prosperous businessmen helped us sponsor this event. My heart bursts with gratitude, watching it all unfold and seeing the beauty and power behind people gathering together and everyone contributing to what they are good at.

I sense Jesus himself smiling in those times, of people working together in unison. The water we will be able to provide to Africa through events like these. Whole villages will be blessed every time we have the funds for one more well! A huge thank you to the wonderful, caring, giving people. We get to do life with amazing people, and to say we are blessed is an understatement.

Prayer Declaration:
Jesus, will you personally bless and reward every single man, woman, and even children who poured out their hearts for You this weekend. May it come back to them many times over.

June 30
Time is Fleeting

Oh, what is as fair as a day in June? How can this be the last day of the month of June already? My favorite summer month of the year. Time truly is so fleeting. I read this quote the other morning, and it made me think. "The biggest mistake we make in life is thinking we have time." Is that true? It could be. Ever since my husband and I are now half a century old, we are more aware of how fleeting and fast time goes.

We try to intentionally take time for ourselves, each other, and our children especially. In fact, today, we are starting to get the camper ready to go camping this weekend. A few nights with just the two of us and a few nights with all of the family. After our busy weekend, this will be just what we all need. Relax. Sit by the fire at the lake. Soak up some beach, sand, sun, and fun.

What do you do for relaxation? What helps you to slow down? Do you have a favorite hobby that helps you unwind or relax, something that helps you put your life into perspective and remember that we won't be here forever? In fact, every day, every hour, and every minute, we are closer to eternity. Psalms 39:4 says, "Lord, remind me how brief my time on Earth will be. Remind me that my days are numbered, how fleeting my life is." All I can say to that is, yes, Lord, do remind us.

Prayer Declaration:
Teach us to be aware, to be in the moment, to live each day as if it truly were our last. Teach us to focus on the things that truly matter in eternity. Jesus, teach us to live with eyes fixed on You, and our hearts set on heaven.

July 1
Better Boundaries

We are still wrapping up our event from over a week ago tonight. Yesterday it was a week since I wrecked my car. It was also a week that I hadn't gone off our property. Now, granted, people have been here off and on from Thursday night to Tuesday afternoon. Still, it's not normal for me, but it has felt so right. I heard in my 'spirit' someone telling me to *slow down.* It also felt right to cancel all my appointments, and I did just that this week. I had lots of healthy naps, watching the sunsets, dinners on the patio, and taking care of my flowers. Some of them almost died of thirst over the weekend because I couldn't keep up with everything.

Another amazing thing I've been realizing is the extra measure of peace I've been feeling and being able to think clearer. At first, I thought it was all my prayer warriors praying over me, and I'm sure that was part of it. However, it's been a little while now since I made myself some good social media boundaries and got completely rid of some.

This explains it. I'm so very grateful for the realization and this exchange of peace for clutter. Proverbs 4:23 says, "Above all guard your heart, for everything you do flows from it."

Social media is amazing, I love it so much, but like a lot of things, too much can be detrimental, especially to our mental health. My husband and I packed up the camper and headed for our favorite lake at the campgrounds, 20 minutes from our house. We took the boat out for a sunset cruise, and that's when he told me he, too, had noticed a positive difference in me. More relaxed and more present. Thank you, Jesus. One of my biggest reasons for making boundaries was to be more present for those who matter the most to me. What is it for you? Do those closest to you feel they have your time and attention? Are you fully present with those who need and want you the most?

Prayer Declaration:
Jesus, help us to truly guard our hearts against anything that will divide our attention and affection from you and our precious loved ones. Teach us how to use the wonders of technology without being devoured by it. We need You desperately in this ever-changing age, Jesus.

July 2
Camping Traditions

Waking up without an alarm clock, no agenda, a slow, relaxing day ahead of me, pure bliss. I'm definitely in one of my happy places. My husband is up early, per usual, sitting outside enjoying his coffee. I brew mine and stay inside, snuggle in my blanket on the couch until the smell of sausage frying draws me outside. This is very strange for us to be camping with just the two of us. It is also very good and much needed after weeks of being exceptionally busy. Tonight, family and friends will start joining us here, but for today, it's just us. We started camping way back when our children were small, tent camping to be exact. It was always the highlight of our year and still is. Yes, now we finally have a nice camper, but I'm again very thankful for how we started out in the dirt. With a tent large enough for us and our six children, talk about togetherness.

Can you think of a time in your life when you, too, started with what you had, and it then slowly and surely grew into something bigger? As you thank God for what He has blessed you with and focus on your blessings, they have a way of growing, especially our family. Our children have grown up and left the house. We have grown in number by adding a son-in-law, 2 daughters-in-law, and two grandsons. I only expect that to keep happening. Praise and thanksgiving can be a powerful thing. I'm so grateful for one-on-one time with my husband today. I'm grateful for the time alone here this afternoon. I'm grateful for the family that will join us here over the weekend. Sitting in the dirt is fine; sleeping on it, not so much: From dirt tent camping to a beautiful camper, "...my heart and cup runneth over," Psalms 23:5. Jesus, thank you for blessing us.

Prayer Declaration:
Thank you for allowing us to enjoy your wonders of nature. Teach us all how to be thankful and count our blessings. Help us to praise and be raised up instead of complaining and remaining the same. Teach us to take every thought captive.

July 3
When Life Comes Full Circle

The family started trickling in late last night. The fireworks show here was already over. It's different now that the children are older and have lives and schedules of their own, but for the most part, the whole empty nesting business is pretty sweet. My husband and I set up the exact same huge tent we used with our six children yesterday afternoon.

Our friends from Idaho, who now have four sons, are in the area and joined us. This truly feels like we have come full circle. Marvin, the dad of this family, used to be like a son to us in some ways when we were still living back here years ago. He was my husband's best worker on his crew, and he was our "driver" because we were not yet driving on our own because we were still Amish. He took us camping many times when our children were small, and now here we are, all back at the same campgrounds. Isn't life just wonderful like this? I'm a very nostalgic person anyway, so things like this are very special to me.

This little family will always have a special place in our hearts. We had a wonderful time around the fire and on the water with delightful food and fellowship. The sounds of children laughing and fires crackling throughout the campfire are music to my ears. There is a camaraderie that is felt among campgrounds. Families outside enjoying each other, the great outdoors, celebrating time off from their jobs, and celebrating our free country. Psalms 119:45 says, "I will walk about in freedom, for I have sought out your precepts."

Prayer Declaration:
Jesus, let that be us, walk about as free people, bringing freedom to our country, to our places of influence, freedom to our families, keeping our own hearts free first of all. It truly is for freedom that You have set us free, we thank you and we praise you forever.

July 4
God Bless America

Millions of Americans celebrate the 4th of July, the day America declared its independence so many years ago. We pride ourselves in our independence and our freedom. I, too, am extremely grateful to live in our amazing America. At the same time, my heart hurts for the many ways we have strayed away from what our forefathers founded our country on. Will you pray with me today for our USA? Pray that we turn to Jesus again and common sense will once again be popular. All throughout the Bible, when people pray and repent, God hears them and answers. We need to get on our knees and cry out to God to save our country. We woke to cloudy skies this morning. We took tents down and made our breakfast outside before the rain chased us inside.

It's cozy and crowded and wonderful. The rain pours down outside, but inside we stay dry. Laughter, games, lots of coffee, and great conversations make up our morning. The children head back home in the afternoon. My husband and I clean everything up before we settle in to read, write, and relax. We have the rest of today and tonight, we're still here. We are so blessed to be able to enjoy this downtime.

As with everything else, this 4th weekend is so much more serious and sobering than it used to be. Do we truly realize how blessed we are to still live in a free country, or do we take it for granted? It is way too easy to do so. 1 Peter 2:16-17 says it well, "Live as people who are free, not using your freedom as a cover up for evil but living as servants of God. Honor everyone. Love the brotherhood. Fear God. Honor the emperor."

Prayer Declaration:
Jesus, thank you for America. Thank you for a free country. Teach us how to honor an emperor we don't always agree with. Teach us what we can do individually to maintain our free country. We repent and we cry out to You for mercy. God, hear our prayers.

July 5
Back to the Basics

Camping restores my soul. Call me crazy, but there's just something about sitting in the dirt and sand, letting the world slow down around you. The lap of the water on the beach, the waves that come in from the wind, and the boats. Family spending time together, fires lit up all around us, and again the laughter of children floating on the airwaves. It's all so therapeutic and delightful to me.

Seeing everything through our little grandson's eyes also adds so much. Things like going to the playground with them, getting on the merry-go-round until we were so dizzy we couldn't walk, training them how to swim with tubes until the rain chased us inside, teaching them how to play the game of my childhood, "Sorry." Whoever came up with camping is brilliant, in my opinion. My heart feels full, and my soul rejuvenated after four nights at the lake.

Psalms 23:3 says, "He restores my soul. He leads me in the paths of righteousness for His namesake." Maybe it isn't camping for you; maybe it's something completely different. What makes your soul feel restored and your world feel like all is well? There's an age-old song, "It is well with my soul." My husband and I had good discussions over coffee this morning about our country. We are so very grateful for our country but also realize we need an awakening. If we want to stay in a free country, we have to work at it. Maybe we all need more time in the dirt and less time on social media and technology in general, back to our roots, back to what the country was founded on, which was a lot more of Jesus and common sense.

Prayer Declaration:
Jesus, save us from our own stupidity. We need You now more than ever. Open our eyes to the truth that will set us free. Save our country, Jesus.

July 6
Worship Jesus

Everything is packed up and cleaned out, food unpacked, and all the towels and laundry done. Another year of family camping is in the books. Nothing is left except some bug bites, sunburns, and precious memories. I posted too many pictures on Facebook this morning simply because my favorite thing about Facebook is the memories that pop up on my feed daily. A picture says 1000 words is an age-old saying. I tend to agree, at least in part. A camping memory popped up yesterday from a year ago of one of our little grandsons, Zion, heartily enjoying an ear of sweet corn. He was short and chubby and so adorable. A year later, he has grown taller and leaner, taking away some of his baby look. Now he communicates in full-grown adult language at only four years old. We are amazed at his constant new words; it's adorable. Zander is right behind him, repeating everything and just as adorable. Seeing them grow up right in front of our eyes is sobering and delightful.

We didn't have Facebook or pictures or cameras or photo albums when our children were little; no baby pictures or birthday pictures to compare from one year to the next. In the Amish, having photographs of people and especially deliberately posing for one is considered wrong. I'm not 100% sure where the verse is found that they base this on. I think it is in Exodus 20:4, which says, "You shall not make for yourself a carved image or likeness of anything that is in heaven above or that is in the earth beneath or that is in the water underneath." There are other verses, too, that warn against having or making idols. If we are honest, we probably all have some idols in our lives we struggle not to bow to. Anything that we exalt above God in our lives is an idol. Let's worship Jesus instead.

Prayer Declaration:
Do we worship idols unaware sometimes, Jesus? Will You teach us what an idol truly is and make us aware if we are guilty of this? Search our hearts, Lord, and reveal any hidden idols to all of us. Thank you, Lord, for convicting us, let us worship and adore You only.

July 7
Be the Community

Foremost on my mind right now is one of my nieces. She has some health issues. My heart goes out to her and her family. My prayers are with them constantly as they seek help and healing. I know God can and He will. As I processed with my mom about this last night, she shared with me how the church is rallying around them and supporting them, bringing in meals for the children at home while mom and dad are away doctoring with the oldest daughter. None of this is easy for any of them, but I'm so thankful that the children have their grandma just down the road a bit. They have a community that cares and helps and will even help with any medical bills. They always do this when someone has a need. This is a trait of the Amish community that is so good, so strong, so right. They take care of each other.

This is a community at its finest and something I miss the most about not being Amish. Whether it's getting ready for church, at their homes, if it's a frolic to raise a barn or a house or a funeral, they get together and help each other. They share their resources, time, food, and, yes, even money. They have no insurance. They are that for each other. They live out Luke 3:10-11 very well, "The crowds asked Jesus what, then should we do? He answered, whoever has two shirts must share with the one who has none, and whoever has food must do the same." Maybe you and I aren't Amish anymore, but we, too, can practice this verse. It might take more diligence on our part to seek out those needs, but this is one rich part of my heritage I want to practice.

Prayer Declaration:
Jesus, show us how, when and who to help to be your hands and feet in our churches, in our cities, towns, and whatever other countries you call us to.

July 8
Trusting Jesus

"I will praise the Lord according to his righteousness and will sing praise to the name of the Lord most high," Psalm 7:17. Sometimes it's easier to do that than other times, wouldn't you agree? No matter how rough life gets, there is always so much to be thankful for, just take a piece of paper and start writing out your blessings. The list is endless. God is good no matter what our circumstances say. I love how Ann Voskamp says we can always be *soul safe.*

Nothing and no one can keep us from a safe place in the shadow of our almighty God's wings or our home secured in heaven after our short time here on Earth. Some days I can hardly wait for that. Till then, there is work to be done and praise to be given to our Heavenly Father. My heart is rejoicing with one of my sisters who was just able to move to a different community.

This community is more modern and spiritually enlightened. I do believe they will flourish there and be well-loved. This is another answered prayer from my prayer closet. It was a long time coming, and now God did it. You know when you pray and ask God for things to happen and change, invite Him into moving in people's lives, we often don't know how He's going to do that. We can get hung up on what looks impossible to us, but guess what? We don't need to know how. Our job is to pray and release God to do the work however and whenever He chooses to. He knows the right times and all the details involved. What do you believe in Him for today? Don't give up. He hears He knows He cares.

Prayer Declaration:
Jesus, thank you for your faithfulness to answer our prayers. Teach us how to pray in faith and be okay with not knowing how You will accomplish our requests. Increase our faith, Jesus, and help our unbelief. Thank you for always working on our behalf and for our good.

July 9
Therapy in Nature

Today is a slow relaxing morning. These are so special. The weather is perfect too. The last couple of days have been mostly cloudy, but this morning the sun is out in all its glory. The plants need water before it gets too hot, so I water them, talk to them, pick off dead leaves, and just baby them. My plants are my therapy. Feeling the lush green grass under my bare feet is also therapy. Praising Jesus comes so naturally to me when I'm outside in his beautiful, wonderful creation. It reminds me of the verse that speaks about the rocks crying out in worship if His people don't. When the Pharisees were upset with the people who were worshiping Jesus, he replied to them, saying, "I tell you, if these were silent, the very stones would cry out loud" Luke 19:40.

Jesus is worthy of our praise, and He will get it one way or another. Colossians chapter one speaks of creation, how even inanimate objects like rocks, mentioned in Luke, were made for the glory of God. No wonder even rocks are so beautiful. Each one has its own unique shape and place, just like humans.

Have you ever really taken the time to listen when you are outside in nature? There is a lot of sound, song, and praise happening all the time. Take a video sometime and then listen to the background. I'm always amazed. Could this be nature itself worshiping our creator? After all, He created not only us but everything we get to enjoy. I encourage you to go outside barefoot sometime and really feel the grass under your feet. Breathe in the fresh air and listen for the whisper of the trees and the breezes. It's all incredible and so good.

Prayer Declaration:
Jesus, thank you for your most beautiful creations. Enlighten in us a deeper appreciation for what we get to enjoy. Help us to give You the worship You so deserve. Thank you, Jesus.

July 10
Alpha and Omega

I love Sundays. They center around relaxing, family, good food, and fellowship. Whether we go to church or gather together as a family for a meal, sometimes both on the same Sunday, it's always a refreshing time. God, in his infinite wisdom, once again knew just what we would need for our upcoming week. Sunday, Sabbath Day, rest and refuel day. Worship was amazing, as always. As we sang Holy, Holy, Holy, and Worthy of it All, among other songs, it felt so right and so reviving.

The message, too, was so good and given by a woman, which is always refreshing for me to hear a message from a woman's perspective. She talked about God being Alpha and Omega, Revelation 1:8, "I am the Alpha and the Omega, says the Lord. The God who is, and who was, and who is to come, the Almighty." Don't you just love this? To me, it all speaks of God being past, present, and future. He was, He is, and He is to come. Can you see that in your own life?

Can you see where God has been and what he's done for you? Can you see what He is currently doing and working out for you? Do you have hope for what He will do in the future? He is faithful in everything. He did it, He does it, He will not only start things as the Alpha, but he also ends things as our Omega. Even a difficult season of life will end eventually. One season ends, Omega, and a new one begins, Alpha. This keeps us from growing stagnant and stale, just like nature and the beautiful world around us.

Prayer Declaration:
Thank you, Jesus, for your plan for us. Thank you that you are both Alpha and Omega, the beginning and the end. Teach us to worship and give you the glory and honor you alone are praiseworthy. Show us how to trust you in the valleys and on the mountain tops just the same.

July 11
Conviction Not Condemnation

Speaking of new beginnings and new seasons, every Monday morning can be a new beginning, a new start. Maybe you fell off the wagon last week in your eating habits. Maybe you gave in to an addiction. Maybe you blew it with your children or your spouse. Maybe all of the above. Today is a new day, a new week. Let it go. Apologize if you need to. Forgive someone, and most of all, forgive yourself. Jesus forgives us instantly when we repent. Why, then, can't we forgive ourselves? Guilt loves to weigh us down and condemn us. Psalms 103:12 tells us this, "As far as the east is from the West, so far, He has removed our transgressions from us," that is good news.

Where do you need to forgive yourself from your own past? I, too, have been there, and sometimes we need to forgive others and ourselves more than once. Sometimes, more often than not, it's not an instantaneous thing, but a walking it out thing, believing the promises of God, believing and receiving His forgiveness first of all. Remember, feeling condemned is not from God. As believers, we will feel convicted, but not condemned.

We still have that small voice, the feeling of wanting to choose a different way. I want to and can overcome this addiction with God's help. Conviction should always make us feel hopeful and not hopeless. Don't listen to the enemy; the devil's accusing and condemning voices. For many years I lived under condemnation and am so thankful it's gone in the name of Jesus. Instead, Jesus continues to gently and continually convict me and invite me into more freedom in Him, one step, one day at a time, physically, emotionally, and spiritually.

Prayer Declaration:
Jesus, thank you for your sweet conviction and forgiveness. Teach us to know the difference as believers between conviction and condemnation. Help us to believe and receive Romans 8:28, "There is now no condemnation for those who are in Christ Jesus." Thank you, Lord.

July 12
Fear Not

With everything that is happening around us in our broken world, are you afraid? Do you lay awake at night, not able to sleep because of worry and fear? If you do, then I have good news for you. Psalms 27:1 says, "The Lord is my light and my salvation, so why should I be afraid?" The Bible also tells us not to be afraid and to fear not. In fact, it says it 365 times. That's enough for one a day. I think perhaps God knew how fearful his people might become, especially in the last days when it seems like or looks like evil is winning; in some ways, it truly never will. Jesus is still on his throne. He will win the war of good and evil. We can win, too, as his sons and daughters. We do not have to live afraid and anxious.

Psalm 73:26 says, "My health may fail, and my spirit may grow weak, but God remains the strength of my heart. He is mine forever." He can be yours forever, too. Remember, nothing that ever happens to you can keep from you your eternal inheritance with Jesus forever. This is what I'm holding on for; will you too? Together we can do this. We can stand strong. We can even use our voices to speak out against evil and injustice. We can raise awareness. We can pray for our country. There is so much we can do to help bring change. Action has a way of pushing back the fear and the darkness. Inaction likes to make us feel helpless and powerless, but in Jesus, we have so much power! Step out in faith today.

Prayer Declaration:
Jesus, thank you that we are always safe with you, our hearts, our spirits, our souls. Teach us to worship when we are afraid and show each one of us where to take action. Give us wisdom on where to make a difference in our world.

July 13
Being Present

A gorgeous, rain-washed morning, once again. How thankful we can be that the rains come from heaven, just as we need them. It's one thing I so love about living in the Midwest. Seldom do we have to worry about drought or watering crops and lawns. After living in the West for eight years, this is another thing I won't take for granted. Our weather has been almost perfect recently, and I'm soaking it all up. These dog days of summer are priceless. They go by so fast. My husband and I had a good chat with our son recently. We were talking about just how fast time goes by. He is the one raising our two sweet grandbabies. He said the last five years feel like a blur. I feel you, son. Children have a way of blending everything together because they need care 24/7.

We discussed the importance of a good routine, boundaries, and, most of all, slowing down and really soaking it up. I was playing with my grandsons the other day. We were splashing in the kiddie pool with a made-up game and some balls. We were laughing and having so much fun; I was completely present.

My husband commented on it. He loves how much I play with the boys versus what I did with our own. It's probably something most of us grandparents do better than we did with our own children, for whatever reasons. If you are in the parenting stage now, you will never regret taking extra time for your children. Back then, I had to work hard to keep up with our simple lifestyle. Amish is simple in some respects but requires lots of physical work. It's a bit of a paradox and complicated, yet it was my own doing. I could have asked for a lot more help than I did. 1st John 2:17, "The world and its desires pass away, but whoever does the will of God lives forever."

Prayer Declaration:
Jesus let us pay attention to the most important things in life. Our precious children. Teach us to slow down and truly live for the next life. Help us to be truly present and enjoy our loved ones, while here on earth.

July 14
Death is the Doorway

We woke up to the news that a dear woman we know who had been fighting cancer for quite some time passed over into glory last night. Her pastor husband wrote on his Facebook page. She is "healthy and free." How I love that, it's so true. Once again, evil didn't win! The evil disease that takes too many didn't win. Heaven won; heaven gained another precious soul. She is "soul safe" in the arms of Jesus. We can only imagine what she is now experiencing. Our hearts ache with the family left behind, but we will all get to go that way sooner or later. We used to sing this song in the Amish singings. *We are going down the valley one by one. If we are soul safe with Jesus, it will be a glorious experience.* Do you look forward to going to heaven or do you feel fear of death in your life, knowing it'll be over one day?

I used to have a lot of fear around dying, but Jesus took it away. Once I understood He is the only way to be saved and free. John 14:6 tells us this. "I am the way, the truth and the life. No one comes to the father except through me." "Acts 4:12 says, "There is salvation in no one else" or "there is no other name under heaven given among men by which we must be saved."

No matter how we die, we don't need to fear death itself. It is but the doorway to our next life, heaven! I do hope and pray to live, to see the next generation grow up, but I will live every day knowing one day will be my last day on this troubled, broken Earth.

Prayer Declaration:
The only way, Jesus, thank you for who You are. Teach us to put all our faith, all of our hope in You. Help us to not fear death, but to live ready to die every day, knowing that death is but the doorway to eternity. Let that be Heaven!

July 15
Leave and Cleave

It was my turn to choose date night this week, but first, we needed to finish up our work here at home. Finishing touches for the BNB guests, mowing lawn, emails, phone calls, writing, reading, and the daily dozens. We could easily work all day, but this is where our commitment to being intentional and spending time together comes in.

We head for Lacrosse mid-afternoon and pick up our twin daughters and head for the good old Mississippi. We rent kayaks, drag them down to the river and climb in. We spend the next few hours laughing, floating, bobbing, paddling down and back up the river. It's a perfect hot day to get wet and splashed. It is so relaxing and fun and good for the heart, soul, and mind. Later, we went out for dinner together at one of our favorite places. The Rooftop. Our son-in-law joined us, and it was a wonderful time. We walked down to the park, where live music was playing, and then down to the water, where the sun was setting. Tranquil. Peaceful. Perfect.

My heart is full as we drive them back home. Life wasn't always like this. In fact, when our children were all small and before we had cars, there was a season in our lives where sometimes we wouldn't see anyone or go anywhere for two weeks at a time, except for the farm my husband was working on at the time. The owners were wonderful people and helped a lot with my loneliness during that time.

I'm so thankful our journey has led us to where we are now. If you are in a difficult or lonely season, trust the process. Ask Jesus, *what do you want me to learn in this season?* Looking back on that season of our life, I can clearly see now that God was teaching me to "leave and cleave." Deuteronomy. 13:4, "You shall walk after the Lord your God. Keep His commandments, obey His voice, serve Him, and cleave to Him."

Prayer Declaration:
Jesus, thank you for every season in our lives. Teach us to learn and grow from each one. Help us to listen to your voice and cleave to You above anyone else.

July 16
Stay Strong

"You gave abundant showers, Oh God, You refreshed your weary inheritance. Your people settled in it, and from your bounty God, You provided for the poor," Psalms 68:9-10. When I checked my email yesterday, there was a beautiful video from Mama Heidi in Mozambique, Africa. She is the one we have partnered with to bring fresh water to the villages in Africa. She sent us a sweet video thanking us and all who support our ministry at Simple Faith. At the end, she prayed the above verse from Psalm over us. Her gratitude blessed us so much. The fact that she took the time out of her busy life to make a video is commendable. Heidi and her husband have made a tremendous difference to the people in Africa. They have been so faithful through it all.

Currently, the beloved home base we love over there and where we stayed is being mostly evacuated. This is so sad to me. Most of us would probably throw our hands in the air, give up and come back to America, but not Heidi and Roland. Instead, they are starting a new base where it is safer, away from the radical terrorism that is happening all around them. Their faith to keep going inspires me. They have faced much opposition and trouble, and yet they remain faithful to God's call on their lives.

Do we know what God is calling us to do? Where does he want us to make a difference? We are blessed to be a blessing. Look around and ask where is that for me? Who and what can you bless with your life, your finances? Together, we can make our world a better place.

Prayer Declaration:
Help us to be obedient to the call, Jesus, even when hard times come, thank you for our many blessings. Teach us where we are called to make a difference. Help us to stay strong.

July 17
Sweet Surrender

It took extra effort to get out of bed this morning. It was so tempting to sleep in. After a long hot shower and a good cup of coffee, things already start to come into alignment. Worship was incredible once again. Seeing my kids on the worship team is always a joy. Dennis drums with his whole body and like I heard someone else say to him after service, you are so anointed, and he is. During the altar call, there was an invitation for families to gather in groups to pray together. We did that. How powerful when families pray together. My heart felt so much lighter on the way home from church than it did earlier that morning. The burdens I had been carrying were less heavy. Are you, too, carrying burdens, questions, and unanswered prayers?

May I remind you, you and I both, that God's got our back, even though things may not look like we want them to or thought they would? God is with us, and He will work everything out for our good. Do you know He can even use our mistakes and mess-ups? He can turn it around for something beautiful. There's a line from the story of Joseph that I love so much. It's in Genesis 50:20, "When Joseph forgave his brothers. He said to them, "You meant evil against me, but God meant it for good." Whatever God allows you and me to go through, He, too, means it for our good. Let's soften our hearts today in sweet surrender. He has a good plan for our lives. His plan doesn't mean we won't ever have trials and troubles to walk through, but that God himself will be right there in the middle of our mess with us.

Prayer Declaration:
Jesus, thank you that you are sovereign. Thank you for always being with us. No matter what we are going through. Teach us to trust you and cling to you no matter the trial. Thank you that your love never ends, and you always have our best in mind.

July 18
Live Ready

A different morning, hot, sticky morning at that, with a heat index predicted to go into the hundreds today. Not normal for our part of the world, but then, not so much has been that normal recently, right? Like someone posted recently somewhere, "Normal isn't coming back, Jesus is." Do you believe that? Yes, He is indeed, but the Bible also tells us in Matthew 24:36 about that day or hour, "No one knows, not even the angels in heaven, nor the Son, but only the Father."

The Bible clearly says this, so what makes people predict it every now and then? Of course, they have always been wrong. The truth is we don't need to know the day or the hour. We just need to live ready every day. Some people are sick and have a long time to think about dying; others go in the blink of an eye. Our cousin's young 18-year-old son died instantly in a motorcycle accident last week. His testimony he left behind was he loved the Lord.

How wonderful. He didn't have time to prepare in that instant. The beauty of that is he didn't have to suffer. People who are sick for a long time often have to suffer. The positive side of that is it gives family and friends more time with them and prepares their hearts for what might come. Let's take inventory of our hearts today. If Jesus called us home today, would we be ready to go? Have we made him the King of our hearts? Could people say of us, they loved the Lord? I want that to be said of me. What about you?

Prayer Declaration:
Jesus, may our lives be a living testimony for you. Thank you for every day You give us to serve You. Help us to live for eternity. Teach us to live ready for eternity every day.

July 19
Above all, Love

A beautiful, cloudy, overcast morning, how blissful. It feels heavenly compared to yesterday's high heat. My husband and I were still enjoying our coffee and connection time this morning when we got another death message. My first cousin was killed yesterday. No details on what happened yet. He lived 30 minutes from us in a large Amish community. We played together as little children in another Amish community years ago before both of our families moved to different places. So, I have long lost touch with his family and especially since we left the Amish. Still, it tugs on my heartstrings to go to the funeral, or at least the visitation, to pay my respects to the family and see cousins I haven't seen in years. It's always a struggle, though. Do I go, or do I stay away? This community definitely practices the "shunning." However, sometimes I just feel this nudge to go be among my former culture, even if it's uncomfortable.

There are always some who are delighted to see me and welcome me. There may be others, though, who might confront me or ignore me. I prefer being ignored over confronted. There's part of a verse in Matthew, though, that always brings me comfort. It's the part that says, "Do not worry about what to say or how to say it" Matthew 10:19. We don't need to have the right answers when we are questioned.

Jesus, too, sometimes didn't say a word. As humans, we too often try to defend and explain ourselves. Sometimes silence and love speak more than any words ever could. Let's make sure we have peace in our hearts about where we are in life; that's all we are responsible for. Walk in truth and love.

Prayer Declaration:
Jesus, thank you that You left the perfect example for us. Teach us when to speak the truth in love and when to remain silent. Help us to walk in humility, love and truth always.

July 20
Judge Not

We had tentatively planned to at least attend the viewing or "wake" as some, especially the Amish, call it. They usually have these two evenings in a row. The first one, the married people of the community, gather to sing and be with the family. The next evening, the young folks gather and sing. Again, the community also brings in lots and lots of food, does chores for the family, and anything else that needs to be done. The Amish culture truly does grieve and mourn with each other; they do it with their actions too. I think it's a beautiful part of their culture. Even the mournful songs they sing at these times are comforting somehow and seem fitting for what seems to be untimely deaths. My cousin left a grieving wife, children, and grandchildren behind when he was instantly killed. A log fell on his head at the sawmill he owned.

However, we never made it over at any time because my mom called and warned me that this particular community might not let us stay even if we decided to go. She had heard the family didn't want any non-Amish people there. Hmm. My first thoughts were wow, that seems a bit judgmental. So, we didn't go.

I contemplated this for a while and found myself asking how people become so fearful or so sure that theirs is the only way. They literally ask others to stay away? Then again, how often have I judged people because I didn't know their hearts? It's so easy to judge and condemn people based on our side of the story or by what we see from our perspective. Yet the Bible clearly says in Matthew 7:1, "Judge not, lest ye be judged."

Prayer Declaration:
Jesus, help us to extend the same grace to others we ourselves long for. Teach us how to see people through your eyes and with your heart. Thank you that you alone get to judge people's hearts. Help us to love the sinner, hate the sin, and leave the judging up to You.

July 21
Bible Study Nuggets

My hair was still in a towel when the first woman showed up for our monthly Bible study this morning. I let her welcome in the others as I quickly went and finished getting ready. These ladies who keep showing up month after month, Bibles in one hand and casseroles, salads, or desserts in the other, are some of my heroes. We all vary in age, but we all have at least two things in common. We all come from either Amish or Mennonite backgrounds, and we are all hungry to grow in God and learn more about who He is. Our daughter-in-law led us in worship once again. We worshiped, prayed, shared testimonies, ate lunch together, and studied the Bible. God met us and ministered to us. We talked about how blessed we are that we can meet on a random weekday to fellowship. We talked about how thankful we are that we came from a culture that values women being, "Stay at home Moms," which also frees us up to make our own schedules.

Even when I was still an Amish mother with six little children to care for, I remember thinking there was nothing I would rather do. I get to do something different every day. Neither do I think it's wrong if a mom wants to work outside the home. Maybe she feels called to a specific job that she is gifted in, that is between her, God, and her husband.

Just because something is a privilege or a blessing for me or you does not mean we should make a law of it out of it for everyone. Again, being able to have stayed at home with our children is something I will constantly be grateful for. Deuteronomy 6:67 tells us of the importance of always pouring into our children, "These commandments that I give you today are to be on your hearts. Impress them to your children. Talk about them when you sit at home, when you walk along the road, when you lie down and when you get up."

Prayer Declaration:
Jesus, show us how to do this consistently, especially when our children are still young, innocent, and like little sponges, thank you for your wisdom and your word to teach and lead us.

July 22
Mourn With Hope

"Brothers and sisters, we do not want you to be uninformed about those who sleep in death, so that you do not grieve like the rest of mankind who have no hope," 1st Thessalonians 4:13. This was a part of the powerful message Bill Johnson shared three days after his wife passed away from cancer. His whole message brought healing to my own heart. It brought answers to my unanswered questions if that makes sense. He started out his message by saying, "The backslider in heart will always judge God by what He didn't do, instead of all that He has done." Ouch.

It hit me hard. How many times do we question God and demand answers when things don't turn out the way we hoped or wanted them? Many of us had been praying for Beni's healing. Yet, God took her home. We don't know why, but we do know we will always live with some level of mystery while we are here on Earth.

It takes childlike faith to be okay with the mystery, to believe despite our unanswered prayers, and to choose God in the middle of our pain. Every loss and disappointment can draw us closer to God, or it can push us into unbelief and harden our hearts. The choice is ours. How beautiful that we don't need to mourn as those who have no hope; that's comforting already. Knowing we will see our loved ones again who were saved and have gone ahead of us. This can fill even our days of mourning with hope.

Prayer Declaration:
Jesus, thank you for your hope and peace, even in the middle of pain and mystery. Teach us how to walk in the humility You showed on the cross. Help us to choose You and humility again and again.

July 23
The Little Things

It's one of those hot summer days with a slower rhythm of life, fresh fruit in season, and sizzling steaks on the grill; my husband makes the best steaks. Hearing our little grandsons giggle with sheer delight during a water gun fight. Somehow I am their favorite target. Dinner on the back porch with my nephew, seeing a beautiful rainbow after the rain, and meaningful conversations, bring life to my heart. Some may call it the little things of life, and maybe they are, but don't you think if we live the little moments well, truly enjoy and thank God for them, they can lead to the bigger moments in our lives? Are we so busy chasing the big things in life we often miss the little things? Are what we think are the little things actually the big things? Most times, I have more questions than answers. When was the last time you sat outside undistracted and only soaked up the beauty of God's amazing handiwork?

The sunsets have been so magnificent recently. Maybe nature doesn't speak to you, and that's okay. What is it for you, the so-called little things that bring you joy and peace? Being busy is such an American cultural thing, but neither do we want to be idle.

Finding a healthy balance is key to our well-being. Let's not be so busy chasing the glitz and the glamor that we forget to live. Often when we lose sight of what really matters, it can hurt our health and our families. Maybe let's do some soul-searching today. Who or what are we living for? Mark 8:36 asks the question very well, "What good is it for someone to gain the whole world yet forfeit their own soul?"

Prayer Declaration:
Jesus, thank you for the millions of blessings we get to enjoy daily. Help us to never take them for granted, but to continually give You thanks. Teach us to take the time to evaluate continually and ask ourselves, are we living for, what really and truly matters?

July 24
Stay Alert

Waking up early and driving to church by myself to practice with the worship team before service is such a privilege, such a blessing, to be a part of. My husband, some of the family, and my nephew join me in time for the service. Worship centered around the goodness of God and how worthy He is of our worship.

The message was about strong marriages and raising Godly children in our current culture. It was such a good message. Great encouragement to the parents with little ones to be ever so careful about what they allow them to watch, see, and hear. It is all beginning to shape their little characters. The advice to parents with older children who might be straying away from their faith is to keep praying for them but, above all, to keep loving them.

We were reminded of the importance of love, humility, and forgiveness for strong, lasting marriages. It was all so good and timeless advice. "Be alert and sober of mind, your enemy, the devil prowls around like a roaring lion looking for someone to devour" 1 Peter 5:8. This verse is truer than ever today. The enemy of our souls would love to wreck our marriages, our homes, and our children. It is our job to stand up against him and say no, not today, Satan! Instead, we will be alert, watchful, and aware and invite Jesus into every part of our lives. His power can change everything. Pray in His blood, His protection over it all.

Jesus, thank you that your power trumps any other power!

Prayer Declaration:
Teach us how to live vigilant, and yet without fear. Help us to recognize the schemes of the enemy and realize we have the power through You to overcome every attack of his.

July 25
Baby With the Bathwater

Never in my life did I expect to enjoy Mondays as much as I do in this current season of life. Looking back on my previous life, Mondays were filled with mountains of laundry, little ones, and my husband going back to work. Getting all the laundry done with an old-fashioned wringer washer and no dryer was a major chore, one I don't miss at all. It's okay to appreciate some things of how we were raised and to not appreciate other things. Laundry would have been so much more doable and made more sense with a washer and dryer. It's okay to embrace the good in cultures, messages, and even people. Let the parts go that we don't appreciate. Like the old saying goes, don't throw the baby out with the bathwater, so true and great advice.

Even today, I feel like people want to put all their hope and trust into one culture or one church, one pastor, or one mentor. But not one person, place, or thing has all the answers; that's actually a dangerous way to live. On Judgment Day, you and I will give account for our own lives. We won't be able to point to anyone else and say it's because of him or her or them. No, we will answer for ourselves. It is up to us today who we listen to and who we let influence our lives, minds, and hearts.

Let's make sure it always measures up with what God has to say about it. First and foremost, Jesus is the only one with all the answers. In Him alone, we put our trust. Psalms 20:7 says, "Some trust in chariots and some in horses, but we trust in the name of the Lord our God."

Prayer Declaration:
Jesus, thank you for being trustworthy. Teach us how to discern what to keep and what we need to weed out in every person, church or culture. Help us to measure it all with your word and your wisdom.

July 26
Healing Soul, Body, and Spirit

Another perfect, peaceful morning as I hustle to get my morning routine done. Work out, water flowers, breakfast, and shower before my first client arrives. I feel so privileged and blessed to be able to have this part-time ministry/job. Another huge blessing is to be able to do it from my home office, looking out into the woods. It's amazing to me how God works out even the details of our dreams. In my culture, growing up Amish, counseling and coaching were not a thing, certainly not a thing we did or valued. If I remember right, it was more looked upon as a negative thing. People who needed any type of help mentally, spiritually, or emotionally were usually labeled as something being seriously "wrong with them," or so we thought.

Who are we to separate mental and spiritual well-being from our physical well-being? Why is it okay to get help for our physical bodies but not for our internal struggles? The Bible says we are, "...fearfully and wonderfully made," Psalms 139:14, indeed we are. Our bodies are such miracles, so intricately woven together, and if one part doesn't work right, it can affect everything else.

Soul, body, and spirit, every part must function properly to be completely healthy. Just as we have doctors for our physical bodies when we need them, so we have doctors, counselors, or therapists for our emotional needs when we need them. If we are constantly judging others, that is often a sign that we aren't completely healthy and secure ourselves. Let's lay down our judgements and get the help and healing we need.

Prayer Declaration:
Jesus, thank you that You are our ultimate healer, but that You also give doctors wisdom and guidance as you also heal through them. Help us to have compassion for each other instead of pointing fingers. Teach us how to think rightly about these things and get the healing we need for ourselves first of all.

July 27
Our Neighborhood

Since moving on to our 100 acres in the country and making our home here, we have been so blessed with the best neighbors. We love our neighborhood. There are seven of us on the same road within a mile or so, yet we all have our own privacy because of the trees, the woods, and the rolling hills. We all know each other. It's quite common for me to meet up with another neighbor while out walking or running. We always stop, chat, and catch up. When our oldest son brought his new puppy home a few years ago, he kept running away. The amazing neighbors brought him back too many times to count, different neighbors at different times. Another neighbor will do our chores for us when we go on trips. He will also plow the driveway and just simply be on call whenever my guys go on their winter snowmobiling trips. This past week, the elderly neighbor's horse got out and was roaming all over the neighborhood. Our Airbnb guests and I took some time to catch him for them and we returned him home. They were ever so grateful, just like I am, too, for the kindness of our neighbors.

We don't take our country, common sense, and neighborhood for granted, but we consider ourselves very blessed and fortunate to have this. We look out for each other. Romans 13:10 says, "Love does no harm to a neighbor, therefore love is the fulfillment of the law." Often, love will actually look like something. Love is a verb. How can you love your neighbor today in a tangible way?

Prayer Declaration:
Jesus, thank you for our wonderful neighborhood. Teach us all to walk in love, to love our neighbor's help us to serve and love each other the way You love people.

July 28
Defend the King

The King is here. The King is here. This song came across my Spotify on my run this morning. My thoughts went to when the people cried out in Matthew 21:9. "Hosanna to the King of David. Blessed is He who comes in the name of the Lord, Hosanna in the highest heaven!" There were crowds ahead of Jesus and behind Him, as he rode the donkey into town. They even laid down palm branches for him to ride over or wave in welcome.

Do you ever wonder where these people were when Jesus was condemned and crucified? Were they the same people? Perhaps. I had this vivid dream one time that Jesus was about to be crucified and I was in the crowd, and I too didn't defend him. When I woke up, it broke my heart. I made a commitment to myself and Jesus that day to stand up for Him, to be bold for Him. Of course, one of the best ways we can defend Him and stand up for Him is to live our lives for His glory. There may be times, too, when you will actually feel called to speak out against evil or to speak the truth, but always in love.

How easily do we get swayed by popular opinion or what the masses are saying? What about when everyone else is crucifying a fellow brother or sister's reputation? Will we dare to speak up and defend them too? Maybe let Jesus speak through us. Do we believe that King Jesus is here? He hears and sees all. Let's make His heart glad.

Prayer Declaration:
Jesus, thank you that you are our King. Thank you for standing for us, even when all forsake you, help us to stand up for You and always defend your name and our fellow brothers and sisters' names. Help us to bold for You!

July 29
Joy vs. Happiness

Yesterday was cool, windy, and cloudy most of the day. Definitely a hint of fall at the end of July. As much as I love fall, this made me feel unsettled. Why? Because season changes are difficult for me. Routine and stability are very important for my well-being with every season change.

New rhythms must be found. Have you ever had that vague feeling where you can't quite pinpoint what is troubling you, and yet it seems to be there with you, perhaps even all day? Maybe it's the lingering effects of depression or anxiety, or you are subconsciously dreading something you don't even realize, which for me, it was probably winter yesterday. I know that might sound ridiculous to you, but coming from someone who craves sun and Vitamin D, our long, cold winters here in Wisconsin are no joke. Unless you are like my husband and you love the cold, the snow, and all of winter. After feeling off all day, my husband and I went for a drive and ate dinner at a fun outdoor place we hadn't before. We talked and he made me laugh, like always. We discussed how it's okay to not always feel perfectly happy.

Maybe our culture puts too much pressure on feeling happy all the time. Trying to discern why we are feeling the way we are, though, can be important. Joy and happiness are not the same thing. Nothing can take away our joy found in Jesus alone. He made our emotions happy or sad, yet we can still choose joy through it all. 3 John 16:22, "Talks about sorrow and joy both. So, also you have sorrow or sadness now. But I will see you again and your hearts will rejoice, and no one will take your joy from you."

Prayer Declaration:
Jesus, thank you for the joy that comes only from knowing you. Help us to hold on to that. Teach us to remember, happiness comes in moments, and it is fleeting, but your joy is forever.

July 30
Women of Wisdom

Yesterday was my mom's 80th birthday. She is the epitome of health, hardly takes even a vitamin, goes on walks every day, still lives by herself, mows her own lawn, and has the most gorgeous flowers and garden. She has always been healthy all her life. Maybe it's her lifestyle of hard work and raising her own food for the most part. I'm not sure.

I do long for those genes of growing old gracefully like that with no health issues. It's also our beautiful daughter-in-law Camille's birthday today. She is such a gift to our family. Quiet, sweet, serious, but can be hilarious. She is a wonderful wife to our third son, Lavon. Proverbs 18:22 says it well, "He who finds a wife finds a good thing and obtains favor from the Lord." She definitely has been a blessing to all of us. She is also very beautiful, smart, works super hard, and is also the epitome of health, just like my mom.

They both live out Proverbs 31:27 very well, "She looks well to the ways of her household. And does not eat the bread of idleness." Again, I'm so grateful for the example that my mom left me in taking care of our home, family, and husband first and foremost. Personally, I still believe it's the highest calling we, as women, have. We have so much influence in our homes and families. We often set the tone whether we realize it or not. What are you modeling for the next generation? Will it matter in eternity, or are we chasing a phantom? Are we trying to measure up to the world standards, building a career, or are we building a legacy that will last for all eternity?

Prayer Declaration:
Jesus, thank you for mothers and daughters-in-law. Both are tremendous blessings from You. Impart to us wisdom to live a Godly legacy. Help us to realize the impact we as women have in our homes. Jesus, help us find Godly role models to look up to, that will point us to You!

July 31
God's Power Displayed

Another month gone just like that, the last day of July. It's also our son-in-law Trent's birthday today. It was the perfect evening to gather at their house and surprise him with food, family, and friends. Quality time is one of his main love languages, so he was happy that our daughter planned this for him. He is such a bright, ambitious, kind young man. We are so proud of him and how he lives life. We gathered at church first, where worship was wonderful and the message was convincing and inspiring out of John 9. It was based on a man who had been blind since birth. The disciples asked Jesus in verse 2 who sinned, this man or his parents, that he was born blind. I absolutely love the response Jesus gave them in verse 3, "...neither this man nor his parents sinned, said Jesus."

This happened so that the works of God might be displayed in him. What a wonderful answer; no one is to be blamed here. Maybe that is more often the case than we realize with situations and trials. Do we assume that someone has sinned or is to blame when they go through something like long-term sickness, struggles, or... you fill in the blanks? It's rarely a sin issue but much more an opportunity for God to show his glorious power as He did in this story.

Jesus healed the blind man. Let's all learn from the disciples and ask Jesus questions before we condemn or judge someone based on what we see. If you yourself are suffering or struggling right now, ask Jesus what is the purpose of this. How will you be glorified in this?

Prayer Declaration:
Jesus, Thank you that you can bring good from every situation we ever face. Teach us to see what you see. Help us to remember to ask You what You want to do through us in this circumstance.

August 1
Now I See

The story continues in John 9: 6-7, "After assuring the people that neither the blind man nor his parents had done anything wrong, Jesus reached down and took some dirt, spit on it, and made some clay with mud and put it on the blind man's eyes. He then told him to go wash in the pool of Shalom." Don't you just love the creativity of Jesus when he did healings? I believe it's an example for us. Don't we love our formulas and rituals and reasonings too much?

If something worked one time, let's just do that again and again and make a doctrine out of it! The Pharisees got so caught up in the fact that Jesus healed the man on the Sabbath that they could have cared less that a man was blind but could now see. That was a miracle, yet they discounted it because it didn't fit their theology.

It's easy to think how narrow-minded the Pharisees were. Yet again, how often do we do the same thing? We judge people because it doesn't fit in our way of thinking, our way of doing things, or the box we may have created for them and us. Maybe we completely miss what God is doing in our midst because it doesn't look like we thought it should or would. I know I've been guilty of that in my lifetime. What about you? At the end of the story, in verse 34, they throw this man out of the synagogue. They had no grid for the happiest day of his life, where he could see for the first time ever. This story is quite astounding to me. Can we start rejoicing with people in their miracles?

Prayer Declaration:
Jesus, will you open our spiritual eyes? Will you take the scales of blindness off of our eyes so we don't judge and condemn others so quickly? Help us remember this narrative when we are tempted to put your word, your works, your power and your might in a box.

Soul Water

It's a beautiful, breezy, sunny August morning. We got a wonderful, delicious dump of rain. We were very dry. The grass was getting so brown in places that even just walking across it with shoes on left tracks. As I looked at those tracks and the brown spots coming across the lawn, I thought of us. God often speaks to me through nature. It's easy to see what happens naturally when it doesn't rain. Things dry, shrivel up, and don't grow anymore. We are no different. We, too, need rain for our hearts and our spirits. The rain of the Holy Spirit. We must continually drink from the fountain of life, or we will also dry, shrivel up and quit producing good fruit. I just unplugged our little water fountain this morning because it's hard to keep it filled with the wind and heat, and I have plans to be gone for a few days.

We need to keep drinking the water of life daily to be at our healthiest, best version. What waters you spiritually? Is it worship? Is it God's word? Is it nature? Maybe it's a combination of them all. Maybe it's like my oldest son Duane says. "I feel God in the woods, alone, hunting or on my motorcycle, rushing through the wind, and a wide-open road in front of me." He's a manly man, and that's normal. Again, let's not put someone else's experience in a box. The point is to figure out what is it for us, what makes us come alive and feel God's presence? Drink deeply from the well that will never run dry above all. John 4:14, "But those who drink the water I give, will never be thirsty again. It becomes a fresh, bubbling spring within them, giving them eternal life."

Prayer Declaration:
Jesus, thank you for this fresh living water. Help us to drink deeply and daily from this source. Teach us to not wait until we are dry, withered and wasting away. You're the Living Water we need.

August 3
Days of Youth

Walking down the lane this morning, I smelled the aroma that instantly took me back to my childhood. The same thing I used to smell, walking to school as a little girl. Was it fall? I'm not sure, but it was a wonderful fragrance, and I inhaled it deeply. It brought more memories flooding back. A one-room schoolhouse only a quarter mile up the road from where our family farm was. Walking to school with neighbors and friends, carrying our packed lunches. Those fresh tomato and cheese sandwiches were so delicious and, to this day, are one of my favorite sandwiches. Sometimes, for a treat, we would have bologna too. When we got to school every morning, our teacher had us all put our little jars of milk on a tray, and she put it in the refrigerator.

I will never forget how cold and delicious my pink strawberry milk would be by lunchtime. We didn't have refrigerators at home in this community. They were against the rules, but because we had an 'Englisher' for a teacher, the school had one. My school days are some of my best childhood memories. We always had three recesses, which was so much fun and where we learned to play softball and many other entertaining games. I will forever be thankful for the two different one-room Amish schools where I received eight good, solid years of education. I have since gone on to get my GED, among other studies.

All these nostalgic feelings and memories reminded me of the verse about our youth in Ecclesiastes 12:1, "Remember your Creator in the days of your youth, before the days of trouble come and the years approach when you will say I find no pleasure in them." Well, I still very much find life to be pleasurable. But life was very simple back then, and my Creator had my life mapped out even back then.

Prayer Declaration:
Jesus, thank you for wonderful childhood memories. Help us to remember and dwell on those. Thank you for even way back in our childhood and youth ordering our steps and our future.

August 4
Learn from Others

I packed up the truck yesterday around noon and drove 2 1/2 hours to my sister's house. Yes, my car is still in the shop, being fixed from my earlier mishap. The inconvenience of not having my car has been good for me. I now have a healthy respect for airbags; having been blasted and bruised by those things twice in one month was painful and scary. You better believe I will drive more carefully than I ever have before to avoid setting them off and getting hurt again. I still have a scar on my leg. Isn't this a lot like life, once again? Some things we only learn through experience. Some lessons aren't learned until it hurts.

Wouldn't it be so nice when we warned our children or people we mentor about certain things, and they would just quickly believe us? Sometimes they do, but sometimes they have to experience the consequences of their choices. Are we any different as adults? Do we listen well to people who have experience and good advice for us, or do we do it anyway? Only after we have learned the hard way do we believe and truly get what we were previously told. Proverbs has a lot of advice about seeking wisdom and advice. Proverbs 13:10 says, "Where there is strife, there is pride. But wisdom is found in those who take advice." It only makes sense that taking, asking for advice takes humility. Let's learn from the mistakes of others. Maybe we'll save ourselves some pain in the process.

Prayer Declaration:
Jesus, will you give us the ability to listen, especially to those with experience. May we choose peace and humility over pride and strife. Teach us to learn from you above all, and your example of humility you left for us.

August 5
Quality Family Time

My sister from Montana traveled in with the Amtrak, and we all met at my youngest sister's house tonight. Four of us. Our oldest sister couldn't come, which we were all sad about. The rest of us walked up to my mom's cute little place at dinner time and completely surprised her. She was mowing her lawn. Yes, at 80 years old, she still does that by herself. Her lavish flowers would win any competition. We planned to surprise her like this for her 80th birthday. The look on her face was worth all the effort. We took everything we needed for food and for the meals, while we were there so she didn't need to cook. This is a treat for any Amish woman to get a break from making meals.

We sisters decided to make BLTs for dinner that night because it was one of our good childhood memories. Once in a blue moon, Mom would go in early from doing our many chores, and she would make BLTs for all of us nine kids, for her and Dad as well, usually on a Sunday evening. This took a lot of bacon, and it was a treat for us. We enjoyed wonderful, quality time together that evening as we sat by Mom's big fire pit until the wee hours of the morning, and we all slept at her house. We sang and reminisced about days gone by and about how much we missed that. Dad's quiet presence still leaves such a big hole whenever we go home. We talked about the verse he always quoted in Dutch. "Un shtill un ruhas levah fuhrta." The English version of this verse is found in 1st Thessalonians 4:11, "Make it your ambition to lead a quiet life and attend to your own business and work with your hands, just as we commanded you." Dad lived this verse out well. Never condemning or judging anyone.

Prayer Declaration:
Jesus, thank you for such wonderful times with family. Help us all to live out the above verse in our own lives. We would be better people to attend our own business at all times, just like Dad did. Help us, Lord.

August 6
Love and Respect

God has done some amazing things for my family. He truly is the restorer of all things. It hasn't been easy since my dad's sudden death from a heart attack. My sister's mom and I talked about his sickness prior to that. He had suffered from diabetes and was in the hospital for quite some time a few years earlier. We knew he had a weak heart, and we knew he would keep going, walking, and working until he dropped. And that's exactly what he did. We talked about whenever families go through a grief journey, it can either separate and drive them apart, or it can draw us together and make us closer than before. Which one do we want?

It truly felt to me like this weekend drew us girls and mom closer together. It was precious and healing, with lots of laughter and tears mixed in. We had holy and healing moments. My own heart, too, just overflows with gratitude. Gratitude for what God has done in all of our lives. Gratitude that I am allowed to be a part of this intimate family gathering. We truly have learned to love, honor, and even respect each other right where we are at. They no longer shun me (at times like these), and I no longer try to change them but respect their way of life. It takes humility and grace all around. Ephesians 4:2 spells it out for us, "Be completely humble and gentle. Be patient, bearing one another in love." I felt that amongst us these days together. What if we lived like this always? Would some of our troubles and drama just melt away? Wouldn't it be worth a try in a world of me, myself, and I?

Prayer Declaration:
Jesus, thank you for your restoration power. Teach us to walk in humility, patience, and gentleness with our families, and all people, teach us how God. We need your help to love well and honor without judgment.

Kneel at His Feet

I'm still recovering from a few nights with only a few hours of sleep, but it was worth every wink of sleep lost. My sister from Montana hardly ever comes in. She and I were so close growing up as little Amish girls. We shared chores, rooms, a playhouse, and many secrets. We drifted apart over the years, both moving out of our home communities and going on our own journeys. We were also both on the hunt for more answers about life and God. We don't see eye to eye on everything, but our closeness has returned, and that is so special to me. After church today, my recliner and a nap felt absolutely wonderful. These deep, relaxing Sunday afternoon naps feel like a slice of heaven. The busyness and any stress of the previous week just kind of melt away. Church was wonderful today.

I'm so grateful to be a part of a church that knows how to host and steward the presence of God. The Holy Spirit was so close and real during worship. I got to help lead, and our son on the drums is always so special. Psalms 95:6 says, "Come let us worship. Let us kneel before the Lord, our Maker," during worship today, this happened. People came to the altar and knelt there. It was a holy moment. It was a moment of deep worship and surrender. What do you need to let go of this morning? What do you need to surrender to the feet of Jesus? Bring it right now. We don't have to wait for church or Sunday. You can kneel wherever you are. And give it all to Jesus; He can handle it.

Prayer Declaration:
Jesus, thank you for your presence and that you are in the middle of our messes with us. Teach us how to surrender it all. Help us to give up control and let You lead us in those we love. We kneel before you in repentance.

August 8
Using our Authority

How do you cope when the pressure is on, and you can't seem to catch a break or a breath? Do you feel anxious, scared, hopeless, like your prayers are hitting a brick wall? Sometimes life is going so smoothly and floating right along until it's not. Sometimes you get a bad report that seems to unleash a chain of events. If that's you today, then take heart, for the Bible says, "We do not wrestle against flesh and blood, but against principalities and powers and the rulers of darkness," Ephesians 6:12. What if we remembered this when trouble comes knocking? As Christians, we have the authority of Jesus to take authority over principalities, powers, and darkness.

This is exactly what I did on my walk this morning. I was feeling the gravity and seriousness of a certain situation. I cried out to God amidst my worship and commanded the darkness to be pushed back in the name of Jesus around this circumstance. I commanded the enemy to take his hands off and to go to hell, where he belongs. After that, I made a few phone calls that impressed upon my heart, and then I felt complete peace. Later in the day, a phone call came with great news. Things had shifted. When we partner with God's heart, and we speak to the darkness in His name, things happen. Remember the authority and power you have the next time you are in a battle.

Prayer Declaration:
Jesus, thank you for the power you release through us when we partner with you. Teach us how to use it over principalities, powers and darkness. Help us to walk in it and release your peace whenever we go, no matter what we face.

August 9
Go with Grace

A coffee date with my friend this morning was just what my heart needed. She is my prayer warrior friend, and we constantly share prayer requests with each other. Not only about ourselves and our own families but the requests we get from others. She was right there with me, battling in prayer for the same situation I was in yesterday. We are both intercessors, so we understand the emotions, everything we feel at times, and the urgency that comes with some requests. Romans 12:6 says, "We have different gifts according to the grace given to each of us." Don't you just love that? We receive grace to go with our gift. How easy, though, is it to step outside of that grace and operate in our gifts, out of striving, or going beyond what we truly have grace for?

That's me, for sure. In fact, just on Sunday at church, one of the prayer team prayed for protection over my heart because I feel so many things deeply. It truly is a challenge sometimes to not come under the pressure of all the human hurt and needs. Beni Johnson's book, "The Happy Intercessor," is an excellent book if you have the gift of intercession. She talks a lot about praying from a place of victory. She also talks about simply asking God how to pray in every situation. She really simplifies it all, and it's such a good resource. It speaks even louder to me since she has joined that great cloud of witnesses and is cheering us on today. Let's go with grace and stay in our lane.

Prayer Declaration:
Jesus, thank you that you give us the grace to walk in our gifts. Teach us how to stay away from striving. Help us to remember to partner with you and pray from your perspective.

August 10
Citizenship in Heaven

The sounds of late summer are all around me this morning. The crickets, the birds, and maybe even already an occasional locust. The sun still feels hot on my skin, which I absolutely love, and the thought of winter coming makes me a tad sad. The trees start changing color in late August here in Wisconsin. As much as I love fall, there's always a little sadness in me to see summer end, but hey, maybe in heaven, we will have endless summer or whatever your favorite season is. Do you ever contemplate what it will be like in heaven, especially? I think about all the different people and religions who don't fellowship with each other here. Especially among my culture, the Amish, yet they all profess to love the same God.

Do you ever wonder if we will know each other in heaven? If so, what if those people we just couldn't tolerate here are there too? Won't that be a bit awkward? Or will that all melt away in the presence of Jesus? I'm quite sure it will. But in my humanness, I wonder and ponder. At times I marvel at the many mysteries about life and death, heaven, hell, and eternity. I hope and pray this can be all of our declaration and desire. "Our citizen citizenship is in Heaven, and we eagerly await a Savior from there. The Lord Jesus Christ," Philippians 3:20.

Prayer Declaration:
Yes, Lord, we do eagerly await your coming. Thank you for making a way for us to spend eternity with You. Help us to remember every day that our citizenship is in heaven. Teach us how to live in that revelation.

August 11
Slower Rhythms

My husband left early this morning for work, which means everything is completely quiet when I get up. The beauty of the morning amazes me. It's only 59 degrees. I open a few windows to let in this cool air and smell the fresh morning aroma. It truly does have a scent if we take the time to notice it. The bubbling sounds of the fountain come through my open windows. The flag flaps lazily in the breeze. I drink it all in and breathe deeply over my morning coffee. It feels amazing after the busyness of the last week. These days I'm all about slower rhythms, being present, and living the life I'm called to live. Ephesians 4:14 says, "So that we may no longer be children, tossed to and fro by the waves and carried about by every wind of doctrine."

By human cunning, by craftiness in deceitful schemes. I'm not exactly sure what that verse all means, but for me, it means staying in my lane, being true to what I know that God is calling me to do, not looking to the right or the left, and comparing myself to others. It also means being aware of the enemies' schemes in our lives. Our strong points can also be our weak points. For example, I love to help people, but I don't always know when or where to stop before I'm exhausted. Just yesterday, my counselor talked to me yet again about having better boundaries with people. We cannot give out empty cups or hearts. Let's make sure we are taking care of our own hearts first, whatever that looks like for you. Often for me, it's as simple as slower rhythms of life, spending time in prayer, and listening for God's voice.

Prayer Declaration:
Jesus, thank you that You never move or change. Thank you that you were always right here waiting for us to come back to you, to slow down and be aware of you. Teach us to live in this place more and more.

August 12
God's Goodness

Delicious cool rain came down in sheets this morning. Thank you, Jesus. We needed it so much, and once again, he is faithful. Do we realize just how faithful our God is? He also answered a prayer request in my personal life and is working out the details of the burden I had for a certain situation earlier in the week (for someone else's pain). I love how Isaiah 59:1 declares, "Behold, the Lord's hand is not shortened that it cannot save, neither is His ear heavy that it cannot hear." This is so true. He always hears our prayers, our pleas, and our petitions. Sometimes He answers quickly and the way we hope. Yet other times, it can take days, weeks, months, or even years. Quite often, the answer won't look like we thought it would or should, and yet it works out beautifully. Have you experienced that in your life? I truly hope so.

It's a beautiful thing and a peaceful way to live when we remember He is God, and we are not. He is working all things together for our good. Too many expectations of God or other people often lead us to deep disappointment. Let's remember people are human, and God is sovereign like Bill Johnson said recently. We work for Jesus. He doesn't work for us. When we remember who Jesus is and how He holds the whole world in his hands, it is especially sweet and special when he does specifically answer a certain prayer, isn't it? Just like we want the very best for our children, so God wants the very best for us, his sons and daughters. He's a good, good Father, even in the times we don't understand why He allows certain things in our lives.

Prayer Declaration:
Jesus, thank you for your loving kindness. Thank you for always hearing us and helping us in the ways that are best. Teach us to ask, surrender and trust simultaneously. Help us to remember You are sovereign and You are always Good.

August 13
Make a Plan

Enjoying a second cup of coffee on the back deck this morning; it's a cloudy, cool, slow, and peaceful Saturday so far. I hear the traffic in the distance on the interstate. We only hear it when it's this quiet and still outside. The hummingbirds are looking for nectar, so I make a mental note to fill the feeder. Pretty sure I'm also seeing a yellow leaf here and there in the woods behind our house. A gentle reminder that fall truly is almost here. Like my daughter said this morning, "I'm ready for fall, but just not winter." Me too, my dear, me too. However, in these 12 years back in this frozen tundra, I have learned to somewhat enjoy them, at least until March and April, when winter often refuses to release its icy grip. We are longing for spring, but instead, we get another foot of snow. It happens a lot here in Wisconsin.

This year I'm planning ahead, though. Isn't that what we should do when we know an area of our life that sets us up to struggle? Let's make a plan to set ourselves up for success. Maybe for you, it's something completely different. Perhaps you love winter and struggle with the heat in the summer? Maybe it's much deeper and more personal than that. Proverbs 15:22 speaks about this in a way, "Without counsel, plans fail. But with many advisers, they succeed." My husband has counseled and advised me to go somewhere warm as often as I need to in the winter for my health, physically and emotionally. Can you, too, find a trusted person or two to help you make a good and wise plan ahead of time before you are in the middle of the struggle or temptation that is reoccurring in your life?

Prayer Declaration:
Jesus, thank you for your love, grace, mercy, and forgiveness, we struggle in areas and from time to time, fail. Teach us to seek wise counsel. Help us to make a good plan to help us get through the difficult places in our lives.

August 14
Our Jon Boy

Our youngest son's 20th birthday is today. Our baby, we named him Jon Lamar. His nickname is "Jon Boy," he is smart, witty, loyal, and tender-hearted. He gives the best hugs; he also has a great sense of humor and loves a good joke! He makes us laugh many times with his dry humor. He probably remembers very little of actually being Amish, but he sure got the work ethic and worked as hard as anyone in our family-owned business. His birth was the best experience out of all six of my children's births. Simply because we listened to the advice of our doctor. I had a wonderful, blessed, and beautiful epidural, pure bliss. We had no such plans, but when we got to the hospital that evening after I went into labor, they asked us several times if we had considered that. Finally, I said to my husband, this feels like a nudge that I should.

He told me it was whatever I wanted. We went into the hospital Chapel and had the most peaceful, relaxing time together. When the contractions started becoming almost unbearable, they gave me the epidural. Jon wasn't born until early the next morning at 5:30 AM. I don't even like to think what it would have been like without the epidural, as he ended up having his head kind of turned back or to the side. It was very hard work bringing him into this world, but with the epidural, I was able to be present, stay focused, and somewhat enjoy the process. His birth story will always be dear to me. How often do we overlook those nudges of the Holy Spirit, especially when someone suggests something several different times from different people. It just might be the Holy Spirit talking to you through them. 1st Thessalonians 5:19 says simply this, "Do not quench the spirit. Yet how easy it is to do this, maybe even daily."

Prayer Declaration:
Jesus, will you give us ears and a heart to hear you? Help us remember that sometimes, you speak through others. Teach us to know You and the Holy Spirit from a place of intimacy, help us to live our lives accordingly.

August 15
Rewards of Pressing On

Our family decided to celebrate all three of the August birthdays together last night. Plus, two of the in-laws also had birthdays in late July. When I told Zion that we were celebrating birthdays (when they were here earlier in the week), he immediately said," we should make cupcakes for them." He has the most tender and thoughtful little heart, so we did. We sat all the birthday participants around the island last night, and they all got their own cupcakes with candles. All the sons and Lorinda went golfing in the afternoon and presented my husband with his gift, a new golf driver. He was tickled, as was Jon with his treasure hunt that ended at the fire pit with his gift. It was another wonderful family night. Camille brought Lavon's favorite salad. I made favorite foods for the guys, too.

We gathered around the dining room table and later around the crackling fire outside. The conversation centered around stories of the past and some reminiscing. Sometimes we actually take turns to talk, but most of the time there's several of us talking, or sometimes all at once. It dawned on me that we are completely out of the teenager stage. I clearly remember having five teenagers at one time, that was an intense stage of life with barely time to breathe sometimes. They all had different paths and interests. My husband and I feel strongly about supporting their individual dreams and not forcing them to all be alike, but, oh my goodness, on nights like last night when we are all gathered round, my heart overflows with gratitude at what the Lord has done! "I will give thanks to you, O Lord, with my whole heart, and I will glorify your name forever," Psalms 86:12. Friend, if you are in an intense season right now, keep going, keep pushing. Your reward will be worth it. Gods got your back, and you can do this.

Prayer Declaration:
Jesus, thank You for our precious family, they are our prize. Teach us how to do family well. Help us to honor You first of all and then one another. Thank you, Jesus, for your strength when we falter and fail. Help us to always remember to look for your divine wisdom.

August 16
Strong in the Middle

There's a phrase that we heard many times in the Amish church. "Behstendiches Middle" meaning, (being strong in the middle). They often quoted it at weddings to the couple that was getting married. We wish you a good "guter anfang," (a good beginning), a "behstendiches "middle," and "Und Glickselichas" end. I assume, I think, the last phrase means, (finishing well). Isn't this just some good solid advice or encouragement for any of us when we start something new? Often, in the beginning, we are so excited, and we think nothing can stop us. Many times, it's also in the middle of something that it feels the hardest. We may falter and quit altogether, but if we give in to that, we won't get to experience the *finishing well* phase, and that is the best feeling ever.

I remember saying this to my husband in the middle of raising our children. I think we are in the "behstendiches" middle. It truly felt like it. We needed to stay strong and keep going even when we were, at times, weary, worn, made mistakes, and failed forward daily. Thank God, children are so forgiving and tend to remember the good times the most, I think, I hope, I trust. So what middle are you in right now? Can you keep going? Can you keep putting one foot in front of the other, just doing the next right thing today, tomorrow, and then the next day? Galatians 4:2 tells us to, "...continue steadfastly in prayer." Only then do we get to experience that blessed feeling of having finished well, whatever it is we are assigned to do by God.

Prayer Declaration:
Jesus, thank you for strengthening us in the middle of our assignments. Teach us to run to You when we get weary. Help us to finish strong and well with your help.

August 17
Soundtrack of Our Subconscious

It's another beautiful, peaceful, quiet morning, but no wind. The lawn is mowed and some of the flowers are at their peak, literally spilling out of their baskets. Everything is healthy, green, and growing; such a beautiful time of year. There's a song that keeps running through my mind this morning, something along the lines of, *my soul sings, my soul sings*, that's all I know, but do know it's a song. It reminds me of Psalms 103:1, "Bless the Lord, Oh my soul and all that is within me bless His Holy Name!" After all, there is so much to bless and praise Him for. Does that happen to you too, where you have this song running through the back of your mind somewhere? It's so much better than those thoughts of fear, doubt, and anxiety.

Can we train our minds to have a positive soundtrack in the background? I do believe we can. Whatever we put into our minds and hearts daily, we will operate out of. Our subconscious stores that it's like a database, just like a computer. Let's be careful what we see, hear, or willingly take in today and every day. Another way of saying this is we are what we eat, both in the natural and the spiritual. If we eat a box of donuts every morning, our bodies won't be too happy or healthy. Our bodies could, however, handle one donut a week or maybe even one a day. Same way with junk for our hearts. We see and hear enough of it without deliberately and willingly taking it through fake news, movies, negative people, or whatever other way we let something influence us. Guard your heart, your soul, mind, and body.

Prayer Declaration:
Jesus, thank you for your goodness. Teach us to subconsciously praise You all the time. Help us to be aware of what we are taking in every day, physically, emotionally and spiritually.

August 18
God's Promises

I woke up to flashes of lightning and rain early. There's just something about a rainstorm coming in, so I decided to get up and watch it. At the same time working on content for a lady's retreat for later this fall, it's cozy in my chair, and the coffee tastes extra good. Our guys head off to work but come back because of the rain. One crew is working inside today. After a while, we look up, and there is a partial, bright, and beautiful rainbow in the morning sky. Wow. They never cease to amaze me and remind me of God's promise to never again destroy all the people.

Sometimes I ponder on that. Was there more evil going on in that time back then than today? It seems hard to imagine, but then again, people were just as driven by their human nature back then as they are today, and evil is still evil, some of my rambling thoughts. Yesterday at our monthly Bible study, we had a time of prayer for our nation. We talked about always in the past, when enough people repented and humbled themselves, God heard their cries for mercy and deliverance. Are we humble and repentant for where our country is at, or are we quick to point to others and who is at fault? What if it starts with us, with you and me? 1st Corinthians 16:13 has some very good advice in it, simply this, "Be on the alert, stand firm in the faith, act like men, be strong." Where do we need to stand firm today? Where do we need to stay strong and alert?

Prayer Declaration:
Jesus, help us, teach us and show us what is our part to play. Thank you for what our country was founded on and bring us back to those principles. Teach us to live alert like this verse tells us to. Help us to make a difference.

August 19
Stay Hungry

A quiet, peaceful morning. I have our 100 acres to myself this morning and love it so much. Our land, our view, our peace and quiet of country living. Sitting outside, it feels and smells heavenly because remember, fall has a fragrance! The goldenrod is already blooming, and a few trees are turning yellow. Fall is my favorite season, but for now, I'm treasuring, relishing, and soaking in these last days of summer. It's so wonderful to be in a season of life where my husband and I both have time to pursue some of our hobbies and things we both truly enjoy doing. Even simple things like finishing our coffee in the morning without interruptions, before it gets cold, lingering a bit longer if we choose to, watching the sunsets together, and consistently going on date nights if we want. These are the overflow for me. The things that are now that weren't possible at one time in our life. Back then, though, we had different blessings.

Yet, even in those busy, intense times, I would long for a slower pace, even though that, too, was a wonderful time of life. One of our sons has a small tattoo that says, *always hungry, never satisfied*; I like that. To him, it means never settling, always going after more of God, and to become the best he can be. He is also a bodybuilder and has some serious muscles! When we stay hungry and on the hunt for all God has for us to do and enjoy, we will never be bored or stagnant. The only way we will ever be truly satisfied is in Jesus. Matthew 5:6 says, "Blessed are those who hunger and thirst for righteousness for they shall be satisfied." Let's make sure we hunger after eternal things, the only thing that truly satisfies, and still stay hungry for more of God's presence and all he has for us.

Prayer Declaration:
Make us hungry for you, Jesus. Thank you that You are good and the only One who can satisfy our hearts. Help us to open our hearts to all You have for us instead of being satisfied and stagnant.

August 20
My Husband, My Rock

Today is my husband's 51st birthday. I barely had time to give him his gifts and make him his favorite breakfast before he left the house at 8. "Just like any other morning," he says. He is a very independent man, solid, steady, manly, and doesn't depend on anyone to make his world go round. There's almost nothing he can't figure out or fix. He grew up with no brothers, so he was lonely, but it also made him part of who he is today. His life hasn't all been roses. He walked some hard and solitary years, even in adulthood, trying to fit in, trying to find meaning in life inside the walls of church and religion, in different ways, groups, and settings.

Thank God he has found what he is looking for, freedom, a solid foundation, and a family who loves him so very much. Without his leadership, I sometimes reflect and wonder where we would all be today. He also has the gift of discernment and prophecy and sees through things or agendas that aren't real or fake very easily. This isn't always the easiest or most popular gift to steward. Some of his stories include having been given up for adoption as a tiny baby, adopted into a loving Christian Amish home, and then much later in his life, being reunited with his birth mom.

It's, again, a wonderful story of redemption of God's mercy and grace. I'm so blessed to be a part of it all. Can you look at your life too and seek how God has written your story? Is He still writing it? When we surrender the pen to the master writer, He will write our story in a way that is so beautiful and in a way that all things work together for our good. Psalms 139: 16-17 tells us this, "You saw me before I was born. Every day of my life was recorded in your book. Every moment was laid out before a single day had passed. How precious are your thoughts about me? Oh God, they cannot be numbered."

Prayer Declaration:
Jesus, thank you for writing our stories. Teach us to trust you and leave the pen in your hands. Help us to let go of our own agenda and let you write the perfect story for us!

August 21
Glorious Bodies

It was midnight when we finally crashed into bed last night. My husband has a truck in a Pullers' association. Last night he was pulling in Colby over in our old stomping grounds. Because it was his birthday, I tagged along; his love language is quality time. It was a beautiful, perfect evening to be outside until all hours of the night, so my alarm woke me very rudely this morning. I jumped up and was completely dressed before realizing I had forgotten to take a shower. I start my morning over, and by the time my coffee is ready and a hot shower is taken, life looks good again.

I make it to church just in time for worship team practice, coffee, doughnuts, pre-service prayer, and worship, filling up the early morning hours. My heart rejoices at this opportunity once again after all these years. Worship team season ended for me about 11 years ago. Now it's back, fresh, new and different. This is what I mean about different seasons. Son Dennis is on the drums this morning and builds up the momentum at just the right times. Worship is incredible. God's spirit is right there and moving in waves among the people. My heart feels light and free. It must be a taste of what we will experience in heaven, *worship day and night, night and day, let incense arise.* That's part of a song, actually. What do you look forward to the most when you think about heaven? Do you daydream about heaven, what we will do, see and hear? Oh, and we will even have brand-new bodies that will be amazing in themselves. Philippians 3:21 tells us this, "Who by power that enables Him, the Lord Jesus Christ, to bring everything under his control will transform our lowly bodies so they will be like His glorious body." This is good news, and some days I can't wait to trade in this "getting older" body, wrinkles, pain, and all for that heavenly glorious body!

Prayer Declaration:
Thank you, Jesus, for the glimpses of heaven you allow us to see and read about in your word. Help us to run our race in a way that is pleasing to You with the hope of heaven as our motivation, teach us to worship you continually, even while still here on Earth.

August 22
Open Hands and Hearts

Sitting at the airport this morning, waiting to board my flight. My kind husband dropped me off so I don't have to deal with the parking garage, remembering where I'm parked when I come home, and just all of the hassle. Check-in and security were smooth and fast, with no long lines to wait in. This allowed me plenty of time to find my gate and favorite fall drink. An extra hot green tea latte is so delicious, especially if you are craving something hot and you've already had your caffeine. Part of me wants to hang on to summer as long as possible. There is another part of me that is ready to embrace fall with complete abandonment. My flowers are losing some of their luster, and I'm looking forward to replacing some of them with beautiful mums. I saw some the other day in all their glory. I said to myself, okay, fall, you are welcome here. Bring on the bonfires, sweaters, apple cider, and all things fall. Isn't it, again, a lot like life?

We must be willing to let go of a current season to be able to fully embrace a new one or the next one God has for us currently. I do still love our hot summer days, and thankfully, they will just gradually fade into fall. Sometimes in life, though, we need to open our hands and let go of the thing we are clutching onto so desperately. Sometimes God is even waiting for us to open our hands and our hearts so He can give us something new. It takes faith, believe me, I know. He even allows good things to come to an end for a season for reasons we don't understand at all. Even then, it's all because He has an even better plan and even greater purpose for you to fulfill in the next new season, He has for you. Encourage yourself with Jeremiah 29:11, "God has plans to prosper you, to give you hope and a future. Psalm 62:8 says, "Trust in Him at all times. Oh people, pour out your heart before Him. God is a refuge for us."

Prayer Declaration:
Yes, you are Lord. In every season, new or old, warm or cold, you are our refuge, our rock, our redeemer, the one we can trust and live open handed and open hearted with.

August 23
Mountaintop Journey

Waking up in the loft of a rustic, cozy cabin on a mountain felt delightful this morning. I can't wait to get dressed, make my coffee, and step outside to breathe in the cool, fresh mountain air. Ah, what a gift. My friends are awake by now too, and we gather around the table on the deck outside for a light breakfast and our first lesson. Last night, six of us gathered here in Gatlinburg, Tennessee, for a three-day retreat. Mountaintop Journey is what it's called. My friend, who is leading this, was inspired by God to start this ministry. After finding healing from her own grief journey, she has lost not only one but two precious grandsons. One was 16, the other one three months old. One died of suffocation and neglect at the hands of a babysitter, and the other died in a car crash when his best friend was driving.

My friend could absolutely drown in her grief, she could be bitter and unforgiving, yet she isn't. She has forgiven time and again, not only that, but she has started a ministry out of her own grief to help others heal from theirs. If that isn't taking something broken and making something beautiful out of it, then I don't know what is. If you have been on this earth for any amount of time, you, too, have probably experienced grief on some level. How could you rise above it and use it for good? Out of our tests come our testimonies. Someone may be waiting to hear your testimony. Your story of overcoming and breakthrough. My friend Jodi's story blesses, encourages, and inspires me to choose forgiveness in every situation. Romans 12:19 tells us," Do not take revenge, my dear friends, but leave room for God's wrath, for it is written it is mine to avenge. I will repay, says the Lord."

Prayer Declaration:
Jesus, thank you that one day everything will be made right. Help us to remember this, to forgive as many times as we need to and trust You to make all things right and new.

August 24
Surrendering Our Burdens

We may have stayed up a bit too late last night, but how do you bring good, deep, life-changing discussions to an end? You don't, so we didn't get much sleep, but we are so eager to head for the mountains again today. We make our coffee and head out. We also bring a cooler with water and a picnic lunch, all put together by our leader and friend Jodi and her assistant Tammy. Having grown up in the Smoky Mountains area, Jodi is perfect for what she does, knowing just where to take us for the best scenery, hiking, and healing. Just being outside in this amazing, wonderful, beautiful place is healing to my soul. We stop along a breathtaking view and drink it all in. We have our first lesson right there, gazing at the mountaintops with the valleys deep below us. Next, we hike back into a beautiful waterfall, well worth it, soaking it up before hiking back down and heading to chimney tops for our picnic lunch.

After lunch, we have another lesson as Jodi instructs us how to start releasing any burdens we are carrying into the water and let Jesus wash them away. We all go find a quiet private place to pray, soak and start the surrendering process. It's so easy to feel the nearness of God's presence here in the quiet, the water rushing down over the rocks of this cold mountain stream. I know exactly what I need to surrender, and with that comes sweet peace. Maybe you, too, have heavy burdens today that are weighing you down. Perhaps you need permission to lay them down at the feet of Jesus. You can do that wherever you are right now. He wants to carry those for us. He is waiting until we surrender them to him. Will you do that today? Contact my friend for your own mountaintop journey experience. You can find her on Facebook.com/mountaintopjourney or mountaintopjourneygatlinburg@gmail.com. Psalms 55:22 Tells us to, "Cast our burdens on the Lord and He will sustain us."

Prayer Declaration:
Thank you, Jesus, for carrying our burdens. Teach us how to release them daily and even hourly, thank you for bringing people like Jodi into our lives at times to help and guide us.

August 25
Moving Mountains

We are all a bit sad that today is already day three and our final day of the Mountaintop Journey. We are determined to make the most of it. We start our last day with coffee, waffles, and all the trimmings on the deck. Surrounded by mountains on every side, it was breathtakingly beautiful. We hiked to another waterfall. We can actually stand behind them and feel the spray of the water, and it's magical. Once again, we find our own spots to commune with God. I find a big boulder, take my hiking shoes off and just soak in the goodness of God. The water all around me and the sun on my skin is all so wonderful. The song, How Great Thou Art, goes through my mind over and over. God, who made all of the universe, such wonders, cares for me and you beyond what we can even grasp! We enjoyed another picnic lunch and a lesson together.

After hiking back down the trails again, we find rocks to rest and release our final burdens. Again, I know just what it is for me. Any stress I had been carrying coming into this retreat has melted away more than ever. I am convinced that God will make a way where there seems to be no way. Maybe you find yourself in some situations that look impossible or even too big for God. Nothing is too big for God. In fact, He specializes in the impossible, the supernatural. If he can turn water into wine and multiply food, heal the sick, and raise the dead, He can move mountains for us too. Asking him to move on our behalf and surrendering our burdens to him go hand in hand in a beautiful, powerful combination. "Truly I tell you, if anyone says to this mountain, go throw yourself into the sea, do not doubt in their heart, but believe that what they say will happen, it will be done for them," Mark 11:23.

Prayer Declaration:
Jesus, thank you for this promise. Thank you for these days of healing, cleansing, releasing, and rejuvenating. Thank you for moving mountains for us as we all go back home, to do what we are all called to do.

August 26
Say Yes

Once again, I'm in the air, sandwiched between two fellow passengers on the plane. I've had a wonderful nap and a cup of coffee, which helped me wake up. We woke up and left the cabin early this morning to catch our various flights across the US. I'm excited to see my family again, but like I said to my friends, I didn't even realize I needed this retreat. My body feels rested, my soul restored, my heart rejuvenated. We ended our time together by attending dinner and a show last night. We laughed out loud a lot; it truly is the best medicine. A delightful facial massage was also part of my package on this retreat. It felt like a treat and luxury. I can count the number of facials I've had in my life, but not very many. We enjoyed spending some time in the hot tub together before heading to bed early to be up in time for early flights.

My heart feels full and light. The last three days with these wonderful women have been healing and amazing. We laughed, we cried, we shared our hearts and our struggles. We prayed, and we healed together. I'm convinced sometimes God knows what we need before we even ask. This is what this trip felt like to me. He orchestrated this all for me. I was invited and asked to come by these ladies. All I had to do was say yes. It would have been so easy to say no, thinking of the time and the money and all the reasons why not to come. God knew, and He helped me make the right choice. Yes, sometimes we just need to say yes. Is there something you could say yes to in your life right now that would have the potential to bless you tremendously? Remember, God wants to bless us. We are, after all, his beloved children. Isaiah 30:18 says it this way, "The Lord longs to be gracious to you. Therefore, He will rise up to show you compassion, for the Lord is a God of justice. Blessed are all who wait for Him."

Prayer Declaration:
Jesus, thank you for your good gifts, your ever extravagant blessings you let us enjoy. Thank you for your mercy, your compassion and forgiveness. Teach and help us to live from these truths.

August 27
Childlike Innocence

Dinner is done and the kitchen is cleaned up. The grandchildren just left a bit ago. So once again, I'm physically tired but emotionally charged up. They always give me reasons to laugh and be in awe of what their little hearts and minds already comprehend. When I picked them up, and we drove past our son Lavon's home, this struck up a conversation. Where did they get their house, Grandma? Before I could think of a suitable answer for a four and a two-year-old, Zion declares, "I think Jesus GAVE it to them." Isn't childlike faith just so precious? In fact, Jesus must have thought so too, because in Luke 18:17 He says, "Truly, I say to you, whoever does not receive the Kingdom of God like a child shall not enter it."

What are some ways we could become more childlike in our faith and actions? We, too, should never quit asking questions and learning, ever growing and learning in our faith, perhaps forgiving as easily as a child does.

Maybe we can be better friends by willingly sharing. This is also something I observed with our little boys today. We can definitely learn from their little innocent, childlike hearts. It is what we need instead of cold and bitter hearts. Rain came down in torrents today. Everything is beyond soggy and sloshed outside, but it's cozy inside tonight with a cup of tea, some candles, and my blanket soaking up the coziness of an early fall evening. I'm thanking God for my many blessings. Breakfast and worship practice with the team this morning was so fulfilling and fun too. God truly does love to give us good gifts and, yes sometimes even a house!

Prayer Declaration:
Jesus, thank you for the example of blameless little children. Teach us to have such childlike faith. Help our unbelief. Thank you for every good and perfect gift you give us to enjoy daily. Help us to live in childlike innocence.

Core Values

Church first, next lunch at one of our favorite restaurants, then a delicious nap before our children start trickling in for the family night. With everyone's busy lives, it's not always easy to make this happen. In fact, daughter Luanne and her husband couldn't make it tonight, but at least we got to see them at church today. Even though it isn't always easy to make this happen, it is important to us. Don't we all make time for things that are truly important to us? It's so easy to say we don't have time for this or time for that, but if it's truly important, we will find the time somehow. One way to figure out what is important to us is by looking at our core values. What are some absolutes that you will not budge from? One of ours is indeed a healthy, thriving, close family, so we put in extra effort to get together and celebrate birthdays, babies, and anything in between.

My husband and sons were all out in the yard playing softball after dinner tonight. The rest of us were sitting outside, playing hide and seek or whatever else the little boys wanted to do. Suddenly this saying came to mind. A family that plays together stays together. The more common saying is the family that prays together stays together. It also reminds me of the song, "The family who prays shall never be parted, the circle in heaven unbroken, shall stand." Matthew 6:21 says, "For where your treasure is, there your heart will be also." What are you treasuring/valuing the most here on your journey through life?

Prayer Declaration:
Jesus, thank you for your plan for family. Teach us what core values to hold on too tightly, help us to make time for the most important things in our lives, things that will have lasting effects on eternity. Help us to choose our priorities carefully!

August 29
Pay Attention

As I was driving along today, my thoughts went to my recent flights. It was so much easier for me to find my way around the airports this time, even with last-minute gate changes and having to go to different terminals on my layovers to get to my connecting flights. This all used to be overwhelming to me, and I pretty much hated airports. It dawned on me that one thing I did differently this time was a big help. Normally, as soon as I would get off an airplane, I would step into the first bathroom that came along. By the time I got out, everyone else had moved on. This time, however, I stayed with the crowd. The one time I faltered and wondered if I was going in the right direction, I simply asked the lady beside me if she was going to the same terminal I was, and she said yes. She assured me we were still on the right track, and on we went. This was a lesson for me.

How often do we wander off on our own? We may be taking care of business but lose our tribe. How often do we travel life's road alone instead of with fellow people whose destination is also heaven? The other thing I used to do was blindly follow my husband through airports, learning nothing. Only when I started paying attention, looking around, and learning was I able to navigate airports by myself. Now they are almost fun. Let's make sure we are surrounded and traveling with people who are on the same journey we are. Let's also be careful, and we are not just blindly following anyone. Think for yourself! Matthew 15:14 speaks about this, "If the blind lead the blind, both will fall into the pit."

Prayer Declaration:
Jesus, teach us to be careful who we follow. Help us to discern at all times where we are going, who and what we are following. Thank you that You show us when we ask and we want the right way that leads us home to you. Thank you for helping us find our tribe.

August 30
God Within Us

Deep, meaningful, soul-searching conversations over coffee and homemade cinnamon rolls with my nephew this morning. He came last night already and continued on his way this morning. As always, his hungry, tender heart is such an inspiration as he finds his way with the Holy Spirit as his guide. This is such new and, at times, confusing territory for him and brings back so many memories of how it was for us when we started our voyage out of the Amish. Searching for more, longing for more, asking, seeking, and knocking continually, just like the Bible tells us to. It also says seek, and you will find. Isn't that so comforting? We talked a lot about how easy of a trap it is to start following a man, a church, or a group instead of Jesus alone.

He alone is worthy of our devotion. He is the only One who has the answers. And if we have accepted Him into our lives and He lives within us, this is good news. We can literally carry Him with us wherever we go. The Bible speaks about this in Luke 17:20-21, "Jesus himself said the Kingdom of God does not come with observation, nor will they say, see, hear or see there. For indeed, the Kingdom of God is within you." Do you believe that? Do you live every day knowing that Jesus is right here, right now? He's within you, and He's with you. (If you have asked Him to be your Lord and Savior). The Pharisees were saying He was only here or there, and they had all these hoops to jump through to get to Jesus. But He's right here with us. Let's let that sink in and soak in it. Let's also quit putting God in a box. Let's just let God be God.

Prayer Declaration:
Thank you, Jesus, you choose to live in us, what a tremendous gift. Teach us how to be aware of this reality and live from this place. Help us to remember this when we are tempted to chase after all kinds of things.

August 31
God is all Everywhere

There's not much that starts my day off better than a good run, headphones, worship songs, fresh, crisp morning air, and the winding road inviting me to run like the wind. Prayer and praises are effortless on these morning runs. Jesus is nearby; I feel Him in the wind, in the cool breezes, I feel Him in the sun, I hear His heart in the songs. It's all enough to make me laugh and sometimes cry, and it clears my head, rejuvenates my body, and fills my heart. Isn't it amazing that we can worship God anywhere? We don't have to wait until church on Sunday morning or go through certain rituals.

Yes, corporate worship on a Sunday morning is wonderful, but learning to feel God's presence in our everyday life is so important too. Psalms 99:5 says, "Exalt the Lord our God and worship at His footstool, for He is holy." I believe the earth is God's footstool. He wants to hear from us. He wants to hear it all. The good, the bad, our highs, and our lows. Talk to Him like a friend. Remember to take some time to listen to what He has to say to you. He still speaks to us today, but we don't always take the time to listen. Maybe it's time to listen more than we talk as we go about our day-to-day. Practice listening and seeing God in places maybe you hadn't before. Like my son Duane recently said, God is everywhere; sometimes, you just have to look for Him. Jesus, thank you that You are everywhere. Help us to look for you in our everyday and normal lives.

Prayer Declaration:
Help us to not put you in a certain box of our choosing. Teach us to see you wherever we are and not wait for a Sunday morning only experience. Open our eyes and our hearts to see you rightly!

September 1
Forever Learning

A brand-new month before us once again; fall is definitely in the air, cool mornings and evenings, beautifully warm during the day. It's perfect, in my opinion. This could stay for three more months or more. It's also the time of year when teachers and students go back to school. Sometimes there's a part of me that misses those days. My school days are among my most happy childhood memories. In a little one-room schoolhouse with no more than three classmates, deep friendships were made. In fact, I married one of them, my husband. Isn't it amazing how God is often writing our stories long before we realize it? Later, after we left the Amish, we tried homeschooling our children several different times. There just wasn't enough time for everything with six children, so after a few different private schools, we sent them to public school.

This made me want to get involved and still be a part of their education and environment at school, so I subbed periodically as my children finished and graduated high school. Subbing was wonderful because I could make it fit my schedule. I will always cherish my years working in the different offices as a secretary. Once again, I made some good friends and learned so much. Now our son Dennis and his wife are homeschooling our little grandsons, and I'm sure I will be a part of that too. Learning is such a privilege. Books, reading, pens, paper, and the scent of a classroom or bookstore are inviting to me. As long as we are alive, we can continue to learn. Would you still like to? What would you still like to learn about? What holds you back? What intrigues you? Proverbs 18:15 says, "The heart of the discerning acquires knowledge for the ears of the wise. Seek it out."

Prayer Declaration:
Jesus, thank you for the ability to continue to seek knowledge and learn new things as long as you give us breath in our lungs. Teach us to be wise and seek understanding and wisdom. Above all, help us to help ourselves by continuing to have a heart for learning and growing as long as we live.

September 2
Honey in the Rock

This phrase keeps floating through my head this morning. There's honey in the rock. Sure enough, there's a verse in Psalms 81:16, "But I would feed you with the finest wheat. I would satisfy you with wild honey from the rock." What does that mean? I don't know, but I sure do like the sound of it. In fact, there is also a song written about this very thing. It goes like this: *There's honey in the rock, water in the stone, manna on the ground. No matter where I go, I don't need to worry. Now that I know everything I need, you've got. There's honey in the rock. There's honey in the rock, purpose in your plan, power in the blood, healing in your hands. Started flowing when you said it was done. Everything you did is enough. I keep praying. You keep moving. I keep praising. You keep proving I have all that I need. You are all that I need. You are all that I need. Yeah. There's honey in the rock...*

These lyrics are so musical and delightful and were written by Brooke Ligertwood. What if we actually lived like we believed these beautiful lyrics? It's easy when everything is going well according to our plans, but what about the days it doesn't? What if the healing doesn't come, or it only comes ever so slowly? What if a few of the prayers feels like we prayed forever and still haven't been answered? What is it that tests our faith the most? Those are the times we choose faith. We choose to believe and we let the honey in the rock be enough for us to continue to walk by faith, trusting, believing your plan is the best plan for us even when it hurts. We all have those days, times, and seasons. Jesus, thank you that you are enough.

Prayer Declaration:
Help us to trust You with everything. Teach us how to grow in our faith in the hard times because that is when we grow. In our lives, knowing that You want to feed us with that wild honey makes it delicious, sweet, and satisfying.

September 3
Love Like Jesus

It's a perfect fall morning. Cool, sunny, fresh, and beautiful. What is not to love about fall? Even though, at first, I struggled and complained that I was not ready for this, here I am, smitten as ever with my favorite season, falling in all its glory. I may even have bought a few mums yesterday. Yesterday was a rough day for me of not feeling well physically and dealing with some relationships that are a little tough right now, but if you are in contact with any type of people, that will happen, right? If dealing with people is also part of your business or ministry, it might happen quite a bit. But take heart. I'm always so encouraged by how Jesus dealt with people. Even when he was falsely accused, at times, he didn't say a word, didn't defend himself, or prove what he could have.

Oh, Jesus, I want to be like that too, knowing that as long as we live rightly before you, that's all that matters. You see our hearts. You alone get to judge people and their hearts. Our job is to love, forgive and then do it some more. Your prayer on the cross, Jesus, will forever amaze me after everything that was done to You. This was your prayer, "Father, forgive them, for they know not what they do..." Luke 23:34. What if we, too, would have such grace for people? Don't you think it would take care of a lot of the anger, strife, and unforgiveness people live with today if we could learn to hate the sin yet love the sinner again like Jesus? He models this for us. Why don't we take a deep breath and try again with the relationships in our lives? Are you willing? And with me? We can do this because of Jesus in us.

Prayer Declaration:
Thank you, Jesus, for your power to rise above and to love people like you do. Teach us how to separate the sin from the sinner. Help us to let your love flow through us to all our relationships.

September 4
Ok to Say No

I'm sitting here at Caribou Coffee. Enjoying a pumpkin chai tea. After all, it's the season for all things pumpkin. Heading to church from here, grocery shopping and a few errands, once again, Sunday isn't always a rest day for me. I take those randomly as my schedule allows me to, like yesterday, for instance. Today, I'm still reaping the benefits. It was a slow, beautiful, soaking-up-the-sunshine kind of day and filled my soul with God's creation all around me. I could have done a million things, gone to different places, and spent time with lots of different people. Sometimes, though, you just have to say no, even three or four times in a row, to protect your space and your peace. Peace came into my whole being yesterday as I read, relaxed, wrote, read some more, walked outside barefoot, nurtured my flowers, and talked to the One who created it all. I only did a few things on my list.

No one came all day, and I didn't go anywhere either. When was the last time you had a date of solitude? Is this something you would even enjoy? Do you have people and needs tugging on you daily? If you say yes, then you have permission to say no to it all and take a day for yourself. Jesus himself knew how to do this. "At daybreak, Jesus went out to his solitary place. The people were looking for Him and when they came to where He was, they tried to keep Him from leaving," Luke 4:42 tells us even Jesus needed to slip away to rest and spend time with his Father. How much more do we need to do this? This morning I feel recharged and rejuvenated.

Prayer Declaration:
Jesus, thank you for the examples You left for us. Teach us that it's OK to say no when we need to have extra time with You. Help us to not feel guilty and remember we must fill ourselves up in order to overflow into others. We cannot pour from empty overwhelmed cups or hearts.

September 5
Family Sundays at Church

After I got to church yesterday morning, I had a nice surprise. It was Family Day, meaning the children were all in the service, which meant I got to sit with my two grandsons all throughout the service. This was so much fun. The children that were old enough helped with the service, some on the worship team, some helped take the offerings, a few shared prayers, and even one shared a vision she had. Our little boys were excited to be able to see Daddy on the drums and kept pointing and saying *Daddy*. It was a sweet, precious, beautiful morning that ended with a church picnic and baptisms. Of course, this took me back to how we did church when our children were small, and we were still Amish. The children were always with us all through the service, three hours or more.

The younger ones often took naps or had something quiet to play with. At some point, a big bowl of cookies and crackers came around for the little ones to snack on. I'm glad they had that for the little ones, but even so, it was a lot of sitting, especially for children. I am thankful it's different for my grandchildren. They get to go to classes and learn about Jesus on their level. Even for today's service, they had colors, pictures, and things for them to do during the service. Hearing from different children reminded me of Psalms 8:2 "Out of the mouth of a child. You have established a stronghold against your enemies." Wow. Yes, truly, what is more, powerful than a child's innocent prayer and worship?

Prayer Declaration:
Thank you, Jesus, for giving us an example. Like children, teach us how to be as pure and innocent in our worship and prayer as they are. Help us to become like a child at heart.

Gifts and Talents

All is still completely quiet here at my son's house. The little boys aren't awake yet. It's cozy and well-kept. Our both daughters-in-law are excellent housekeepers. Elise had an early appointment this morning, so we decided it would be easier if I came over this morning instead of waking the boys up early to come to our house. The guys are off to work after a long weekend with Labor Day yesterday. Do you have fun family traditions for holidays or weekends, or do you like to be completely spontaneous?

Planning things on the spur of the moment is so fun for some people, and it used to be us when the children were little. Now, as they have lives and little families of their own, it takes some strategic planning at times. One tradition our family is trying to establish is floating down the Chippewa River on Labor Day. We did it again yesterday; it was relaxing, wonderful, and extremely fun. We hooked our tubes and coolers together, made a giant circle, floated, talked, and laughed. It's amazing the conversations that can happen when everyone is relaxed and not in work mode. We ended the day with a bonfire and dinner here at our son Dennis' house.

On the way home, my husband thanked me for planning this day and continuing to fight for family time. I thanked him for being so good at what he does; providing a wonderful business opportunity for our family. We talked about how well things flow when we all do what we are good at and when we walk out our strengths and gifts God has given each one of us. If you are married or in any of your relationships, can you see where your strengths complement each other? Proverbs 17:17 says, "Friends love all the time and kinfolk or family are born for times of trouble." I love when families can pull through the hard times and lean on each other; that's a beautiful thing.

Prayer Declaration:
Thank you, Jesus, for blood and spiritual family. Help us to always draw closer to each other when hard times try to tear us apart. Teach us to lean on each other and You.

September 7
God's Comfort

The Bible study ladies came again today, this time carrying bags of baby gifts and lots of food to set up a charcuterie board. There was excitement in the air as we scurried and hurried to set it all up before the "Mama to be' arrived. We wanted to bless and surprise this single mother, and by the look on her face, we accomplished it. Her life hasn't been easy by any means, and so today, we wanted her to feel loved, celebrated, and cherished. We ate lots of good food. She opened all her gifts. We read the scriptures over her. We gathered around and prayed a blessing and favor over her and her pregnancy, that sweet baby girl. Two of the ladies brought the same verse found for her in Isaiah 66:13, "As a mother comforts her child, so will I comfort you. Isn't that a beautiful reminder of God's heart toward us, His children?"

Just as we as mothers try to comfort our children when they are sad or hurting in any way, God wants to comfort us. Will we let him? Maybe your life, too, has had valleys of disappointment. Another lady shared Psalms 23, the well-known Psalm. We talked about how *the valley of the shadow of death* can be anything hard we go through and not just death itself. Again, Jesus promises, I will be with you. We really and truly are never alone. There are so many verses that tell us this. God is the best parent and friend we'll ever have. He longs to comfort us.

Prayer Declaration:
Jesus, thank you for your comfort and the fact that you never leave us nor forsake us. Help us to remember this truth even when we are sad, lonely, or afraid to remember you are just a prayer away. Bless all the single moms tonight too and be their husband, be close to them, and bring them a helpmeet.

September 8
Fly or Fall

God is within her. She will not fall. Psalms 46:5. This was one of my verses for the single mom yesterday. It's a short yet very powerful verse, and it was my life verse for this year. At the beginning of every New Year, I like to ask God to highlight a verse, a phrase, or even just a word for the new year. The above verse has helped me many times already this year. Especially the times I felt overwhelmed, inadequate, and in over my head. This verse keeps me centered on Jesus. Just this morning, as I met with another new client, I had to remind myself that Jesus in us is the only way to make a lasting difference. Because of him, we will not fall, and even if we would fall, He will catch us. As the saying goes, if we fall or step off the cliff, Jesus will either teach us how to fly, or He will catch us! Where do you need to be reminded of this in your life?

Are you in over your head too? Maybe it's your marriage? Your finances, health issues, raising children, whatever, you fill in the blank. Can you stop and say this verse out loud? Two or three times. Say it until you feel it. Say it until you believe it. God is within me; I will not fall! He wants you to succeed; He is your biggest cheerleader. This is what we want for our children, right? Tell God exactly how you feel. He wants to hear from you. Tell Him your fears, your hopes, your dreams. He wants all of us, even our messy, broken parts. He is the only one who has it and holds it all together.

Prayer Declaration:
Jesus, thank you that you are within us, and you will protect us from falling. Help us to believe this and remember it when we are feeling overwhelmed. Teach us how to live from this revelation and listen for your voice and not the condemning negative voices that try to crowd out you, Lord.

September 9
The Harvest

What are you harvesting these days? With fall comes the harvest. What a blessing. Melons, pickles, tomatoes, and sweet corn are among our favorites, but my gardening days are over, I believe. I'd much rather go to the farmers' market and patronize the produce stands. However, we did many years of gardening when the children were still small. Planting, weeding, tilling, hoeing, harvesting, canning, and freezing. We did it all. As with many other things, I'm thankful for the knowledge that my children learned through this. Pretty sure they could grow their own food if they had too. There is, however, another kind of harvest Jesus speaks to us about. In Matthew 9:37-38, "Jesus said to his disciples, the harvest is plentiful, but the laborers are few. Therefore, pray earnestly to the Lord of the harvest to send out laborers into this harvest."

Jesus was talking about the people who needed Him. What about us? Are we willing to help with this kind of harvest? If the laborers truly are few for this harvest, let's look around. What can we do about it? Where is your influence? Who can you talk to about Jesus today? Always preach the gospel and use words when necessary. That's my husband's mandate. Someone is always watching your life. You have influence whether you are using it for good or evil. Will you choose with me today to help bring in the end-time harvest? Many people are waiting for hope and good news. Let's share the best news they will ever hear, Jesus Christ and his great love for us!

Prayer Declaration:
Jesus, thank you for reminding us of the great need for laborers in the harvest. Help us to know what that looks like for us. Teach us how to bring the gospel to people in a way that they can accept it for themselves and choose You.

September 10
Redeemed and Healed

A gentle rain is coming down all morning. This makes for a cozy morning inside. I had planned to run a 5K this morning at a local event. Because of the rain, I decided to go to my friend's house instead. She invited me and a handful of other ladies to come over to start watching 'The Chosen' series together. So, coffee in hand, we curl up and start watching. We watched two episodes, and I'm already so drawn into it. I won't even try to explain it because I can't do it justice. However, this one scene keeps replaying in my mind when Mary Magdalene met Jesus for the first time. How Jesus called her by her real name and told her she was redeemed! He pulls her into a warm embrace, and she is never the same.

She is healed, set free, and delivered from the demons that tormented her until that glorious day when she met Jesus. Luke 8:2 is one of the places you can read about this miracle. She had tried everything else, and nothing worked. She was sad, lonely, and tormented. What a glorious story! Seeing it played out in a physically live scenario just made it even more real to me. So where are we today? Do we, too, need healing and deliverance from things in our lives? One embrace from Jesus can change everything for us, too; let's pray.

Prayer Declaration:
Let's come to Him just as we are like Mary Magdalene did. Jesus, you know us by our names. You know exactly where we are hurting, addicted, afflicted, and rejected. Heal and set us free from anything that would hinder and hold us back; thank you, Jesus.

September 11
The Jesus Life

Where were you when the world stopped turning? Do you know this song by Alan Jackson? He wrote this country song after what we now call now 9/11. That day when a jet crashed into the World Trade Center, many lost their lives; it's been 21 years already. In a lot of ways, life has returned to normal for many of us. Not so for the many who lost their lives that day, people trapped inside the center and the heroes trying to rescue them. Some even jumped out of the burning towers to their death below. It's sad and sobering to this day. Yet life goes on, and people learn how to cope and find new normal, routines, and patterns, even without the loved ones they lost. We all say, may we never forget, and I say may we continue to pray for the hurting left behind on that fateful day.

May we continue to pray for change and take it one step further and 'be the change' our world so desperately needs. What can you and I do, you might be thinking. Sometimes it's as simple as asking yourself, where do my passions and my gifts collide? Could that be where you are called to make a difference? Don't underestimate the power of that combination combined with the power of God on your life. One question we heard at church this morning was, "Is living 'the Jesus life' worth it?" Just because we are saved and living for Him does not mean our life will be free of trouble or a walk in the park. For me it's an absolute and easy yes, because no matter what goes on around us, eventually our inheritance is Heaven. We will rule and reign with God. Our hope is rooted in Jesus alone. These thoughts come out of 1st Peter 1:3-5, "Praise be to the God and Father of our Lord Jesus Christ! In his great mercy He has given us a new birth into a living hope..."

Prayer Declaration:
Jesus, help us always remember why we chose the 'Jesus life.' Help us keep our focus on You and eternity and, at the same time, bring heaven to earth, with our assignments from You. Teach us where our place to make a difference is. Thank you that anything we face here will be worth it, most importantly, our inheritance is heaven for all eternity!

September 12
A Link in the Legacy

I'm the planner in the family. My daughters help more and more since they are older and also value family time. It's a lot of work and texts in our family group messages at times to plan things. Just yesterday morning, as we were getting ready, one of our sons plans to come to church fell through at the last minute. Of course, I was disappointed. It was something out of his control. I was sitting there thinking about the effort it sometimes takes to plan things so that it works for all 15 of us. That's when I heard the gentle whisper of the Holy Spirit, *it will be worth it*. It is worth it. What you are doing will last long after you are gone. You are building your legacy.

Ah, thank you, Jesus. I needed that. And maybe you do too! See, one of the areas I feel called to is *family*. Seeing strong, connected, healthy, happy families who actually enjoy being together starts at home. It has to start with us. We can't go out in the world and accomplish things we haven't been faithful to behind the scenes at home. Being faithful in the mundane and ordinary, yet remembering it's about the long-term, is the legacy we are leaving. In the afternoon, we gathered at our daughter's place for a food fellowship and a wonderful surprise they set up to tell us, "We're pregnant!" My mother's heart soared and leapt with gratitude. There were tears and rejoicing and hugs all around. Another link in the legacy. On the hour drive back home, I kept smiling. I feel the last part of Psalms 28:7 deeply, "My heart leaps for joy and with my song I praise him."

Prayer Declaration:
Jesus, thank you for another new life that will be added to our family. We are completely grateful for your wonderful plan for families to grow and multiply. Teach us how to build a strong, Godly legacy that will last through eternity for all of us.

September 13
His Love Never Fails

September is marching by ever so quickly. These cool, crisp mornings are so perfect to go running and get those 30 minutes of exercise in. Soon enough, it will be too cold to run outside. Listening to music motivates me to run much longer and faster. *'Your love never fails'* by the Newsboys touched a spot deep inside my heart and took me back about 12 years. It was the last Sunday our family would lead worship together at this church. We felt we were being called to a new season with our family, which meant letting go of and laying this one down. We didn't know exactly what God had for us next, which made it even more difficult for me. Oh, it was so bittersweet that last Sunday as our son Dennis led this song from the drums, tears streamed down my face in gratitude and surrender.

We moved back east to civilization soon after that and focused mostly on raising our children. That was the one thing we felt God was asking from us, to focus on our children. We started from scratch in many ways. I won't pretend it was easy. For the first time ever, we weren't associated with any Amish/Mennonite church. However, what God has done for us and in us since that time would take pages to write; that's another book! There were times of hopelessness crashing in and times of feeling lonely, at least for me. My husband was already much further in his journey with God, so he felt more freedom than struggle. But God.... He was and is always faithful. Sometimes He takes us to the wilderness so we can truly know that He alone is enough. Looking back, that was what He wanted to teach me! What is uncomfortable in your life today? What do you think He wants to teach you through it? Psalms 138:8 simply says this, "The Lord will fulfill His purpose for me. You can declare this out loud every day and encourage yourself. Even on the days it looks impossible to you and me. He is still working on His plan and His purpose for us."

Prayer Declaration:
Jesus, thank you for this truth. Teach us to trust You and to hold on to your hand even when we don't know what you are doing. What's next in our lives? Help us to remember all the other times in our lives You have been so faithful.

September 14
Shout for Joy

"Be glad in the Lord and rejoice, oh righteous, and shout for joy all you upright in heart, "Psalms 33:11 Wait, what? Shout for joy? Who does that? When is the last time you shouted with joy over something God has done in your life? When is the last time I have? I'm asking myself the same question. There's also a song that goes something along these lines. *Shout to the Lord all the earth let us sing, power and majesty praise to the King.* What if we lived like this, shouting to God because of sheer joy of who He is and what He's done? He definitely deserves it. We can yell, scream and carry on at a sporting event, but if we do this at church, people might look at us and wonder if we are crazy. Now granted, I have been in close proximity with people shouting in church and it can be very distracting to those around you. So maybe practice doing this at home, maybe even when you're home alone.

The point is, do we get this excited about God? Or do we take his goodness, His mercy, His provision, His millions of blessings every day for granted? Why is it that we find it so much easier to whine and complain and point out what's not right with our world instead of all that is right? Most of us are among the most blessed people on the planet, but we don't realize it. There is this question. If you woke up tomorrow morning and only had what you thanked God for yesterday, what would you have today? The next time you are tempted to complain about something, start shouting for joy about all the good things in your life. Change the narrative, and it will transform the atmosphere around you. It will revolutionize contagious joy; shout it out!

Prayer Declaration:
Jesus, you know many of us at times may lack the joy that comes from deep inside. Help us to be aware of your many blessings, teach us how to live joyful and grateful, and yes, even shout our praise out loud.

September 15
Two Chairs

The grandbaby boys came at 7:30 this morning and I had them until 5 in the evening. Last night I told someone you use brain cells you normally wouldn't, which is a very good thing. No wonder they say your grandchildren keep you young. They also make you laugh a lot. A cute story about a four-year-old. Today he noticed the little stool I put in one of the bathrooms. He asked me, "What's this in here for, Gramma?" I paused for a few minutes, wondering if he would grasp if I told him the truth. He's pretty smart and very observant, so I explained to him that I like to envision Jesus sitting on that little stool and talk to me while I'm in the bathroom. Now, I know that might sound like an awkward place to meet Jesus, but it totally works for me, and those moments might as well be put to good use. Zion thinks about this for a few minutes.

His only response was, "I think... I think that chair might be a little small for Jesus." I love his view of Jesus! So, I only agreed with him. This concept is something I learned at 'Mountain Top journey.' Our friend and leader, Jodi, taught us this. Several minutes of communing with Jesus in the morning with eyes wide open, imagining Him sitting right there in that tiny little step stool (my dad made for me) is powerful. I can't fully describe it, but if you would like to learn more about it, there's a book called 'Two Chairs' by Bob Beaudine. God truly does long to talk to us today. Will we take the time to listen? Start with two minutes of stillness. You will be amazed. I love John 10:27, "My sheep hear My voice and I know them, and they follow Me."

Prayer Declaration:
Jesus, thank You that you still speak to us today. Teach us just how that looks like for each one of us to be able to hear your voice. Help us to know your voice. Thank you for being our Good Shepherd who longs to speak to us, your sheep.

September 16
Rise Above

My to-do list looks daunting this morning. How was I possibly going to accomplish everything that needed to be done today? Do you know that feeling? I'm sure you do. Especially if you are a wife and mother, maybe even a grandmother. As always, when I can't see my way through, those feelings of overwhelming want to take over. I wish we could sit for a cup of coffee together and share ideas and strategies for how to overcome those moments. To top it off, we had a semi-truck stuck in our lane this morning, leaving ruts and ruined grass. Nothing centers me more than a good run, so off I go, headphones on, and just run it out.

Did you know physical exercise has emotional benefits? After thinking clearly, I asked myself, what is a bit of ruined grass in light of a relationship? My husband was very kind and helpful to the driver of the semi, who simply failed to turn wide enough into our driveway and thus ended up in the ditch. Plus, we are super thankful for the product he brought so the guys can continue with work. Now, hours later, both houses are clean, laundry is almost done, office work is caught up, and grocery lists are made. Our guests are arriving later tonight, which allows my husband and me time to go on a date before we host the rest of the weekend. This, too, centers me. Feeling connected, both our love tanks filled before we served others. This is a mandate we try to live out in our marriage. So truly, what is it for you that makes you feel calm, cool, and collected? Of course, for me, above all else is staying connected to my Heavenly Father through the highs and lows of everyday life.

Psalms 118:7 says it best, "The Lord is on my side. He is my helper." He is on your side too, friend. He will help you rise above it all as well. Let's look at our 'To Do List' in light of eternity. Will it matter then, especially the ruined grass and the potholes? Rise above.

Prayer Declaration:
Thank you, Jesus, for your help and perspective. Teach us to see things from a heavenly perspective. Help us to live out of this truth and let You lift us up above it all when we are overwhelmed.

September 17
Parenting With Purpose

Our guests arrived late last night, all the way from Ohio. They are good friends and colleagues in business as well. Last spring, at one of our events, we auctioned off a weekend of wining and dining at our Airbnb. The proceeds all went to Africa for water wells. This couple bought the weekend. We start the day with coffee and brunch before we pack up their four children, and we all head to an apple orchard for caramel apples, picking pumpkins, hayrides, and all things children love to do. I was amazed at all the parents there just simply spending time with their children. There were lots and lots of children, happy little voices, and laughter everywhere. This warmed my heart, and I wanted to tell all the parents they are doing a good job, investing quality time into their children.

We talked about this with our guests, too, and discussed the importance of it. In fact, our mentor used to tell us *if we want to get to our children's hearts, we need to make what's important to them important to us.* That's something I've never forgotten, and now I want to do that with our own grandchildren too. This makes them feel valued, important, seen, and known. Don't we all want to be known? Deep down, we do. It's a God-given desire to want to feel valued, cherished, and known. What if we could provide that for our children at a very young age? Perhaps they would grow up more established and not look for their identity and worth in all the wrong places. Of course, teaching them about their identity in Jesus is the most important of all, but these two go hand in hand. This is a good declaration to have them memorize; Psalms 139:13-14 a wonderful affirmation verse, "I am the wonderful creation of a loving God. He knows everything about me..." What if our children grew up realizing this as soon as they could talk and walk.

Prayer Declaration:
Jesus, help us to speak life over our children from the time they are born. Teach us the importance of investing into our children with words and time. Thank you to the many parents who do realize this already.

September 18
Standing Steadfast

We ended our day yesterday by driving up to a beautiful lookout above the Mississippi River. We sat and soaked up the view before heading back home, where we enjoyed a steak dinner on the back patio. Next, we watched the sunset from the living room windows. Everyone was tired from our day out and about, but it was a fun and fulfilling day out in nature. Different times, I realized our friends that were here were very aware and attentive to their children. The dad would find a few spare minutes and be outside in the backyard pitching balls to his three sons. The mom was very capable and made it look easy to care for her three sons and cute baby girl. Watching these parents brought so many memories of when our children were that age and in the same order, three boys and then a girl. Except then, we had two girls (twins!).

It was good to talk about parenting, among many other things. It's always so fun, refreshing, and inspirational to see parents in tune with their children. Our friends left the Amish culture, too, and are on their own God journey. It was a blessing to reminisce together about where we've been and what God has done. How the road forward is definitely not always easy, but always worth it. Maybe you are in a difficult place trying to move forward. Remember, just because it is difficult right now doesn't mean it's not God's heart for you. Sometimes He allows us to be tested along the way. So, keep your eyes on Him and that thing He is asking you to do; keep persevering. You can trust Him to lead you right! Surround yourself with people who understand and will cheer you on, if possible. 1st Chronicles 16:11 simply says, "Seek the Lord in His strength. Seek His face continually."

Prayer Declaration:
We can look to You day and night; thank you, Jesus, knowing you will lead us rightly, in your way, with your will. Teach us to know your voice and be careful what other voices we listen to. Help us to stand steadfast even when it's hard and uncomfortable.

September 19
The Next Generation

Our guests left around noon yesterday. We had another meal together made by my wonderful husband. He's the best cook, better than me. Our son Dennis and his little family joined us, and the little boys all played together so nicely. With dishes done and everything cleaned up, I turn on worship and have a nap before daughter Luanne and her husband come home. She and I have quality time to talk about all things baby. This is so wonderful and exciting. We don't even know what they are having yet, boy or girl, but that doesn't keep us from dreaming. We talked about everything from how big my baby bumps were, to the baby shower, to the baby register, and everything in between. Our husbands are having their own conversations about roofs and all things football and business.

We enjoy warm apple crisps and ice cream before they leave for home. I will send leftovers home for their lunches tomorrow. Luanne works full-time, so she is a busy little wife. We also discussed the message from church this morning, all four of us. It was so good and encouraging. My heart rejoices at my daughter and son-in-law's hearts for Jesus and the thought of them teaching their children about Him.

Psalm 78:6 talks about continuing to pass on God's goodness and works for generations, "So that the next generation might know them, even the children not yet born, and they in turn will teach their own children." Mamas speak, sing, and pray over those babies, still in the womb (like our daughter's baby). It is not too early. Their little spirits pick it up just like they can pick up trauma in the womb. Let them pick up God's goodness.

Prayer Declaration:
Lord, will you bless even the babies not born yet, still in the womb, that even now they'd be spoken and declared to, about all your goodness. Jesus, thank you for Godly children and for all you've done in our hearts and lives. May we never stop speaking and declaring your greatness. All of us. Do it again, Lord.

September 20
Expect the Miraculous

Waking up to rain showers this morning made me want to snuggle deeper under the covers instead of getting up. However, that was not an option. Instead, I linger over my coffee a bit longer, trying to find and waiting for the motivation to go on a run. Finally, I realized I must just go and hope it finds me somewhere along the road. That's exactly what happened, as Spotify brought me just the right songs. I like to think the Holy Spirit selects them for me because He knows exactly what I need. He knows what you need this morning too. Have you asked Him, or are you pushing through on your own strength? That can make us so tired and so weary. Sean Feucht and his wife are one of my heroes in the faith currently. Facing opposition, ridicule, and even death threats, they travel around the US and do massive worship/revival events.

It's one of the biggest revival moments I know of currently, and it's all outside of the church. One of his albums is finally out on Spotify, and it's called 'Standing on the Rock.' It's so good. It's fresh, it's fire, and it's motivating. As I listened to it this morning, I felt my own faith rising once again. He sings about prison doors opening and being in a den of lions, the timeless Bible stories, and the miracles Jesus did in those stories. You can read them for yourself. The Book of Daniel Chapter 6 tells his story. Act 16:25-28 tells the story of Paul and Silas praying at midnight and how suddenly the prison doors opened. Incredible, miraculous stories! Do we believe that God can still move like that today? Do we believe He can open our own prison doors we find ourselves in? Can He save us from the things that would devour us, yes, even hungry lions. Where is our faith level today? He is still the same God He was back then. Let's expect Him and let him be that God for us.

Prayer Declaration:
Jesus, thank you for those powerful stories. Lord, will you increase our faith levels? We ask you expectantly, Jesus, to forgive us for our apathy and unbelief in trying to do things in our own strength. Teach us to ask for your miracles in our own lives.

September 21
Conflict in Relationships

Conflict is a part of life, it seems. A part that I wish would just magically go away forever. Wishful thinking, right? How do you handle conflict? Were you taught how to do that gracefully or in a way that issues get resolved? Or do you just sweep things under the carpet and hope it goes away? I myself am on a journey with this, trying to do conflict better, trying to remember in the middle of a conflict that a relationship is more important than being right, and yet we all need and want to feel heard, and our opinions are valued. We ought to use our voices for what we believe in or stand for. This can be a tall order. Again, there's an amazing book out on this called, "Keeping your love on," by Danny and Sherry Silk. It's very helpful for any type of relationship conflict. Whether in business, church, your family, or in marriage.

The challenge is to follow the concepts they give us in that book, but I dare say it is the best way to resolve conflict. There's also this short but powerful verse in Romans 15:18, "A gentle or soft answer turns away wrath, but a harsh word stirs up anger." While we would do well to remember these simple words during the conflict, one thing I know is conflict is inevitable as long as we are surrounded by other humans. But we do have a choice in how we engage or respond to it. It's also okay to say, "I need a timeout." It's okay to take some time to sort out your thoughts and feelings when the pressure gets to be too much. Our world, in general, needs a revolution in this, but once again, it starts with us, it starts with you, and it starts with me.

Prayer Declaration:
Jesus, you are again the best example when it comes to conflict in relationships. Teach us how to model you in Proverbs 15:1, "A soft answer turns away wrath..." Help us to not give in to anger and saying words we will regret in the heat of the moment. Thank you for your guidance in this matter.

September 22
Speaking Up

Now that we have established a soft and gentle answer, it is the best way to deal with conflict. There is also another side to communicating that might be needed at times. Let's take a look at Matthew 12:34. Jesus proclaims, "Brood of vipers..." to a certain group of people, "How can you, being evil, speak good things? For out of the abundance of the heart, the mouth speaks." Wow, we might think that's a bit harsh. This was directed at the Pharisees, the ones who found fault with Jesus when He walked here on Earth. No matter what miracle He did, it was always wrong somehow. Jesus healed the blind and the mute man. All the Pharisees had to say was, "This fellow does not cast out demons except by Beelzebub, the ruler of demons," Matthew 12:22-24. This fellow, huh? Wow. Can we blame Jesus for His response to them? I imagine He had just about enough of their religious charades. Do you know people like this? If you do, maybe there is a time to call them out just like Jesus did.

Perhaps we've had experience with leaders who operate like the Pharisees. Nothing is ever quite right or holy enough for them, and they are quick to condemn, shun and make people feel like they will never measure up or attain their requirements or perfectly follow their many rules. I know of different situations that are both saddening and maddening, even right now. I believe we would be wise to separate ourselves from leaders like that. Maybe that's where you are today. Maybe you need to separate yourself from condemning controlling leadership. Or, at the very least, call them out on their sin, just like Jesus did. Maybe even use a bit more honor than calling them vipers! However, there's a time to speak and a time to be silent. Ask Jesus, in each situation, do I speak up or stay silent? He will show you.

Prayer Declaration:
Jesus, thank you for your wisdom. In whatever situation we find ourselves with people, it can be so hard to know what to say sometimes. Teach us how to honor and yet always stand for righteousness and the truth. Help us to know what to do in our situations.

September 23
Peacemakers

Would you consider yourself a peacemaker? Or are you rather a person who likes to stir things up and rock the boat a little bit? Is being right more important to you than relationships? Have you ever seen or been in a situation where both parties were clearly at fault? Yet, both had part of the truth. It is quite often like that, no matter what relationship it is. In fact, did you know that every story has not only two but three sides? Your side, their side, and then the actual truth? None of us has all the answers or gets it right all the time; we would do well to realize this. "I've been pondering over the verse where it says the blessed are the peacemakers, for they will be called children of God," Matthew 5:9.

So, let's take it one step further and explore a little bit of what a peacemaker actually is or does. When I looked it up this morning, it said this; a peacemaker is a person who brings about peace, especially by reconciling adversaries. Wow. So, it's more than just keeping the peace or being a peaceful person yourself and in your own life. It is the ability to help others reconcile their differences and possibly even restore friendships and relationships. It's so easy to cut people off or even out of our lives when conflict and hard feelings arise. While there is a time for boundaries and putting space between ongoing difficult people, what if we first tried the peacemaker approach? Look around at your circumstances and see where you can apply and practice being a peacemaker today. Yes, me too.

Prayer declaration:
Jesus, thank you for enabling us to be peacemakers, even choosing to be intentional. Help us to humble ourselves and take that first step to restore peace and relationships. Teach us the importance of living like this, for then we will be called your children.

September 24
Chilly and Chili

Our 70-to-80-degree weather left us almost overnight. Suddenly we have lows in the 30s and highs in the 50s to 60s. It's accompanied by rain and lots of wind. Perhaps we are getting the tailwind of the hurricane in Florida. I'm not sure why the quick change, but I do know it is chilly indeed. What do you do when it's chilly? You make chili. Homemade chili is the best. Chopping onions, frying meat, blending up fresh tomatoes, and adding plenty of chili powder and seasonings. Next, I dump it all into my large crock pot and simmer it for hours. Anyone that comes through my doors gets a sample. We enjoy it all day, and a large portion goes into the freezer for a future day or event I'm hosting. It's tasty, steamy, spicy, and just delicious. It's all rather therapeutic for me. And will be the first of many batches for this 'chili' season.

It's a little like the saying when life gives you lemons, make lemonade. What is your life giving you these days? Is it lemons? Or maybe you are still in the season of late-blooming flowers and roses. Enjoy them while they last. I'll be the first to admit it's not always easy to look on the bright side and make the best of our circumstances. But it is possible because *how we respond* to what happens to us is usually *more important than what happens* to us. Eventually, we will even see things like beauty for our ashes and joy for our mourning. Praise for the spirit of heaviness. In the last part of Isaiah 61:3, He says, "They will be called oaks of righteousness, a planting of the Lord for the display of His splendor." Wow, what a promise, what an exchange.

Prayer Declaration:
Jesus, today we bring all our burdens, disappointments or whatever is weighing us down, and we exchange it for what you want for us. Teach us how to surrender and receive your will every day.

September 25
Increase and Decrease

He reigns, He reigns, He reigns forever. He reigns, He reigns, and His name is Jesus. These were some powerful lyrics we sang at church today. The people came alive as we declared this over and over. It was healing, holy, and moving. The last line is 'ruler of everything.' He truly is, and that just brings me peace. Where do you need him to rule and reign in your life? Where or what do you need to let go of and trust Jesus? It's a constant struggle for me not to try and fix things for people as a counselor/slash coach. That can be so hard for me sometimes. It's so easy to see what needs to change in situations, but it's almost never easy for people to make those changes. Letting go and letting God is one of my mandates, but not always easy to do.

There's a verse in John 3:30 that goes well with this. He must become greater and greater, and I must become less and less. These were the words of John the Baptist, I believe. He modeled this so well, always preaching and always speaking about the One who is to come, the One whose shoes I am not worthy to tie, he said. Wow, what if we practice this kind of honor and humility in our relationships, especially in our relationships with Jesus? Not exalting our ways of thinking and our ways of doing things over His. Letting him work things out in people's lives, and our own lives, in His timing and not our time. Where can you practice living like this in your life and relationships today? Let's let Him reign above it all.

Prayer Declaration:
Thank you, Jesus, for this reminder today of your supremacy. Teach us to partner with what You are doing and leave the rest for your timing. Help us to become less and let You become more every day and in every situation.

September 26
Me and My House

But for the grace of God, there go I. Those are my thoughts almost every time I pass a horse and buggy on the road. I slow way down, too, because I know just how unpredictable a horse can be. They have a mind of their own and can easily veer to the right or left with no warning. On my way to Rochester, MN, I passed two different ones. It always takes me back to those days, and I wonder and ponder once again, why me, God, why did you bring me out of that culture? That could so easily be me in that buggy, just like it was for half of my life. The only thing I know is perhaps the dangerous little prayer I prayed many times and still do to this day. God, if there is more of you to experience, I want it. We want it.

As for me and my family, we want it. I still pray this on behalf of our ever-growing family. I love how Joshua declares in Joshua 24:15. At the end of verse 15, he says it boldly and declares it over them, "But as for me and my house, we will serve the Lord." Don't you want that, too, no matter the cost? Just the other day, I was having this conversation with someone who is having difficult situations and yet praying this prayer. God, if you have more for us, we want it. Will you show us? I reminded this person that often, the answer to these prayers does not come on silver platters but through difficult or even costly times. Sometimes He may even call you away from all that's familiar to you or those things you put in His place. He may even completely take you out of your comfort zone. But if you still say yes, your rewards will be worth anything you leave behind for His sake.

Prayer Declaration:
Thank you, Jesus, for giving us hearts to choose you above all else. Help us to leave our comforts for your cause. Teach us to know your voice and follow your will in leading our lives. Help us to remember that You never ask us to leave something or lay something down unless You have something much better for us.

September 27
Heavenly Perspectives

Proverbs 13:20 says simply, "Walk with wise and become wise, for a companion of fools suffers harm." That's talking pretty straight, isn't it? So much truth to this, though, and I feel like I've just spent two days learning from the wise. A couple times in the year, a church about 2 hours from us holds these amazing leader's conferences. Such a wonderful blessing to me every single time. The main speaker, this time, calls himself a 'hope dealer,' and he does it ever so well. One of his main messages is about renewing our minds. Philippians 2:2 says, "Complete my joy by being of the same mind, having the same love, being in full accord and of one mind." To me, that means to think like my Heavenly Father thinks. Renewing our minds does not happen overnight, or the minute we get saved.

It takes time and commitment and being intentional about what we put into our minds, as well as getting rid of old mindsets that no longer serve us. Even just yesterday, someone prayed over me to not be so hard and judgmental of myself, right on track. Even though I feel like I've come a long way with that, I believe it's a lifetime of learning to live under grace and not the law, especially if you were raised under the law mentality like a lot of us have. One thing for you to take note of today is your inner dialogue with yourself. How do you view or speak to yourself? Would you say these things to your best friend? No. Then give yourself the same kind of grace. And most of all, see yourself the way your loving Heavenly Father sees you. We truly are often our own worst critics. It's time to renew our minds and align our thoughts with heaven's perspective of ourselves.

Prayer Declaration:
Jesus, thank you for your gentle reminders of where we still need to grow. Teach us to believe and receive how You see us. Help us to forgive ourselves of our past, just like You have forgiven us, Jesus. Renew our minds. Help us to think like You think and speak like You speak.

September 28
Perfected Sanctification

Hebrews 10:14 says, "By one offering he has perfected forever those who are sanctified." Does that mean we can be perfect like our Heavenly Father? Is that how He sees us? That would almost be 'heresy' in the culture I came from. So, what does this all mean? I think sanctification is a big part of our Christian walk. After we give our lives to Jesus, now begins the sanctification part becoming perfect, just as our Father is perfect. We will never think that about ourselves. But is that how He sees us? With good hearts, doing the right thing over and over. Choosing to turn the other cheek or giving our coat to our neighbor, returning good for evil again and again. Constantly wanting to become a better person and dealing with sin issues He convicts us of. This is an idea of what the sanctification process could look like.

Choosing the right thing over the wrong thing, even when it's hard. Jesus paid the ultimate price, the one offering with His blood, His body, and the sacrifice of His life. Choosing the right road over the easy road is sanctification. This will propel us toward how Jesus already sees us as 'perfect.' That is our inheritance in Him and with Him. We can also do this with our relationships. What if we started speaking the truth about who people are over them? Your children, your husband, your in-laws? Don't you think they would be motivated to become all the good things we declare over them? Look beyond the human flaws and see them how God sees them and call that out in them. Call out the valuable, the gold in people, so to speak. Anyone can find dirt in people. Let's be people who find and magnify the gold, the good in people and see what happens in our relationships. Let's practice having Jesus's eyes and mouth.

Prayer Declaration:
Thank you, Jesus, for once again teaching us the power of our words. Help us remember the ways we speak matters. Help us, Jesus, to embrace sanctification in every situation, knowing it will make us more like You with every right choice.

September 29
Build on the Rock

A beautiful, majestic, sunshiny morning. It feels especially welcome after our cold nights. We had a hard frost the last two nights, 26 degrees to be exact, pretty cold for late September. The last several evenings, I spent quite a bit of time outside, covering up some of my prettiest plants and bushes that we didn't want to freeze just yet. It worked, they made it through, and now we get to enjoy them for a good while yet, probably. Just like the people in Florida prepared for Hurricane Ian, wise people will prepare for things they know are coming. It reminds me of the parable of the wise man building his house upon the rock. You can read the story in Matthew. It was one of the many parables of Jesus.

We know how the story goes. Mathew 7:24-27 says, "The man who built his house on the sand, his house didn't stand but collapsed when the storms came." What about us? Where is our house or foundation built upon, sand or rock? Are we prepared and equipped for the storms of life? Will our foundation survive? Just like my plants were covered and survived the last several nights, are we covered and protected from the things that would hurt and destroy us? The armor of God is the best way to be covered and protected. Simply ask God for that protection every day and invite your guardian angels to do their job. I laughingly say I keep my guardian angels very busy. They don't have time to get bored. It's true.

Prayer Declaration:
Thank you, Jesus, that we can be protected and prepared through You and in You. Give us your wisdom to prepare ahead of time. Teach us how to build our foundation on You, the Rock, that will stand for all eternity.

September 30
Bearing Our Fruit

Another beautiful fall morning. No frost this morning, just clear and cold. I'm so thankful we can check the weather the night before and plan accordingly. It wasn't that way growing up, but we usually had the milkman or the feed man or a driver we hired to drive us around tell us. Or maybe we just knew too. I don't remember, but I do know that it's very nice that my phone now tells me the low temperature every night, and it is very accurate. My husband and I decided to take advantage of the beautiful evening last night and went to a nursery to pick out some trees. We knew what kind of trees we wanted. What we weren't prepared for was the many different varieties of each tree. Like a maple, oak, or pine tree, no one can say a tree is just a tree.

There are many, many different kinds, shapes, sizes, and varieties of each kind of tree. So many, in fact, we didn't even buy any last night. We needed time to think and plan and talk about which ones will work for our space, budget, and everything else. Once again, so much like us humans, right? We, too, come in different shapes, sizes, nationalities, and varieties. Yet we all have the same DNA from our Heavenly Father. Are we producing the fruit that we are made of, made for, or are we busy wishing we could be another variety of trees, so to speak? Do we believe that God made us exactly like He wanted us to be for the place He has called us to be and produce fruit for Him? Let's not waste our time comparing ourselves to others. Jesus said about the unfruitful fig tree in Mark 4:28, "If it bears fruit next year, fine, but if not, cut it down."

Prayer Declaration:
Jesus, we don't want to be unfruitful or cut down before our time. Teach us to be thankful for how and who You made us to be. Instead of comparing ourselves to many others, help us to dig deep and let our roots grow deep in who we are in You, and out of that, bear the fruit that only we can, according to how You made us.

October 1
The Blessing of Children

Thirty years ago today, our oldest son Duane was born at midnight. He was a month early, and we didn't even have a diaper in the house. Where I come from, they didn't throw baby showers for each other. We did give each other small gifts, though, after our babies were born, partially because we didn't know what we were having ahead of time. Our first son Duane was only 5 pounds when he was born. We had him at home with midwives, completely natural, with no pain meds of any kind. The back labor was very intense, as many of you mamas can probably relate to, but oh, was it ever worth it, every bit of pain and labor! What a relief when he was finally born and what a gift. Is there any feeling quite like your first child coming into this world? It's a perfect miracle; every birth is.

We were only married about three months before we got pregnant with our son, but we wanted a baby and were so thrilled. 1 Samuel 1:27 says," For this child I prayed, and the Lord has granted the desires of my heart." Today, our tiny firstborn is a grown man with an amazing, tender heart. He's still bringing us joy, even 30 years later. Maybe you are longing for children too? There are so many ways to love children today. Foster care and adoption are very near to our hearts. Perhaps you have lots of children in your Sunday school class or your class at school. Possibly, your way of being a mother looks a little different, but it is perfect for you. Children do fill a special place in our hearts, whether adopted, biological, foster, or however you are pouring into the children in your life.

Prayer Declaration:
Jesus, thank you for our son. Thank you for bringing children to all who are longing for that, lead and guide each one of us to our family and the ones who need our love.

October 2
Heart Alignment

My heart was heavy as I drove to church this morning. Discouragement was nipping at my thoughts and emotions. I turned on some soft, soaking music in an attempt to bring peace to my turmoil of thoughts. Disappointment, questions without answers, and feeling extra tired all had me feeling down. I grabbed a cup of coffee and found my regular spot right in the front row. The worship team started to play and soon the glory came down. The one line we declared for quite some time was, *I will see your goodness in the land I'm living in.* My heart started believing it once again. My mind came to a place of rest. I was able to let all of the hurt and disappointment of the previous week go. Following an amazing time of worship, the pastor's wife had a powerful message again, just what I needed, and she talked about some of the exact things I had been going through. I went up for prayer at the end of the service, and my tears flowed in surrender and hope. I walked out of church feeling so much lighter than when I walked in.

All I can say is thank you, Jesus. Can you remember a time when you were encouraged in a matter of a few hours? Sometimes it's just as simple as letting people into the battle with you. We don't have to fight alone. One thing in the message today was, don't even engage with the negative thoughts and voices. This develops our spiritual muscles. Sometimes we need to let someone speak the truth over us. It is the struggle that makes us stronger, that doesn't always feel good at the moment. Let someone pray for you today, my friend; you are not alone. Above all, let's align ourselves with God's word, "For the word of God is active and sharper than any double-edged sword, it penetrates even to divide soul and spirit, joints and marrow, and judges the thoughts and attitudes of the heart," Hebrews 4:12.

Prayer Declaration:
Jesus, thank you for your word, for your brothers and sisters in Christ to help bring us into alignment, in those times when we feel weak or discouraged. Help us to humble ourselves and ask for help and prayer when we need it. Teach us to believe what You say about us.

October 3
Triune Beings

My once-a-month massage was due today. Perfect timing. Now that my heart is back where it's healthier since yesterday, it's time to align my body too. She told me my neck and shoulders were extra tight, no surprise to me, as that seems to be where we, as women, carry our stress right on our shoulders. If you don't believe me, just start taking notes several times a day. Are your shoulders relaxed or scrunched up? Practice consciously relaxing them throughout the day. This might even help you if you have lots of headaches like I used to. Being aware of our bodies and simple, purposeful actions can have an effect on our health. It truly is all connected, soul, spirit, and body. We are triune beings. I love the prayer in 1st Thessalonians 5:23, "I pray your whole spirit, soul and body be preserved blameless unto the coming of our Lord Jesus Christ."

Yes, we will get brand new bodies in heaven. Even so, it is important to take care of our earthly bodies. I believe it is honoring God when we do take care of our earthly bodies. It is hard to do what we are called to do. Even though our spirit might be healthy, an unhealthy body can affect our quality of life. Coming from someone who used to not take very good care of myself, this is quite a change for me. Where are you with your health today? Where do you long to make changes? Is it your physical body, or do you need to change something in your spiritual life? It is okay to take care of yourself. Invest in your health, whatever that looks like for you. Start today. If you aren't sure where to start, ask Jesus. He will bring something to mind.

Prayer Declaration:
Jesus, thank you that You care about all of us. Teach us how to take care of our physical bodies so we can be healthy and whole. On all three levels, spirit, soul, and body.

October 4
Encourage Yourself

Isn't it just wild how discouragement can cloud your vision? When you start listening to the lies of the enemy of your soul, it leads nowhere good. What if we would learn to pull ourselves out of those places quickly? I must say, most times now, it's much quicker for me than it used to be, but I still have my days, just like last weekend. There is so much to be said about these difficult times, and so much we can learn during or from these periods. Suffering and trials make our roots go deeper in God if we allow them to. It is in the struggle that we become stronger, sometimes it's physical, and sometimes it's mental. Both can be very difficult. What if we could see or imagine ourselves getting stronger in those times? What if we could learn not only to survive but to thrive during those times?

In Psalms 42:5, David encouraged himself, "Why my soul, are you down? Why so disturbed within me? Put your hope in God, for I will yet praise him, my Savior and my God." Don't you just love how David starts out by asking himself some good questions? We would save ourselves some pain, too, if we would ask ourselves, is this true what I'm believing? Is that hurtful thing they said about me true, or is it just their opinion? Let's learn to ask ourselves questions and cut off the lies we believe right away before they manifest and become many more. Let's rearrange our minds and hearts around the truth like David declares; we will yet praise you, our Savior and our God.

Prayer Declaration:
Jesus, thank you for your truth that sets us free. Help us remember that we have the authority to take every thought captive and separate the truth from the lies. Teach us to know the difference and renew our minds.

October 5
Trees, Leaves, and Us

Fall in Wisconsin is breathtaking right now. There are vibrant colors of red, orange, yellow, and lots of green. Throw in my plants that are still blooming, and you have more reds, yellows, and soft orange, even purple and pink. It truly is all so very beautiful. If you are a nature person like I am, you know exactly what I'm talking about. There is almost this urgency to soak it all up to the full before it all goes frozen and dies or is dormant for the winter. I read this quote the other day. Something about the trees showing us how to let things go is so true. They are at their most beautiful, and then they lose all their leaves. Hmm, I wonder how that correlates with our lives. I'm not exactly sure, but I do know that we, too, have seasons with a lot of beauty.

We might also have seasons where we can feel so barren, like we are stripped down to our very soul, just like the trees. Maybe just like the trees need to lose their leaves in order to get fresh, brand-new ones, we, too, need to let go of the old and make room for the new. Sometimes, while we wait for the new, it can feel bare, empty, and uncomfortable. Maybe this is partially what pruning feels like for us as humans. Isaiah 18:5 is only one verse that speaks about pruning before the harvest, "As soon as the bud blossoms and the flower becomes a ripening grape, then he will cut off the sprigs with pruning knives and remove and cut away the spreading branches." This sounds painful, yet it is necessary not only for plants and trees but, yes, as humans, we need to be pruned too. Ouch, but yes, at the same time,

Prayer Declaration:
Jesus, thank you that you know exactly what we need to grow to our full potential. Help us to trust You through every pruning process. Teach us to even embrace it, knowing it is for our good.

October 6
Own Your Story

Sitting at Caribou this morning, savoring a hot pumpkin latte made with real pumpkin, it's so much better than the fake syrups. My day is filled to the brim with last-minute errands and things to do. My heart beats with anticipation and deep gratitude this morning. Tomorrow afternoon, the weekend finally starts. A dozen or so ladies will gather at my house for a short weekend of food and fellowship. We call it a ladies retreat. It's exclusive in the fact that you must have been born and raised Amish. These are my people and where my heart is. For years after we left the Amish ourselves, I struggled with knowing where I fit in. What can I do with only an eighth-grade education? I felt inadequate, lonely, and sometimes lost in knowing what I was supposed to do with my life. For the first time, I had options.

Thankfully, I was still raising my children, so that took up most of my time, but it didn't keep me from dreaming about the possibilities. There was also a time that I'm not proud of when I didn't want anyone to know we used to be Amish, silly, I know. One day God spoke to me and said, "This is your story." When will you own it? It stopped me, and since then, God has also shown me that I'm largely called to my own culture. He gave me Isaiah 61:1 as a mandate, "The spirit of the Lord is upon me because the Lord has anointed me to proclaim good news to the poor." He has sent me to bind up the broken hearted, to proclaim freedom for the captives. And release from darkness for the prisoners." Have you specifically dared to ask God for your mandate and calling? Do it today. He has an assignment for you.

Prayer Declaration:
Thank you, Jesus, that you still speak to us today. Teach each one of us to know what You are calling us to do. Help us to walk it out. With your grace, your help, and your anointing.

October 7
Different Languages

Just a few hours until the ladies start trickling in for the retreat, I'm ready, excited, and anticipating a wonderful weekend with like-minded women. I'm sure there will be some speaking in Dutch going on and maybe some speaking in tongues as well. Who knows? We are fluent like that, being able to speak two languages, or three if you count speaking in tongues. It's a blessing and a privilege. All of our six children can speak and understand Dutch just fine too. It, again, was one of those good things we chose to keep from our inheritance. Some of the younger ones speak it a bit broken, but I love to hear them, and it's super cute. On my run this morning, the song *"Million little miracles"* came on.

Oh, my heart, I love that song. It's my life in a song. *Miracles and miracles, 1,000,000 little miracles 1,2,3,4, I can't even count them all*; that's the chorus. It's so true, and it's true for you, too, whether you are aware of it or not. What if we were as quick to count and verbalize what is right in our lives rather than what is wrong? Let's change the narrative of what we verbalize, and we just might add even more blessings to our lives. I've been to underdeveloped countries a few times, and I'm always convicted, humbled, and amazed. The many, many things we take for granted are mindboggling. We should be some of the most grateful people on the planet, especially as Christians. We should be setting the tone for the rest of the world. Psalms 107:21-22, "Let them give thanks to the Lord for His unfailing love and His wonderful deeds for mankind. Let them sacrifice thank offerings, and tell of His works with songs of joy." Yes, Lord, we do and we will.

Prayer Declaration:
Thank you, Lord, for the privilege of speaking several different languages. Teach us to let praise and worship be our first language above anything else.

October 8
Redeemed and Rejuvenated

We had a wonderful dinner around the table last night before we headed to the woods for a bonfire. We lugged our jug of fresh wassail back with us so we would have a hot drink to enjoy. As we fellowshipped around the fire, it was a cool but calm evening and just perfect for sitting outside bundled up in our hats, jackets, and blankets. My husband had slipped back to the woods earlier, started the fire for us, and turned on the string lights. It was the perfect setting for our conversations. It was centered around Psalms 107:9, "For He satisfies the longing soul and the hungry soul He fills with good things." What a promise. We all shared what we are currently longing and hungry for in this season. Now I'm asking, do you believe the above verse? This verse is for you, too, for all of us.

The first step is to let God know what that is, and the next step is to share it with someone safe who will help you contend for your deepest longings. We also had times of wonderful worship where we felt the tangible presence of God. Have you ever felt that, or would you like to? Again, that would be the first step. It's longing for that. In the afternoon, we all piled on the back of a hay rack with hay bales, and my husband drove us around the block and through the woods. The fresh air, wind, sunshine, and laughter were invigorating. We gathered for another meal together before our evening session and more worship. We finally hit the hot tub before bed, late and tired, but souls and hearts refreshed and rejuvenated.

Prayer Declaration:
Jesus, thank you for hungry hearts and redeemed women. Thank you that you heal our deepest wounds, help us walk out our healing and our freedom to extend forgiveness to those who have hurt us, teach us to forgive like you forgive Jesus.

October 9
Beloved Daughters [and Sons]

We started gathering for coffee early this morning and finally gathered around the table for one last meal together before everyone headed back home to their precious families. We read out of Psalms 37. Such a powerful psalm. We also shared testimonies. I dare say we all settle deeper into our inheritance as daughters of the king this weekend. We sang songs about how good of a father He is, how His love is unconditional, and how when we make mistakes, He longs for us to run to Him instead of from Him. Just like we long for our children to come to us when they make mistakes, do we want them to be afraid of us, or do we want them to come to us? To have a relationship where they know we are a safe place, how much more is our Heavenly Father a safe place for us, His beloved children?

John 1:12 says it so beautifully, "To all who believed Him and accepted Him. He gave the right to become children, sons, daughters of God." He rejoiced in the fact that we are His beloved daughters. If you have accepted Him as your Savior, this is your right and your inheritance too. There are many more verses that speak about this wonderful truth. You can look them up for yourself and let the truth wash over you too. Sometimes even though we have heard or known these things, it is so good and life-giving to set some time aside and let it go deeper into your heart, perhaps even with an amazing group of women, just like I had the privilege of doing this weekend.

Prayer Declaration:
Jesus, thank you for brave, strong and yet surrendered women you bring into my life. What an amazing blessing. Help us to remember all the God moments and truths we learned this weekend. Teach us to hear and live from our place of your precious daughters.

October 10
Prayers for My Culture

My husband had business to take care of close to where my Amish family lives today. So, of course, I took the opportunity to tag along and drop by my sister-in-law's house. Her sister from Iowa, who is also my good friend, was here to visit, so we had a few short hours to catch up and snuggle their newest baby. The next stop was at my sister's house for coffee, pastries, and sitting in the sun. Again, only a short but sweet time. My heart is full, and I'm so thankful my family allows us to drop in like this. As my husband and I drove the five hours round trip, it provided time for me to catch him up on the previous weekend. Some of the women's stories are heartbreaking. I couldn't tell him the whole of it. My heart literally hurts for what some of these dear ladies have been through, often suffering silently. No one knew what they endured until years later when they got married or left the Amish.

Most of them have come a long way in their healing journey, and this weekend was another layer I trust, as they had a safe place to share and process. The rest of us gathered around them to pray and build them up and anoint them with oil for healing. We talked about what is brought to light as having no more power over us. "For nothing is hidden that will not become evident, nor anything secret that will not be known and come to light, Luke 8:17." While the plain communities have a lot of good in their culture, there are also hidden, evil things that happen just like any other culture. God is no respecter of persons, and judgment will come one day to all nations, no matter our culture or color.

Prayer Declaration:
Jesus, I cry out today especially for my culture. Especially those who are being abused physically, emotionally or spiritually. Hear my cry, my prayer, Oh God.

October 11
He Still Speaks

My heart is still overflowing with gratitude and thanksgiving to Jesus for all He did this past weekend. This morning was the first time I had to breathe and bask in it all, looking through pictures the ladies were sharing in our group. Reliving the precious moments of worship, fellowship, tears, and laughter. It is amazing to me what happens when the hunger in our own hearts and Holy Spirit collide. There is something special that happens in those moments. God honors our hearts and cries for more of Him. He is faithful to meet us when we gather to seek Him and listen for His voice. What a privilege it is to be able to host a space for women to come and be themselves and seek His face together.

The theme for this retreat was our identity and inheritance as God's daughters. Also, we leaned into learning to hear His voice. We talked about where the Bible says, "His sheep hear His voice..." John 10:27. 1 Corinthians 2:16 ends by saying, "But we have the mind of Christ," meaning, of course, if we are saved and Jesus is our Savior. What a privilege to be able to listen to his voice, never loud, rude, demanding, or condemning, but rather still gentle and sometimes convicting. Some people have heard the audible voice of God. Maybe you have too. If so, then I am jealous. I do know He still speaks to his children today. He is the same yesterday, today, and forever. Take some time to quiet your heart and be still today. You might be surprised. He wants to whisper to only you. Receive and believe the best encouragement straight from him, your Heavenly Father.

Prayer Declaration:
Jesus, thank you that You still speak to us today. Teach us to truly know your voice. Help us to trust You inside of us. Teach us to be still and know that You are God.

October 12
Faith in Suffering

It's our Bible study day today. Yay, a rainy, cool, cozy day to stay inside and explore the Bible together. There's always delicious food and good worship. I often remind the ladies that we are some of the most blessed women on the planet. We are able to gather on random days of the week. Our men provide for our families, and very few of us need to work outside the home. Seeing our daughter-in-law and our now pregnant daughter choosing to stay at her mama's, brings my heart so much joy. Another blessing from our culture that we are choosing to keep. Today we study the entire book of 2nd Timothy. So much goodness and admonishment packed into those four little chapters.

Paul was writing to Timothy from his jail cell. He said he is chained like a criminal languishing in his cell, basically waiting to be put to death. We discussed how did Paul know his end was near? Was he weary and tired from all the persecution, ready and longing to go? Would we be? In different places, he talks about being willing to suffer for the sake of the gospel. 2nd Timothy 1:12 says, "I am not ashamed because I know whom I have believed and am convinced that He is able to guard what I have entrusted to Him for that day. What about us? Are we ashamed? Are we willing to stand for what we believe, even if it costs us something, even if we lose some followers? My husband reminded me this morning our social media followers are not like real friends, yet many take delight in the number of followers they have. Friends, let's be much more concerned about following the One who gave his life for us, to follow Him and no one else.

Prayer Declaration:
Jesus, forgive us. Help us to have a faith like Paul. Teach us how to stand steadfast for You. Yes, even in hardship and persecution.

October 13
Healing is Available

Sitting here with my favorite hot fall drink, well, one of them. This is an oolong tea with red pepper, turmeric, sea salt, cinnamon, and sweet cream. I would much rather have another coffee drink, but this one is actually good for me. It's hot, filling, and very nutritious. I'm also just sitting here listening to the wind whipping around outside and embracing the fact that our cold weather is here to stay. Indian summer is over, and the trees are losing their luster. I'm finally ready to accept it and move on to the next season. I wrote a song at one of the lowest seasons in my life. One of the verses goes like this. *Seasons come and seasons go, but you're not alone. I'm your cornerstone and I will make you strong again.* He has indeed made me strong again.

I am convinced more than ever that we can go through any season with Jesus by our side. When my health plummeted at the age of 40, I had no idea what was going on, but God did. He met me at rock bottom. He truly has healed me and set me free from sickness, physically, emotionally, and spiritually. He worked through other people a lot, too. Therapists, mentors, doctors, you name it. Jeremiah 30:17 says, "For I will restore health to you and your wounds, I will heal, declares the Lord." Our body keeps score, and if we do not deal with our emotional wounds and hurts, it may very well show up in our physical bodies. Do not hesitate to seek the help and healing you need and deserve. It is available to all of us. God sees us. He cares and weeps over your wounds with you.

Prayer Declaration:
Jesus, once again, I come to You for healing, help, and wholeness for each one of us. Help us find the right people to walk with us. Teach us the benefits and the wisdom of healing the soul, body, and spirit from the inside out.

October 14
Treasures in Heaven

Yesterday, my husband's mom, who adopted him at two weeks old, would have been 91 years old. We miss her dearly. She was the best grandma to our children, just an extraordinary woman in many ways. As much as she loved music and singing, I have no doubt she is on the worship team in heaven. She has passed on to her heavenly home for many years already. I find it ironic that we are traveling to Iowa this weekend to put the gravestone on my husband's dad's grave so close to Mom's birthday. I could not have asked for better in-laws. After we left the Amish culture, they never turned their love off, but seemed to understand, at least in part, why we did what we did. They even took parts of our freedom journey with us, and we had some very happy years together at a church we helped start together. My mother-in-law was one of the most contented people I ever saw.

She demonstrated Matthew 6:19-20 very well, "Do not store up for yourselves treasures on earth, where moths and vermin destroy and where thieves break into steal, but store up for yourselves treasures in heaven. Where moths and vermin do not destroy and steal." What about us today? What treasures are we laying up for ourselves? Are they earthly treasures that will completely vanish away one day? Or are we laying up those heavenly treasures, living in contentment, knowing this world is not our home? That was one of her favorite songs. *This world is not my home. I'm just passing through. My treasures are laid up somewhere beyond the blue.* Thank you, Mama-in-law, for the beautiful example you left for us, your children.

Prayer Declaration:
Thank you, Jesus, for such wonderful in-laws we had. Teach us to live out the beauty of our legacies. Help each one of us find, remember and model the gold and good examples from our parents.

October 15
True Love of Family

It's snowing this morning. My goodness, this is early for snow, even in Wisconsin. Thank God we brought the plants inside yesterday. We also picked the apples and kind of prepared for cold weather this weekend, but snow? No way. Of course, my husband is delighted with the snow. Me, not so much. We got everything taken care of, packed up the car, and started out for Iowa. Naps and beautiful scenery pass the time as we wind our way South. Such a beautiful time of year to travel and see the trees. At times the white snow, the green trees, and all the colorful trees were breathtaking. Huge fluffy snowflakes came down until the ground was covered at home, but we drove out of it and arrived at our B&B on the lake by early evening.

My husband's sister had found this beautiful setting. We had some time to rest and go on a walk before our step-family from Indiana joined us for dinner and the night. Close to twenty of us all together under the same roof was a lot of fun. Even though this family is still old-order Amish, they are so joyful and fun. We had many laughs as we all sat around visiting until midnight, tears too as we reminisced, all the loved ones gone on ahead of us. Their family has had more than their share of sorrow, yet their hearts are tender, loving, and so completely accepting of us, even though we left their way of life. Luke 6:37 declares, "Do not judge and you will not be judged. Do not condemn and you will not be condemned. Forgive and you will be forgiven." They inspire us, and we are so grateful for them in our lives.

Prayer Declaration:
Thank you, Jesus, for family, blood, biological and adopted. All of them! Teach us all to live and love like You do and let You be the judge of how each one of us chooses to live out our faith for You.

October 16
Relationship vs. Religion

We enjoyed breakfast together and walked down to the lake before we all traveled on down to the community where my husband and I met and married. It's always so nostalgic to go back, drive through the community and see our old home places. Things have changed quite a bit since we lived there. We met at the graveyard, dug a small hole, mixed up the concrete, and placed my husband's dad's headstone at the base of his grave, right next to his dear Mom. We lingered a long time, all of us just sharing memories, singing Dad-in-laws favorite song, how beautiful heaven must be. Discussed if we would know each other in heaven. Again we cried and laughed together. It was precious, sacred, and peaceful. I kept thinking; this is the last thing we can ever do for Dad except live out the godly legacy he and Mom both left for us. We had lunch at a cousin's house then, where more of them had gathered.

All of them left for home late afternoon. Our work together was done. My husband and I lingered until noon the next day, meeting with more family and friends over coffee and food. We slept in our old hometown. My heart aches for some of what happens in that community. In the name of religion, rules have gotten stricter and longer. Fear and control seem to be rampant. My heart hurts for those who are caught in the grip of it all to the point where there is almost no hope at times. In fact, I remember feeling like that. I'm so thankful this is part of my testimony. When hard pressed, I cried to the Lord. He brought me into a spacious place. Psalms 118:5, "If you find yourself hard pressed or in an impossible situation, cry out to him. He hears you. He will make a way of escape at the right time."

Prayer Declaration:
Jesus, thank you for your spacious place, hear the cry of my fellow brothers and sisters who may be hard-pressed under a religious spirit to set them free, Lord.

October 17
True Freedom

Religion will always make you feel like if you only tried a little harder or did a little bit more, maybe you could then attain God's love and man's favor or whatever it is that is being withheld from you. It's such a lie. God's love is available to all of us. All we have to do is accept His free gift of salvation. He already paid the price with His life. We don't have to perform or earn His love. Romans 5:8 tells us, "He demonstrated His love for us even when we were still sinners. While we were still sinners, Christ died for us." I sometimes wonder what God's thoughts are when He sees people taking His free gift and adding so many rules and regulations, most of all, their own agenda to it. Another verse says that, "…it is for freedom He has set us free" Galatians 5:1. It talks about not letting ourselves be burdened by the yoke of slavery.

Again, slavery could mean different things. I believe we could be slaves to addictions and habits. We could also be a slave to man-made rules or fear of man. We probably all know deep down where our own areas of slavery and bondage are. The good news is once we receive that free gift of salvation, Jesus is more than willing to set us completely free. We only need to acknowledge our need for help and let Him change us from the inside out. Don't you want that true freedom that truly sets us free? I know I do. I am so thankful for the areas that have already happened for me. Why don't we invite God to come and clean us up completely? Let Him into every corner of our hearts. Give Him the key to all those locked rooms in our hearts.

Prayer Declaration:
Jesus, only you can set us free in every area. Would you come and set whole communities free? Start with us, we say even more. Lord, we want to be vessels of freedom and love for You.

October 18
Wise Counselors

A cold, rainy day that turned into snow towards evening. Seems too early for snow, but what do I know? The weather in Wisconsin can change very fast. I do know that. My day consisted of lots of rest and ended with a session with my counselor, such a wise woman who speaks life and hope. She helped me process the heaviness I've been feeling ever since our weekend in our hometown. Having been made aware of several different situations among my people and culture, my heart just felt so heavy and burdened. There's a part of me that is very much a rescuer, and sometimes I make situations worse by trying to help prematurely. My counselor also helped me understand that I may be taking false responsibilities that aren't mine to take. My shoulders feel so much lighter than they did this morning, and once again, I'm so grateful for mentors and counselors.

There is much to learn from those who have walked this road of life much longer than we have, someone who can help. They call out what they see in us and help us fix it, and also speak the truth over us of who we are. It's all so powerful and healing and does my heart so much good every time. Proverbs 19:20-21 says, "Listen to advice and accept instruction that you may gain wisdom in the future. Many are the plans in the mind of a man, but it is the purpose of the Lord that will stand." Don't we all long for more wisdom? Who better to seek wisdom from than Godly people, experienced, seasoned women and men? God, first of all, of course.

Prayer Declaration:
Jesus, thank you for your plan for us to grow in wisdom and healing all the days of our lives. Teach us who to go to and instead of listening to the masses, teach us to know your voice and then who else to trust with input into our lives and the path You have for us.

October 19
Release Your Burdens

"From the end of the earth, I will cry unto thee. When my heart is overwhelmed, lead me to the rock that is higher than I," Psalm 61:2. How well we would do to always call out to God first and foremost when our hearts are overwhelmed. Yet it is also important to process with people who you trust and who will speak life and hope into your situation. Nobody has a perfect life; we all go through valleys and discouraging times. The secret is not to stay there but to grow through those times. My five-hour round trip to Madison today gave me lots of time to think and process my own life. Some of the things I myself have been through, and I know others are walking through. Being a counselor/coach is mostly emotional work. The main struggle is to not carry the things my clients are going through.

This is part of the reason I love still having my own wise counselor. She helps keep me centered and sees when I'm carrying things I shouldn't. My guess is if you and I were to have a cup of coffee or tea this morning, I'd tell you, too, are carrying burdens not meant for you to carry. Are you hurting for your friend, your family, your spouse, your clients? What is that for you today? You are allowed to lay those down, take them to the feet of Jesus, and let's together not pick them up again. We can still pray and intercede for circumstances, but not carry them around everywhere we go, become burdened and bogged down to where it now affects our lives too.

Prayer Declaration:
Jesus, thank you that your shoulders are wide enough to take on all our cares, worries and burdens. Teach us how to let go and let You help us. To trust You to work out all things for good, even when our road gets rocky, at times, winding and we cannot always see the way You can. We thank you for that.

October 20
The Blink of an Eye

It's a cold yet clear October Day. I can hear the wind blowing outside. Just a few short weeks ago, it was still warm enough to sit outside to write. How can it change so fast in a few days or weeks. Just like life sometimes changes, things can come in the blink of an eye. Maybe it has for you. Perhaps tragedy has come to your life and your family, and things were never the same again. We reminisced about that over the weekend with our stepfamily. Their dad and my husband's mom and my dad all died from almost instant and unexpected heart attacks. Neither of them was that old, in our opinion. We definitely still needed and wanted them here. It seemed unreal and unfair, but there was nothing we could do to change the cold, hard truth. They are never coming back until Jesus himself comes back. What do you do when something like this happens, and you can't even think straight yet?

You must go on. You have to pick up the shattered pieces of your family and continue on with life. You have to find a new normal and a way to grieve in a healthy way, you do, and you will. You will laugh again. You will even feel joy again as you rebuild your life, traditions, and routines without your loved ones. Is it easy? No. Is it possible? Yes. Reach out to someone who knows how you feel. Let's live our lives today so we have no regrets if life changes forever, even in the blink of an eye, as 1st Corinthians 15:52 speaks about, "In a moment, in the twinkling of an eye at the last trumpet, the trumpet will sound, and the dead shall be raised incorruptible, and we shall be changed." What a day that will be. Until then, let's carry on. Jesus, thank you for your steadfast love and mercy, even when change comes, or tragedy strikes in a moment.

Prayer Declaration:
Teach us to live with no regrets. Help us to rebuild our lives and remember this world truly is not our home, and to be ready when that trumpet sounds.

October 21
Firm Foundation

Christ is my firm foundation, The Rock on which I stand when everything around me is shaken; I've never been more glad. Seriously, who sings such lyrics? As Christians who trust God, we can! We can sing with such confidence and gladness, even when everything around us is shaking. I don't know what it is for you. Death, divorce, homelessness, a job that didn't work out after many years of pouring your heart and life into it. I don't know what you are facing today, but I care. *When there's all the bad news reports and people who are proclaiming all the bad that is coming. Fear wants to creep in, cripple and paralyze us at times, doesn't it?* The above song came out of Matthew 7:24-27. Jesus is our firm foundation. That is good news in a sometimes-gloomy world.

The second verse goes like this. *I've still got joy in chaos. I've got peace that makes no sense. I won't be going under. I'm not healed by my own strength. Because I built my life on Jesus, He's never let me down. He's faithful through every season, so why would he fail now, He won't.* Aren't these lyrics just so comforting? Aren't we so thankful that our God is faithful in every season? Yes, even when we go through hard and painful seasons, He is still right there with us. He's suffered while on this Earth too, so he is well acquainted with grief, suffering, and rejection. Once again, I invite you to bring it all to Him. Tell Him all about it. Let Him carry and heal you until you can be glad again. Jesus, thank you for being our Rock and our firm foundation.

Prayer Declaration:
Teach us to run to You and stand steadfast. Help us to trust You no matter what we feel or are facing today. Carry us, Lord, heal us.

October 22
Fight for Your Priorities

Sitting at a lake in Wisconsin, beautiful, peaceful, sunny, and 65 degrees. What a gift. These last several sunny days have felt like a bonus and even a bit redemptive since last week's early snow. A few quiet moments to relax and rest after a busy morning feels good. I had a client this morning before my husband, and I packed up the car and left our house at noon. We have a beautiful Airbnb on the lake, three and ½ hours; it's a jaunt but well worth it. It's "family time" this weekend, with our entire family coming, one more camping getaway before winter settles in to stay. Our BNB at home has guests in it too this weekend. It's always fun to go and explore other people's and get ideas. This particular BNB sits right close to the lake with a cute brick walkway right out to the water and a massive fire pit with plenty of chairs for all of us. The sun still feels nice and warm on my face, but it's also sliding down in the sky very fast.

This trip didn't just happen. Once again, we had to plan it out multiple weeks in order for everyone's schedule to be clear. Many things came up, wanting to crowd this out, but we had it on the calendar; we had the house booked and planned around this weekend. Quality time with family for me is worth protecting and planning for weeks in advance. What are you fighting for? Maybe it's your health, your marriage, or tackling a mountain of debt. The list could be endless, but you can absolutely do it. Prioritize and make it happen. You are not just doing it for yourself but also for the generations coming behind you in your family name and lineage. Psalms 33:11 is encouraging, "The counsel of the Lord stands forever, the purpose of His heart to all generations."

Prayer Declaration:
Jesus, thank you for your beautiful plan for your family. Help each one of us prioritize in our lives what's important to us. Teach us how to choose things that help advance your Kingdom on this Earth, not only for us, but for the generations to come.

October 23
Fumbling Forward

We were all a little disappointed when we discovered our checkout time was already at 10:00 AM. How did we miss that? We just expected it to be noon, the same as our Airbnb. However, we decided to make the most of it and just got up a little earlier, so we still had time to linger over coffee and one last breakfast. Waking up to one of our sons stirring up breakfast in the kitchen was fun. Cleaning up was easy, too, with everyone pitching in to help. We were all done and ready to leave before checkout. Even the drive home was so beautiful, with lots of pine trees and lots of foliage still in their beautiful fall colors too. Arriving home in time to sit in the 70-degree sunshine, watching it go down into an awe-inspiring sunset tonight, completed this wonderful Sunday. It was so special to have the whole family together under the same roof for two nights and parts of three days with plenty of beds and bathrooms, and space in general. This is how memories are made, with food, family, fellowship, fun, sun, golfing, games, and life in Jesus. My heart feels full and very thankful tonight.

There were many years as we were fumbling our way forward in life, raising our little ones. With our journey out of the Amish culture, we didn't have the time, energy, or resources to do a weekend like this. We started with simple fire pit dinners in our yard on a weekend evening, then we started tent camping, and finally, we graduated to a camper. Now these occasional lake houses, we love all experiences. We can all start doing small things. Starting with baby steps as we grow and dream our way forward. What are you dreaming about or pursuing? What slight steps can you take in this season to move forward, to move toward it? Proverbs 21:5 has some wisdom for all of us. It says, "Plan carefully and you will have plenty. If you act quickly, you will never have enough."

Prayer Declaration:
Jesus, thank you for caring about our dreams. Will you breathe on them and bring them to life? Help us to live out our dreams with eternity ever on our mind.

October 24
A 3- Cord Strand

It's a warm and partly rainy day, much like our wedding day 31 years ago. It seems like a lifetime ago, and in some ways it is. We were two young, naive teenagers who thought love would fix anything, and we were partly right. If you have been married for any length of time, you know it also takes a lot of working together, commitment, communication, forgiveness, and choosing each other again and again, or, as some people put it, falling in love with the same person over and over again. We got up early that morning and went on a walk back to my prayer rock before breakfast and got ready for our big day. We had our ceremony out in my dad's shop. It was an older building, and the cement was cracked and stained even after we thoroughly washed it. We had a very traditional Amish wedding.

The reception was in our house, no glitz, glamor, and not even one photo of our wedding. We chose to sleep in the room that I had as a girl on our wedding night. Honeymoons, or even going away for that first night, were not encouraged back then, and so we didn't. We got married on a Thursday, and by Saturday, we moved to my husband's family farm in their backyard in a used mobile home. We got right to work helping with chores and farm work for our rent. My husband also worked at a day job. Our marriage wasn't always easy, but I'm thankful for what God has brought us. I'm thankful for what He has done for us and how He has added to our legacy. We've learned many lessons about life and love along the way, and one of my favorite verses about marriage is the one where it says, "A 3-cord strand is not easily broken" Ecclesiastes 4:12. Marriage can be challenging even with God. I can't imagine how people do it without God.

Prayer Declaration:
Today, Jesus, would you simply bless marriages? Help all couples to choose You, that third strand that holds it all together, teach us the importance of choosing one another again and again.

Vitamin D and Sea

The season change is here to stay now, and I'm feeling it, complete with body aches and a headache today. I wish I could just effortlessly breeze from season to season without it affecting me like this. I was processing this very thing with a client recently. We searched for words on how it makes us feel. Unsettled is one word I would use, sometimes accompanied by a somewhat foreboding feeling. If you experience seasonal depression or mood swings with season changes, then I have so much empathy for you. Give yourself a lot of grace. Find new rhythms in the new season as soon as possible. For me right now, that means switching up my workout routine, as it will be way too cold to walk outside very soon. Our appetites can change too, and we can easily crave comfort food that might not be as healthy for us. It gets dark so much quicker at night, so there goes our sunlight and vitamin D.

The good news, all of these things can be adjusted. It takes time, close to a month, at least for me. Good supplements are very helpful, especially generous doses of Vitamin C & D in the winter. My favorite remedy is large doses of Vitamin SEA which can also be helpful. However, I realize that is a luxury that can't happen too often. Perhaps you can also find yourself a good wellness doctor who can help you through your toughest times. Mine isn't only my doctor, she's also my friend and truly cares about me, which is a tremendous blessing. Above all, spend extra time reading, prayer, or whatever it is that brings you comfort. James 4:8 says, "Draw near to God and He will draw near to you." Isn't that a comfort God wants to draw near to us? Let's invite Him into our difficulties.

Prayer Declaration:
Thank you, Jesus, for helping us navigate our seasons well and teach us how to make new, healthy rhythms quickly. Help us to remember to draw near to You and let You be our comfort, our rock that never changes no matter what we are going through.

October 26
Broken and Beautiful

Beautiful, cold, but sunny outside, and just seeing the sun lifts my spirits. The leaves are coming off the trees fast. Some of the trees are already naked and bare. Others still have brown ones that will stay till spring with the sun and wind route. Right now, they look orangish and gold and much prettier than they actually are. Just like when we let the SON shine on us and into our hearts, He makes us beautiful too.

Even though there are parts of our lives right now that may feel bare and exposed, like we have no leaves or fruit to share, we are still beautiful in other areas because of the sun. He loves all of us, the broken and the beautiful. In fact, He loves to take the broken and make it beautiful. Where in your life do you feel less than beautiful today? Maybe you even feel extremely broken, bare, and exposed. You are probably not alone. I was just processing with the client this morning about how many of us try to hide and avoid our pain. Instead of reaching out to someone in our pain, what if we were all just honest with each other about what we were going through?

What if we got rid of the lie that if we struggle, there's something wrong with us? Why do we feel like we should have it all together all the time? It's such a facade. The older I get, the more I don't want to be like this. And here's a funny saying I like, "The moment I think I have it all together, I forget where I put it." Even in our pain and brokenness, we have verses like Exodus 15:2, "To stand upon the Lord is my strength and my song, He has given me victory. This is my God, and I will praise Him."

Prayer Declaration:
Jesus, thank you for being our strength and song not just when things are all well, but in our hard seasons and days too. Help us to remember your goodness and faithfulness. Teach us to cling to You. Broken yet beautiful, we let You shine into our hearts to heal us.

October 27
Joy in the Journey

It's another clear, sunny, frosty, cold morning. I'm excited because my grandbaby boys are coming today, and we are going to have a baking day. They are bringing the little pumpkins I gave them earlier this fall. We are turning them into bars, cupcakes, and who knows what else? It truly is the season for all things pumpkin spice and hot drinks, as some say, sweater weather. Despite anticipating today with joy, my heart is also still longing in other areas. Burdens of unanswered prayers that I must surrender to the Lord over and over again. Psalms 55:22 tells us to do this, "Cast your burdens on the Lord and He will sustain you. He will never permit the righteous to be moved. He will sustain you."

I like that. He has, He does, He will, for as long as it takes for our prayers to be answered. Maybe you have unanswered prayers that want to gnaw at your heart and very soul until you are so weary and worn out you just want to quit, but what would that gain us, really?

Instead, let's look for the joy in our lives in spite of our sorrow. Did you know we can actually have both at the same time? It is possible to feel joy and sorrow at the same time. It is not a sin to struggle in your Christian walk. Some people seem to think the minute you become a Christian. Your life will magically be all good all the time. It's simply not true. What is true is because of Jesus, we can have joy that comes from deep down inside, and only He can help us feel and sustain that in the hard seasons of our lives. There can always be Joy in the Journey!

Prayer Declaration:
Jesus, thank you for your joy that no one can take away. Help us to always look for and hold to that. Teach us to thank You and praise You, even when it's a sacrifice of praise.

October 28
Rest and Re-evaluate

The Lord has promised good to me, His word my hope secures. He will be my shield and portion be, as long as life endures. Ah, these beautiful words washed over my aching soul this morning during my workout. Soothing, so full of promise! His word, my hope secures. Yes, it does when we open His word and meditate on and read it. There is so much hope. On those sacred pages, as I did just that this morning, I was drawn to Isaiah and then came upon this verse and had been meditating on it. "This is the one I esteem He who is humble and contrite in spirit and trembles at my word," Isaiah 66:2. Would we be humble and contrite if we never had struggles? Would it be easy to forget and start taking for granted the many blessings in our lives?

It is easy to start coasting or going onto autopilot when everything goes well and always as we want it to. Is that also maybe when it's the easiest to become lukewarm? Maybe our trials are meant to bring us back to the basics and the feet of our Father. Maybe we can use them like a reset for us. Maybe it's a good time for us to reevaluate our lives and ask ourselves, is there anything I can do to make this situation better, or is it out of my control? God often does work through people, so he may give you an assignment. He is delighted when they are willing to be a part of the solution and partner with him for breakthroughs in our lives and the lives of those around us; just ask Him.

Prayer Declaration:

Jesus, thank you for your strategies that You sometimes share with us when we take the time to ask. Teach us to have humble, willing hearts ready to partner with You and bring healing and hope to our broken world around us.

October 29
Heavy Pruning

My husband and I cleaned out the garage this morning. We took care of all the recyclables, trash, cardboard, all of it. It was long overdue, so it feels even more clean and orderly. I always bring my plants into the garage to either flourish or finish dying. I'm able to save some over winter.

Usually, I wait to trim those down until they start to look sad, but this morning I was on such a cleaning, purging spree that I thought, why not trim these before they make a mess and dead leaves are everywhere. The next thing I knew, I was even cutting off the geraniums that were still blooming. Still can't believe I did that, but that is when I had this revelation. Oh, my goodness. Maybe this is why God, too, prunes back even things in our lives we think are still beautiful and bearing fruit.

I knew if I cut those geraniums way back now, they would grow back fuller, thicker, and even more beautiful by spring and grow even nicer and more flowers than what I cut off. There have been several times in my life where God pruned or cut things off that, in my opinion, were still working just fine. In fact, it feels like I am once again in one of those seasons. It's not fun and it's uncomfortable, but we can trust He knows what He is doing even when we don't. What if we looked at pruning as an act of love, Proverbs 31:2 tells us, "The Lord corrects those He loves, just as if Father corrects a child in whom He delights." Let it be a sweet sound to His ears.

Prayer Declaration:
Thank you for loving us enough to prune and correct us. Help us to trust You and remember it is for our own good and growth. Teach us how to embrace being refined instead of fighting it. Here I am, Lord, prune me. Make me all that you want me to be.

October 30
Our Lifeguard Walks on Water

I remember that you reign. The man who walked on water is walking over my storm. These spontaneous worship lyrics came across my YouTube tonight from a home group during the pandemic. We can read the story in Matthew 14:22-33, verse 25 says, "Shortly before dawn, Jesus went out to His disciples walking on the lake water." Yes, this same Jesus walks over our storms, and He walks with us in our storms and through our storms. Nothing is too difficult, too big, or too messy for Him. He can handle it. In the same story, Peter wants to try and walk on water, and he does until he sees the waves and gets terrified, and takes his eyes off of Jesus. Only then does he sink. Even then, Jesus rescues him. What a good lesson for us to keep our eyes on Jesus during our storms.

Worship at church was wonderful today. We sang of His power and might, turning seas into highways, dry bones into armies, shame into glory. He's the only one who can. Yes, He is. His presence was tangible once again as we worshiped Him together, bringing Him the honor and glory He deserves. Being on the worship team with our son and his wife was extra special today. Quick hugs and kisses from the grandsons before and after they went to their class. It was special to have my nephew here too. After church, he and most of the family gathered for lunch. Life isn't perfect by any means, but I love celebrating the perfect moments and dwelling on those when they do happen. So today, let's allow Jesus to walk over our storm, and let's keep our eyes on Him and celebrate what is right and not sink into our storm.

Prayer Declaration:
Jesus, thank you that You are bigger than any storm we will ever encounter. Teach us to keep our eyes on You and not the waves. Help us to dwell on our many blessings.

October 31
Do Your Research

Today is Halloween. This is quite a controversial subject, especially among Christians. Growing up, we never acknowledged it in any way. I still prefer it that way. There was maybe once or twice we took our children trick-or-treating in our little neighborhood after we left the Amish. It was more just to visit the elderly with the three youngest. They dressed up in fun costumes; we always said no evil or dark costumes. We don't celebrate darkness, but we do celebrate the Lord of the harvest. I think everyone has to decide for their family what they want to celebrate. We did have a sobering message at Church yesterday about some of the history and practices behind Halloween, a Holiday many celebrate or participate in without giving it a second thought. I don't get or understand the decorating or dressing up in skulls, spiders, witches, or all the things you see nowadays.

Perhaps dressing up in a good character could be harmless. Again, you must decide for yourself in your house. Ephesians 5:11 says, "Have nothing to do with the fruitless deeds of darkness. Rather expose them," but then again, those deeds of darkness aren't only in certain things, like perhaps some Halloween rituals and traditions of some cultures, but they can creep in anywhere. Anytime we dabble in willful sin, it can be classed as deeds of darkness. So, whether you choose to celebrate Halloween or not, above all, do your research on what it's all about and then decide accordingly. Ask God, what do you want for us and our family legacy? Jesus, help each one of us seek your wisdom first of all and then educate ourselves also.

Prayer Declaration:
Teach us how to search out the truth for ourselves and not just go with the masses or what is popular. Thank you that You have all the answers we need when we come to You and ask.

November 1
Forgiveness

Forgiveness is powerful. It is such a vital part of life in relationships. Why, then, can it be so hard at times? This morning I was processing this with a client, and we talked about the fact that it is our choice whether we choose to forgive or not. Either way, our choices will have consequences. Matthew 6:14-15 makes it pretty clear for us, "For if you forgive other people when they sin against you, your Heavenly Father will also forgive you. But if you do not, forgive others their sins, your Heavenly Father will not forgive your sins." That's straightforward, isn't it? Ouch. So, it really boils down to do we want our Heavenly Father to forgive us for our sins. If so, we will do well to choose to forgive those who have hurt us too.

If we choose not to forgive, we will hurt ourselves more than the person who hurt us in the first place. I'll be the first to admit that it's so easy to hold a grudge instead of moving forward with forgiveness, but it is so worth it. Is there a time you can remember in your life when you consciously chose to extend forgiveness? Maybe you told the person, or maybe you just did it between you and God and then showed the person. People can sense whether we have forgiven or are holding grudges. The more grudges we hold, the heavier our burdens and often our countenance gets. But oh, the sweet relief that comes with surrender and choosing forgiveness. Now we've given the offense back to God. Now he can deal with it as he sees best, but He probably won't as long as we keep holding on to it ourselves. Friends, let's choose forgiveness today! It doesn't mean that what was done to you wasn't very wrong or that the person will get away with it. It just means now we can have peace again. It also means we step out of the way so that God can get to the person.

Prayer Declaration:
Jesus, thank you for your forgiveness and for showing us the way. Your way is always better than our way. Teach us to follow your example. Help us to give our offenses to you and let you God.

November 2
Redemption

I woke up in the night and couldn't fall back asleep for hours. That hardly ever happens anymore, but recently it's been several weeks of not sleeping well. I snuck out to my chair in hopes of not waking my husband, but here he came, not far behind me, wondering if I was okay. We talked a bit about what could be disrupting my sleep like this again, and then he went back to bed. I put on my headphones and listened to Bible verses with soft music in the background. Listening to the precious promises of God is so soothing, especially in the middle of the night when you really need to get back to sleep, it works every time. But while I was lying awake, for some reason, I had this thought of how I grew up with four brothers. We got along for the most part and also fought like most siblings probably do. I'm pretty sure I took them for granted and didn't realize I would miss them when we moved away from our families.

Now today, since we have left the Amish, we very seldom see or have anything to do with my four brothers. Sometimes that makes me sad, but in the night, God reminded me.... Now you have four sons, four strong, handsome sons who would do anything for me, protect me from anything, and stand up to anyone for me. They all have a sense of humor. And often make me laugh too. God has a beautiful way of reminding us of our blessings and redeeming our pain. God has redeemed so many things in my life that I've had to give up or leave behind. He wants to do the same for you. Tell him where you are hurting. Psalms 111:6-9 talks about how God provided redemption for His people, He still does that today. Let Him hear your heart and tell Him what you need.

Prayer Declaration:
Jesus, thank you that you are a God of redemption. You never ask us to leave something unless you have something better for us. Help us to trust you in the pain of our process.

November 3
Birthing New Things

Sitting by my office window, watching the sun come up over the woods, enjoying a second cup of coffee, breakfast, and writing. I woke up way too early again. It may very well take a few more cups of coffee to get through my day. As soon as my Airbnb guests leave, I need to clean that. I have an evening flight with a friend to leave for the weekend, flying to Atlanta, GA. We will meet up with my husband and son and more of our friends for a weekend of fun. Because sometimes that's just what we need. My husband calls it the neutral zone that helps us relax. He is much better at it than I am, which is why he handles stress so much better than I do too. The past month of my own struggles, as well as carrying those of others at times, has been a hard month. I'm ready to embrace this carefree weekend to the fullest.

Yesterday was a wonderful experience. I had the beautiful opportunity to have a group therapy session with some beautiful women. I do believe God just birthed a new passion in me once again. The day before, my daughter-in-law and I had a therapy session with someone. It was also something new and brought incredible breakthroughs. So, listen carefully the next time you feel crushed and squeezed and discouraged, and you cannot figure out why God is allowing you to struggle and hurt for so long. He just might be birthing something new in you. A new passion, a new ministry, a new assignment. Just like physical labor pains are painful and intense, it can feel emotional and spiritual when God is birthing something new in and through you. So, take heart. Hebrews 12:11 tells us, "No discipline is ever pleasant at the time..."

Prayer Declaration:
Jesus, thank you that most times you allow us to be disciplined and feel pain, it truly is for a greater purpose. Teach us how to partner with You quickly and ask what it is You want to teach us or birth in us?

November 4
Dig Deeper

A beautiful, hot, sunny day here in the South, soaking up the sun, sitting around with friends. It's all so relaxing and definitely what we both needed. My husband and I both after our very busy schedules at home. My friend and I got in late last night. We were exhausted, but we made it safe and sound, even riding several different sky trams to find our rental car and getting off at the wrong spot at least once. But we did it. We were proud of ourselves for figuring it all out because it was a maze. Once again, I learned something. It seems like airports always teach me something, just follow the signs. If you do get lost or confused, just ask someone. Not just anyone, but someone who is qualified to give you the right answer instead of a random answer.

The signs don't always make sense unless you stop and really understand what they are saying. Sometimes you could take it several different ways. Doesn't this sound a lot like the Bible? Our road map for this life. We don't always understand what we are reading the first or even the second time. Sometimes I think it's even like 3-D. You really need to dig deep sometimes, and at times it is easy to misinterpret what we are reading.

Once again, if we ask for help, it becomes clear to us, and we can adjust our thinking accordingly. Asking the Holy Spirit to help us understand is the best source for us, but we can also ask people we trust and admire for their opinion. Let's be willing to change our thinking and belief system when we do get a revelation of a verse or an entire chapter in the Bible. I truly believe this is how we continue to grow and learn in God's word. I never want to be like the verse that talks about "...always learning but never able to come to knowledge of the truth" 2 Timothy 3:7.

Prayer Declaration:
Thank you, Jesus, that You teach us the truth when we ask. Help us to always read with the Holy Spirit as our guide. Teach us to let him guide us in all we do and into all truth.

November 5
Golden Rule

It sure doesn't feel like a Saturday today, but that is what the calendar says, so I choose to believe it. My husband and I slept late and made coffee, and took it outside to enjoy the cool, misty morning. With our friends camping all around us, they soon start trickling over to sit with us. One of the guys brings a whole pan of fresh monkey bread he made, still warm from the oven. This is what these events are all about for me, the friendships and the camaraderie that has formed among our class of 2.6 diesel trucks. We all pull in the same class, and in some ways, many of them have become what we call our pulling family. Of course, also, the thrill of my husband and sons' wins!

Yesterday morning, some other friends invited us over for a delicious breakfast they cooked outside their camper, complete with cheesy, creamy grits. The southern hospitality is so much fun, and we love to hear the Southern drawl. Okay, they might break out their homemade moonshine down here every now and then, but they also pray unashamedly before the truck pulls long, heartfelt prayers, just real down to Earth, southern folks, red dirt tracks, and roads. It just all feels like home somehow. It's our favorite and final truck pull of the entire year. This class has something special in the way they look out for each other. Most of them would give the shirt off their back to each other, so to speak, helping each other fix and figure out things, all while competing against each other in the actual pulls. It's a beautiful example of the golden rule. "So, whatever you wish that others would do to you, do also to them, for this is the law and the prophets," Matthew 7:12.

Prayer Declaration:
Thank you, Jesus, for this short little rule when followed has the potential to make any relationship beautiful. Teach us to apply it to our marriages, our families, our friends, and all of our relationships. Help us to live it out all day, every day, and enjoy the fruit of it.

November 6
Memories and Blessings

The pull was rained out last night. The whole clan huddled in our trailer, just talking and hanging out until they finally made the call that they must cancel for sure. Rain came down in torrents, and not only did we get wet before we ran for shelter, but the red Georgia dirt now turned to clay really fast and stuck to the bottom of our shoes, boots, sandals, or whatever else we were wearing. Once again, I felt the camaraderie of these die-hard pullers and us, their wives. They were a disappointed bunch not to be able to get their second pull-in, but no one complained. Just took it in stride. As I was walking back to our camper in the mud and rain, I couldn't help but think this is how memories are made. Not when everything just goes as planned, but the unexpected. The rain, the mud, the clay, all of it. I loved what the announcer said at the end. "We can't control what the good Lord gives us." Words of wisdom to live by.

We packed up this morning and headed out. Our son and girlfriend were driving home a truck for one of our other good friends. Lo and behold, this morning, it wouldn't start. Another unexpected delay, but the most amazing thing was happening here. We were in a random part of town in Tennessee, and these wonderful worship songs were being blasted across the whole town. One good song after another, all songs we knew, and next, a message and a heartfelt prayer. And then more worship music. This went on all the while we fixed the truck in the Tennessee heat. We still don't know where it came from, but to me, it was a kiss from God. Maybe the church truly isn't always inside the four walls. This surely wasn't a traditional church this morning, but oh, how it blessed my heart and soul this Sunday morning. 2 Chronicles 2:6 says, "Who is able to build a house for him? The heavens cannot contain Him." So true. A house or church can never, ever contain all of Him. We may as well quit trying to fit Him in our boxes and churches.

Prayer Declaration:
Jesus, thank you for who You are and where You surprise us at random times. Teach us to see you in unlikely places. Help us to see how big and powerful You are and that You're everywhere.

November 7
Keys

An unexpected morning at Starbucks somewhere in the middle of Illinois. Once again, when life gives you lemons, you make lemonade, or in this case, I'm having my first peppermint latte of the season. It's

delicious and hot and just the perfect combo of chocolate and peppermint. Somehow our keys got locked inside our truck that was already running. So, while my husband figures out that problem, this gives me some time to catch up on writing. Once again, hidden blessings inside our delays! Yesterday morning when I was waiting on the guys to fix a friend's truck, I saw a random key lying in the parking lot. We also thought it might be the key fob battery that the other truck wouldn't start. All of this key business is making me think, okay, God, are you trying to speak to us? God will use random things to get your attention sometimes.

However, keys are pretty significant because they unlock things. Think of the importance of keys. How many do you use on a daily average? Your car, your house, anything that's important to you is probably locked, right? Keys unlock things. They are an important thing we use almost every day. Jesus is the key to our lives, any situation we find ourselves in. He has the answers, the solutions, and the key! In Revelations 1:18, He tells us, "I am the living one, I was dead, and behold, I am alive forevermore and I have the keys to death and hell." Wow. That's a powerful yet true statement. Only Jesus has those keys. Sometimes He will show us what the key is to unlock someone's situation or our own two. If you are in difficult circumstances, feel free to ask Him. Jesus, what key do I need to unlock? A closed heart will require a different key than a broken heart. God knows and He loves when we partner with Him and ask Him for strategy and direction.

Prayer Declaration:
Jesus, thank you that You alone hold the keys of heaven and hell. Teach us more about the power and significance of keys. Help us to understand how to use them and how to partner with You to unlock situations and hurting hearts.

November 8
Your Voice and Vote Matters

We finally made it home last night, a whole day later than our plan. We arrived in time to watch the most magnificent sunset. Bright reds and pinks spread across the West and Southern sky. It seemed like a good welcome home. Home felt wonderful after a weekend of camping, but weekends like this are so good for us. It always reminds me of everything I take for granted in my normal daily life. Maybe most of all, a good cup of coffee, fixed just the way I like it. It tasted heavenly this morning. Next, we went down to our local town and voted. I love how my husband encourages our whole family to vote. We grew up not voting at all. The Amish, in general, don't vote. I'm not sure why, but it was always like that. I think it has something to do with not mixing church and state, but what if all Christians took that approach? As well as supporting the military. If no one would fight for our country and vote for the right things, we certainly wouldn't still be enjoying the freedoms we currently do.

Someone is paying the price for our free country. Much like Jesus paid the price for us. *Freedom is never really free.* I've heard my culture say we don't get involved; we just leave it up to God. Well, that sounds good and holy, but what if God is depending on us for Godly change? Think of the difference the votes of all the thousands of Amish communities would make. But again, it is their way, and because we presently live in a free country, it is also their choice. As for me, though, I'm thankful we as a family have learned it is right for us to use 'our rights' and vote for what's right. "Open your mouth, judge righteously to defend the rights of the poor and needy" it's confirmed in Proverbs 31:9.

Prayer Declaration:
Bring your true freedom back to our country, Jesus. We are grateful for your freedom and the rights You have given us as sons and daughters. Teach us to use our freedom and rights in a way that is pleasing to You. Help us to be a voice for those who are hurting, oppressed and persecuted. Our voice and vote matters.

November 9
Choose Carefully

Another superb, sunny, warm fall morning. 60 degrees is predicted for today. I'm overjoyed and marveled at our extended, spectacularly long fall. With that first early snowfall in mid-October, we thought surely, we were in for an extra-long winter. I'm so happy we were wrong. Things are not always as they seem, are they? That snow is long gone, and we've had several Indian summers since. The trees are almost all completely bare now, and there are leaves on the ground everywhere. Growing up as a little Amish girl, fall was a very busy time on the farm. My mom was the queen of canning. She canned many jars of chili and vegetable soup, lots and lots of applesauce, and pie fillings; you name it, she did it. Her chili was the absolute best.

To this day, I still use her recipe as well as her pumpkin pie recipe. Another memory I have in my younger years is coming home from school, grabbing an apple, and riding on the wagon back to the field to husk corn by hand. Although I'm not sure how much I actually helped, it was fun. Raking the endless bushels of leaves was my least favorite task of all. It seemed never-ending and overwhelming, but I'm pretty sure we got every last leaf. Now I just let them deteriorate over winter, and the wind blows most of them away. Neither do we preserve food anymore. It's freeing to have a choice. I tell my children the same thing. It is now your choice for your generation and family. I love how 1st Thessalonians 5:21 asks us to examine everything carefully and hold fast to that which is good.

Prayer Declaration:
Thank you, Jesus, for giving us the freedom to examine/decide what we want to hold onto. Teach us to choose wisely and carefully. Help us to keep and cherish all the good and important things.

November 10
God's Plans are Perfect

'I've never seen the righteous forsaken, and He won't stop being faithful now. These are song lyrics from my worship and workout time that stuck with me this morning. Perhaps this comes from Deuteronomy 4:31. For the Lord your God is a compassionate God. He will not fail you, nor destroy you, nor forget the covenant with your fathers which he swore to them." There are many more promises of God's compassion and faithfulness to us. They are all so comforting. If you have been reading this devotional up until now, you know that we have two grandsons we absolutely adore. They are two and four already, no longer babies, but still so much fun. It is only natural that I was longing for a little granddaughter as well. You can imagine my delight and gratitude over the news that we are getting a granddaughter this summer!

Our daughter Luanne and her husband Trent called us this week to tell us the news. Would we have been happy with another boy? Undeniably, but isn't it so wonderful when God answers your secret or desired prayers? When we were done having our six children of four boys and two girls, I often wished for another girl, and now it's happening. But once again, just not like I thought, God truly does never fail, you or me. Neither will He answer our prayers the way we think He should, and often not in our timing because He knows what's best for us. We can trust Him in that. Just like the Bible tells us over and over, He won't fail us. He loves us enough to answer our prayers according to what's best for us in the right season of our lives at the right time. Keep praying and let God work out the details only He can. He will, and it will be perfect.

Prayer Declaration:
Jesus, thank you that You never fail us. Teach us to trust You in every season and in every predicament we're in. Help us to remember that even when our plans fail, You never do.

November 11
Planners and Pencils

Slowly savoring an extra hot peppermint white mocha latte at a bookstore. Two of life's basic pleasures for me. Lovely aromatic blend gusts in from the minute you enter the bookstore found nowhere other than a bookstore with a coffee shop combined. Someone should invent an air freshener with this scent. Our weather changed drastically overnight. This morning it was time to pull out long sleeves and boots. I even saw a few snow flurries. It's been a full morning of odd jobs and errands. Because it's Friday and the weekend, the traffic was swamped this morning. I missed my exit, which made it even more chaotic. So this little reprieve feels wonderful here in my nook. It's been a long time since I've had time to do this; it feels extra good and well-appointed.

One of the first things I'm planning to do is pick out a new planner for next year. I always do it this time of year because there are already dates and things that need to be written down. Do you use a planner? Why or why not, I wonder? It's something I implemented after leaving the Amish, where perhaps life was slower-paced and more predictable. Now I would hate to do without it. It's almost next to my Bible for me. I've also learned a good trick, and that is to write your plans in pencil. Pencil that can be erased. When plans change, as they often do, you can simply erase and rewrite. Your planner stays much neater. My non-negotiable plans are written in red. Even those are crossed out and canceled sometimes. Proverbs 19:21 tells us, "Many are the plans in the mind of a man, but it is the purpose of the Lord that will stand."

Prayer Declaration:
Thank you that your purpose always stands and is our top priority, Jesus. We welcome your plans for us. Teach us to pencil time with You in our planners first and foremost. Help us to be flexible and obedient to your leading in spite of our carefully arranged days.

November 12
We Are All Called

One thing I love about the transition into cold, winter and the days feeling short is simply what feels like slower rhythms for my husband and me. We have most of our fall work done and are pretty much ready for the snow to fly. We took the liberty to go on a spontaneous breakfast date this morning and grocery shopping together. Later, I had a soothing nap, then food prep for dinner tomorrow night when the kiddos come home. I love days like these where there's no strict schedule or awaiting agenda. Days like this help me catch my breath, to breathe deeply and consciously, transitioning into winter and possibly slower rhythms. I also had a long conversation with our daughter, who is in Belize for her nursing capstone currently. This Mama will breathe better when she is back on US soil.

Although I do know experiences like this are rich and rewarding for her, it doesn't mean it's easy. She is homesick, among other things. I'm enormously proud of her and for what she is doing over there. Walking house to house to do physical checkups in the villages as well as working in their hospitals. The heat is constant, and their water is limited. As always, going to an underdeveloped country is eye-opening. If you've never been, I would encourage you to go at least once. Maybe you just want to go to visit. Maybe you too will go as a doctor or nurse. Or maybe you feel called to go and do what Jesus says. In Matthew 28:18-20, "Go and make disciples of all nations, baptizing them in the name of the Father, Son, and Holy Spirit, teaching them to observe all that I have commanded you." We don't exclusively have to leave our country to do that, and yet it says *all nations*. We are all called somewhere for God's purposes. Ask Jesus if you are unsure of yours.

Prayer Declaration:
Jesus, we recognize the different gifts and callings You have given each one of us. Instill within us to be obedient to those gifts and help each of us to know what it is for, where You want us to use them and serve YOU!

November 13
Be Fruitful and Multiply

The house is quiet again tonight. The children were here for family night. It's always a good time. Food, fellowship, games, lots of talking and laughter. The little grandsons are always in the middle of it all, and we can't imagine life without them. We talked a lot tonight about the fact that we are adding two more babies to the family this summer. Yes, two. Our son Dennis and his wife just told us they are also expecting another baby. This will be their third, and we all have a feeling it will be a girl this time. But we could be so wrong too! Isn't God's plan for family brilliant? Way back in the beginning, in the Book of Genesis, when God said to Adam and Eve, "...be fruitful and multiply," Genesis 1:28. It's especially precious for me to see our sons and daughters choosing to start a family or adding another.

Growing up in our culture, any type of birth control was considered wrong; consequently, there were times when babies came almost faster than we could handle physically or emotionally. But now I am appreciative of every single son and daughter we have. Would I have chosen to space them? Yes, probably. Sometimes your body barely recovered before you were pregnant again. I personally don't believe that is God's heart for women. I believe God expected us to use common sense as we are fruitful and multiply. But that's only my opinion. You must follow your convictions. Perhaps your body is much stronger than mine.

Prayer Declaration:
Jesus, thank you for sons and daughters and families. Teach each one of us to hear your heart on how many babies we should bring into this world. Help us remember to care for their emotional and spiritual needs, not just their physical needs. Impart instruction to know what to do. Give us wisdom, to discern the difference.

November 14
God's Timing for Change

A follow-up lab appointment with my doctor today. Fasting was part of the orders to prep for it. I decided against no coffee at all instead of just black. I was super grateful my husband had time to come with me and drive because it was early, and there was no coffee! After my appointment, we went to The Cheesecake Factory next door from the clinic. He got breakfast, I got lunch, and we shared a piece of white chocolate raspberry cheesecake. The huge hot steaming cups of coffee tasted extra flavorsome after the delicate and delicious sweetness. Especially having missed my coffee this morning. On the way home, we chatted, laughed, and talked about doing more fun and spontaneous things together during the winter season. I realized then winter has a silver lining because particularly my husband's schedule is quite a bit less demanding than it is in the summer. We are also in that empty nesting season of learning how to do life with only two of us most days.

It is amazing and can be challenging too. Learning how to cook for two people has been difficult for me. I still end up with leftovers for most meals. Furthermore, there are issues we now have time to work on that maybe we never took the time to resolve. Like our pastor always says, if God dealt with everything in our lives at once, we couldn't handle it. But He is gracious enough to be gentle with us, yet at the right time in our lives, He gives us the grace and puts His holy hand on areas, and says, *it's time*. Time *to overcome* this toxic pattern you have had forever. Time *for change*, time to *give this up* or *make that right*. Time to *forgive this person*. You fill in the blanks. What is He doing in your life? What area is He refining, pruning, and making better, more wholly healed, and redeemed? When He shows us an area, He wants us to work on, and God will also give us the grace to do so. We don't have to do it on our own.

Prayer Declaration:
You are gracious with us. You are persistent, yet perfectly patient, merciful, continually dealing with things in our lives. Thank you, Jesus. You love us too much to leave us the same. Help us to realize this and embrace what You are doing.

November 15
White as Snow

What is it about that first real snowfall you almost know is here to stay awhile? We woke up to about 2 inches piled flawlessly, just where it landed on the railing of the deck, small ledges, as well as every tree branch. It looks magical and puts me completely in the Christmas spirit. But we have a tradition we abide by, and that's no Christmas decorations until after Thanksgiving. Today, it's hard to stick by that while the snow is still coming down softly and gently. Some of the words that come to me are purity, beauty, frosty, and captivating when I see the fresh white snow.

There's also this charming poem we used to write in each other's autograph booklets in Amish culture. It went something like this. "Your future lies before you like a blanket of new snow. Be careful how you tread it, for every step will show." So true, isn't it? I don't know about you, but I know I have muddied and messed up my snow many times. I know I've sinned willfully and unintentionally. I've left smudges, dirt, and ugly things along the way, and I've hurt people, too, numerous times. We have all sinned, and we are all broken. *But God...* (Scripture's way of introducing intervention). Thank God for his forgiveness. I am reminded of the song. *Oh, precious is the flow that makes me white as snow. No other fount I know nothing but the blood of Jesus!* Wherever you have smudged and messed up the purity and whiteness of your life, ask Jesus today to come wash it away with the crimson red of His precious blood. Isaiah 1:18 says, "Come now, let's settle this, says the Lord. Though your sins are like scarlet, I will make them white as snow." What a beautiful promise! Choose Him today. He is waiting for you too.

Prayer Declaration:
Jesus, how do we ever thank you enough for what you do for us. Thank you for covering up our messy and muddy tracks. Thank you for letting your blood run red and erase it all. Thank you, Lord Jesus, we honor You, we worship You and we serve You for the rest of our lives!

November 16
Receive and Believe

The snow is still falling, ever so softly and gently. The woods behind our house looks like a calendar picture. The crooked branches and ugly brown leaves look beautiful under this fresh layer of snow. Again, just like us, Jesus' blood makes us beautiful too. He covers our unpleasant places seamlessly. He calls us righteous, forgiven, and cleanses us from all our sins. Where we are dirty, He makes us clean. Where we are dreadful, steeped in sin, He pulls us out and makes us appealing, pure and spotless, ever blameless before Him. I know it's considerably much to grasp. It's a lot to believe at times. It's a gift. Let's unwrap it and live in it, receive and believe it. There were many years when I wasn't certain of this. Even after I was saved. I didn't believe all that Jesus did for me.

I still struggled with guilt and fear. In the Amish culture, largely, you are taught that you can only hope to go to heaven. Granted, some verses do indeed read like that, but there are plenty of others that are different and say we can know we are saved. John 3:16 is as timeless and simple as it gets, "For God so loved the world that He gave His only begotten son, so that whoever believes in Him shall not perish but have everlasting life." The Book of Romans has many promises of salvation for us additionally. If you have any doubts, I encourage you to search them out for yourself. Discover, read, and receive until you believe all that God has for you and all that He says you are. Open your heart and accept all of it today. Run to Him, not from Him. He wants all of you and all of me. We are not too much for Him.

Prayer Declaration:
Jesus, what You have done for us is so unbelievable and such a tremendous gift that sometimes we struggle to receive and believe. Will You touch each heart today and help us to believe? Will you teach us to know the depths of your love for us and help us to live fully loved from that place?

November 17
Seek Wisdom

More snow. It came down most of the day again. Big, oversized flakes. Breathtakingly stunning. In spite of all the snow, the Bible study ladies all made it safely. One of the ladies brought her brand-new tiny baby girl along today. She was the center of attention. Our Ladies Group has three more babies on the way. We talked about the fact that although the world is in turmoil, the miracle of life in babies and families continues. It was a perfect day to be nuzzled up inside with good food, good fellowship, lots of coffee, worship, and God's word. We always have the best discussions.

It's such a blessing to have all different ages attending, as it brings different perspectives. It's always a pleasure to hear from older women, especially, they are remarkably wise. We discussed Titus 2:3-5 quite a bit today, "Likewise, teach the older women to be reverent in the way they live, not to be slanderers or addicted to wine. But to teach what is good. Then they can train the younger women to love their husbands and children, to be self-controlled and pure, to be busy at home, to be kind and to be subject to their husbands so that no one will malign the word of God."

What if we simply came back to some basics of the Bible and applied them? I truly believe we can all benefit as women and men by having older people in our lives. They have a lot of wisdom to share, and it's biblical. Maybe you have them through your church, but if you don't have anyone, I encourage you to reach out to someone you admire and trust. We need those who have walked before us and have seen and experienced more than we have.

Prayer Declaration:
Thank you, Jesus, for reminding us of what's important in your word. Help us to find those older, more mature people in our lives. Teach us to be humble and ask for their advice and guidance when we need it.

November 18
Dressed for the Occasion

Even more snow is coming down this morning. I'm adjusting to the cold gradually, deliberately. I dug out my thick winter jacket last night. Because one thing I have learned about our Wisconsin winters is this: they are only half as miserable if you dress appropriately. Hats, boots, gloves, scarves, and thick jackets are all a big part of my winter wardrobe. Growing up working outside on the farm, we wore what we called long-johns under our dresses. We also wore something called an "unarok" under our dresses. This was like a soft sleeveless, homemade garment that reached almost to the bottom hem of our dresses.

On the coldest days, we would wear a "zichtuch," which was another scarf tied around our face with only our eyes and forehead showing. We walked to school almost every day of the winter. These two items helped keep us snug and warm as we did our share of the daily chores and walking to school. Wouldn't you say if we are dressed properly for the occasion, we can handle almost anything? Wouldn't that also apply to our spiritual life? The Bible talks about putting on the full armor of God in different places. Isaiah 59:17 is one of my favorites, "He put on righteousness like a breastplate, a helmet of salvation on His head. He put on garments of vengeance for clothing, and He wrapped Himself with zeal as a mantle." What if every morning, before we fully started our day, we would dress ourselves with these truths? We would enter the day dressed for the elements, for whatever comes our way, physically and spiritually. Search out the other verses on what we can put on for our spiritual armor daily.

Prayer Declaration:
Jesus, thank you for the clothes You give us to do both, physically and spiritually. Prepare us to be dressed and ready every morning. Guide us towards standing strong no matter what weather comes our way every day.

November 19
Abundant Thanksgiving

Cooking pumpkins and cleaning my two stoves feels kind of a normal, ordinary Saturday. Can I tell you a secret, though? I've learned to look for joy in the mundane or even create little pockets of pleasure in the otherwise daily chores that can be less than fun. Nonetheless, while my next pot of pumpkin is cooking and the snow is again flying outside, surely, I can slow down and enjoy this weather. I made my husband and I steaming cups of fresh pumpkin spice chai teas from scratch with fresh pumpkin and molasses for the sweetener. It tastes delightful! Reading a good book is next on my agenda. The sun is trying to peek out, but it's only 19 degrees outside. So yes, a good day to hibernate. Drink hot tea, relax, and count my blessings.

Getting the updates from our daughter in Belize is a stark reminder again of how easy it is to take things for granted. I'm also very thankful she is coming home tomorrow evening. I'm thankful we have unlimited fresh water, hot showers, and plenty of food. I'm thankful for good doctors and nurses, including our daughter, a nurse. The list of things that I tend to take for granted is endless. However, it's the 'thankful' month, November. I encourage you to write up your own list and dwell on all that you do have. I never realized the power of gratitude and thankfulness. Colossians 2:7 says, "Rooted and built up in Him and established in the faith just as you were taught, *abounding in thanksgiving.*"

Prayer Declaration:
Jesus, thank you for our abundant blessings. Teach us to live with thankful hearts every day. Lead us to dwell on all we do have instead of what we think we don't have. Show us to be abundant in our Thanksgiving.

November 20
Watch and Pray

The snow finally stopped coming down after three days, and this morning was clear, sunny, and cold, with a low of 2 degrees predicted for tonight. Winter in Wisconsin is not for the faint of heart! On the way to church this morning, as we passed several Amish farms, their horse was hitched to the buggy, ready to take them to church, no doubt. The Amish very rarely cancel church because of the weather. The horse with their sharp shoes can pretty much travel on any road. Of course, this stirred up a host of memories for us as we reminisced about those days of our youth when we traveled by horse and buggy. Yes, even on chilly mornings like this. I remember having especially cold hands and feet long after getting to church sometimes. But as the song goes, *what doesn't kill you makes you stronger!* I'm joking, but maybe there's some truth to it. I'm only now learning to actually enjoy and embrace wintertime, which took quite a few years for me.

Church was empowering and life-giving today. Matthew 24:12-13 was part of our message, "Because of the increase of wickedness, the love of many will grow cold, but the one who stands firm to the end will be saved." This is very meaningful to me. Our pastor expounded on the fact that we need to be willing to suffer for Christ's sake. As the end of this age draws closer, persecution of the saints could very well be possible again, yes, possibly here in America. He talked about the explosion of wickedness and immorality that already seems to be starting. However, it will be a win in the end for us as His saints because we get to spend eternity with Jesus forever. While we don't need to dwell on what may be coming, it is important to be aware and watchful and keep our love for Jesus burning, our lamps trimmed and filled with oil. As the wise virgins in the Bible did, this will help us not to grow cold when persecution comes. Jesus will be strong in us when we abide in Him!

Prayer Declaration:
Help us to be those who stand firm until the end, Jesus. Be strong in us where we are weak. Thank you once again for making a way for us. Accurately show and communicate to us how to hold steadfast until your return.

November 21
Everything in Moderation

A splendid, perfect winter day reminded me of our winters out west of 30 degrees with no wind. Yes, we lived in the Wild West for almost 8 years. There are parts of that beauty I still miss. I wish we could plant mountains! Their elegant, rugged beauty is hard to beat. It's a good day to be out and about getting groceries for Thanksgiving. I may have started Christmas shopping. What a fun and festive time of year. My monthly massage was due today. I'm still dealing with a lingering frozen shoulder issue. It's manageable now, and I'm thankful for a talented massage therapist. They work really hard.

I was aware of a deeper peace today. Peace that passes understanding. Ah, it is truly blessed and so, well... peaceful. Remember the peace I experienced when I got rid of Instagram? I'm slowly cutting back on Facebook as well [unless my readers contact me, then I'm there]. There is noticeably less clutter in my mind and head. It's easier to be present wherever I am and whomever I'm with. While I love social media, the way it can connect us to multiple people, and how we can talk to people easily, social media doesn't always love me back. I believe anything in moderation is okay unless it's a sin; it's my goal for Facebook. What is your current struggle? What consumes too much of your precious time? Do you waste time? You can absolutely rise above it and not let it rule you like Timothy expresses, "For God gave us a spirit not of fear, but of power and of love and of self-control." 2 Timothy 1:7, With God's help, we can do hard things and live with self-discipline. We can be obedient to the things He asks us to give up. Because remember, when it's Him, He will also give us the grace to follow through.

Prayer Declaration:
Impress in us the desire to live fully present, aware, and in tune with your spirit. Help us to be mindful of the people around us to always give them our best! Jesus, thank you for your deep peace that comes with clearing the clutter, making more room for You. Help each one of us know what that is for us.

November 22
God's Amazing Love

All is quiet except the hum of the furnace. Peaceful and relaxing after an exciting full day. One day closer to Thanksgiving. Today I'm thankful my to-do list is getting shorter. My afternoon was brightened up considerably when the grandbabies popped in while daddy went hunting. It's always a delight, and the weather even allowed us to be outside for a while, which was a treat this close to December. Today, as I was watching and listening to the boys playing, also feeling extravagant love and pride for them, I was suddenly reminded of God's love for us, his exorbitant love. He looks at us lovingly, fondly, and with so much adoration for us, his children. Today I'm super thankful for God's sacrificial love for us as humans.

It may not sound like something new, but I love these times of having a reminder or a revelation on the depth of His love for us, which we won't ever truly be able to grasp while on this earth! Being around innocent children can teach us so much. Ephesians 3:18 is my prayer for every human being, "And may you have the power to understand, as all God's people should, how wide, how long, how high, and how deep His love is." How amazing to be so loved by our Heavenly Father that He made way for us to be saved from our sins and to be with Him forever.

Prayer Declaration:
Once again, we thank you, Jesus, for what you've done for us. We are eternally grateful. Thank you for loving us even when we act unlovable. Engraft in us your deep, high, wide, love, consume us and make us more like You every day. Help us to live from this place of being 'so God-loved' by you.

November 23
Highs and Lows

There is so much to do before tomorrow. Pies to bake, among a list of other things to get ready for Thanksgiving tomorrow. I know better than to skip my work out because when the adrenaline starts to kick in and the sweat starts to drip, that's when everything starts to make more sense to me. My brain clears itself, so I can go about my day much more productive. It's a beautiful thing, but it doesn't happen without consistent habit and pushing through. In spite of the effort, it's always worth it. It almost never fails. I get a good nugget from what I'm listening to. This morning, it was a song from Hillsong, 'Highs and Lows.' *Tell me, where could I run from your light? Where could I hide? Within your precious thoughts, there's no hiding from your love. Highs and lows.*

You are with me, either way it goes. Should I rise or should I fall, your mercy is an even flow. You're too good to let me go. This song is just like a balm to my heart this morning. It also reminds me of the verse in Psalms 139:8, "If I go up to the heavens, You are there. If I make my bed in the depths, You are there. So, in other words, in the highs and the lows, He is right there with us." No matter where we find ourselves. Maybe you, too, feel a little weary today. Possibly while the holidays are still festive and fun, they are also strenuous in some ways. Perhaps your extended families are gathering, but you are not invited. That is the case for many of us who have left our culture. It's called 'shunning.' Maybe you are invited and choose not to go. Whatever your pain or struggle is today, in this season, just know God sees, He hears, and He cares. He's right there with you in the depths or wherever you find yourself.

Prayer Declaration:
Jesus, thank you that we cannot go anywhere, that You aren't there. Thank you that your mercy is an even flow. Thank you that you are too good to let us go. Help us to rest in that today.

November 24
Thanksgiving Day

My husband got up extra early to smoke a turkey for Thanksgiving lunch. I'm so grateful for him and all his talents. I'm appreciative of how he loves early mornings and provides so well for us, among many other things. I'm also thankful we can meet with his sister's family and friends today, then tonight, we have our children home to celebrate some more. Thanksgiving Day has arrived. I'm grateful that we set one day aside out of the whole year to be thankful intentionally. It's just a wonderful privilege and one I don't take lightly. Yes, we are thankful every day. Or we should be.

Thanksgiving Day is special. The Bible talks a lot about Thanksgiving, praise, and gratitude. Psalms 7:17 says, "I will give the Lord thanks due to his righteousness, and I will sing praise to the name of the Lord most High." Psalms 95:3 declares, "For the Lord is the great God, the Great King above all Gods. There are too many verses to talk about here, but I love how these two expound on being thankful to Him for who He is and what He's done for us. Now let's think of all the other blessings we get to enjoy. Our lists of thankfulness could be almost endless. Let's live aware of how extremely blessed we are today, even though our lives aren't perfect. We may also be dealing with pain and trials, but we can still be grateful at the same time. There is always something to be appreciative of if we look around ourselves.

Prayer Declaration:
Thank you for all our wonderful blessings You pour out on us daily. Teach us to live more aware of them today and every day. Help us to live from overflowing hearts of gratitude today and every day. Jesus, thank you for You most of all. Amen.

November 25
Healthy Traditions

Some of the family wanted to go shopping this morning for Black Friday sales, or should I say, we girls wanted to go, and we persuaded the guys to come with us. We may have bribed them with lunch and coffee. They came, we shopped along with all the other people. Way too many people for my comfort. In fact, I told my daughter, who is pregnant, that next year Dad and I will stay home and babysit, and they all can go shopping. We did have fun, though, and a scrumptious lunch afterwards. The weather was almost perfect, 50 degrees. Everyone left for home later this afternoon, and once again, the house was quiet and in order. The children all gathered here last night; we had our tradition of putting up our huge tree and decorating it together. It's always a fun, cheerful, loud, and chaotic time, but that's precisely how some memories are made. Some stayed the night again.

What are some traditions you have with your loved ones throughout the year and for special holidays like Easter, Thanksgiving, and Christmas? Growing up, I remember a few. Traditions like certain kinds of candy are still my favorite to this day. My mom made the best turtles and rice krispies and also went to our relative's home for meals. Traditions can be a good thing as long as we don't make a law out of our own traditions and hold them above God's commands. Mark 7:8 warns us about this, "You have let go of the commands of God in our holding on to human traditions." Granted, this is talking more about the rules and laws we make, on how to live, based on our perception of the Bible. Other people's traditions may look very different from ours, and that is a good thing. I believe each family should make their own traditions that are important to them and what they feel is pleasing to God for them.

Prayer Declaration:
Jesus, thank you for this blessed and joyous time of year. Help us to keep You first and foremost in our traditions and celebrations, teaching the next generation about You and why we celebrate. May we create a custom that glorifies you.

November 26
Sign of the Times

It's one more splendid, sunny day. It feels like spring. Indeed, the snow has mostly melted again. It feels like our weather is confused at times, like so many other things in our current world. I can assure you the weather isn't confusing. We have lived in a fallen world since Adam because God orchestrates everything. He is still on the throne. He has power and dominion over all the confusion and folly down here. He won't force us to trust Him, ever, but goodness, life is so much better, blessed, and peaceful when we do so. Luke 21:25 does speak about some signs on the Earth. As we get closer to the end times, it says, "There will be signs in the sun and moon and stars on the Earth. Dismay among the nations, in perplexity at the roaring of the sea and waves." Luke 21:11 tells us, "And there will be earthquakes and in various places, plagues and famines, and there will be terrors and great signs from heaven."

I won't even pretend to know what all that means. However, when our weather patterns are so strange and unusual, you do hear of earthquakes, dreadful unrest, and rumors of war at times. Doesn't it make you wonder if we are unquestionably in the end times? How do you feel about that, scared, excited? Maybe, like me, a mixture of emotions? As much as I enjoy my life on Earth, there are also definitely days when I would be ready in a heartbeat for Jesus to come back. What an incredible and exciting day that will be. Let's live ready for that moment.

Prayer Declaration:
Help us to live heavenly-minded, Jesus. My prayer is for every soul to be saved before You come back. Guide us to help make that happen. Teach us where You want us to proclaim Your good news every day.

November 27
First Love

"You have persevered and have endured hardships for my name, and not grown weary," Revelation 2:3. "Yet I hold this against you. You have forsaken the love you had at first," Revelation 2:4. This was a part of our message scriptures at Church today. Isn't it something how you can hear a verse many times and suddenly one day it resonates with you? I like to say it slides from your head into your heart. Head and heart knowledge are two different things. I grew up with a lot of head knowledge about the Bible and who Jesus was, but the beautiful absolute truths are still finding their way into my heart, slowly but surely.

Transforming thoughts, actions, and beliefs, I do believe this will be an ongoing experience as long as I'm alive and hungry to know and learn more. So how do we keep that first love alive? It takes intentionality, that's for sure. We can cultivate our hunger and passion for Jesus by feeding on His word and His presence. Those are two of my favorites.

Another favorite way is reading devotional or inspirational books that expound on Bible verses. Do you remember what your first love for Jesus felt like? Maybe take some time to remember and think about how pleasing your first love for Jesus felt. Now let's boldly ask Him to bring us to our first love for Him. Once again, let's ask Him to stir up fresh hunger in our hearts. He wants to do that for us.

Prayer Declaration:
We need you more than ever, Lord. Jesus, will you stir up our faith and fresh fire in our hearts for you? Teach us what to feed on that will enhance our appetites for You and our first love. Help us to not get caught up in all the distractions the world has to offer.

November 28
Keep Going!

Once again, our alarms went off extra early. We hustled out the door and headed for the airport 2 1/2 hours away. Early morning flights are not my favorite thing to do, but life is a lot of doing what you need to in order to get what you want to do. I want this 10-day vacation my husband and I have coming up. It feels like it's overdue for just the two of us; I'm excited for quality time together. I'm anticipating slow days of sun and sand, celebrating our anniversary from earlier this year. We are also celebrating our anniversary from 2020, as we were limited then because of the pandemic. Currently, we are about to land in Miami, FL, where we will be for five days. One of our sons is with us for this portion of the trip. We will gather many other friends, colleagues, and team members of ours. It's always a rich and rewarding time, as well as a fun time to rest, relax and celebrate our year-end accomplishments. We look forward to this trip the whole year. Our family business is a wonderful blessing, but it doesn't always come on a silver platter.

My husband and four sons worked very hard to achieve their goals and these trips for us. There's a verse in 2 Chronicles 15:7 that speaks about rewards and perseverance, "But you take courage. Do not let your hands be weak, for your work shall be rewarded." Don't you just love that promise? You too, whatever it is you are currently pushing through in life, your job, your relationships: You will be rewarded, so encourage yourself with this today. Pick your head up, put your shoulders back, take some deep breaths, and then go back to work. Determine your goals, your dreams and tell Jesus about them too. He cares about our deepest heart's desires.

Prayer Declaration:
Thank you, Jesus, for your reassurance we can always find in your word, teach us how to seek personal encouragement and strengthen ourselves in You. Help us to not give up even when our path gets intense, messy or hard, but help us to keep going, with your strength.

November 29
Worship and Wait

"Wait for the Lord. Be strong and let your heart take courage. Wait for the Lord," Psalms 27:14. This verse also reminds me of the song, "I will worship while I'm waiting." What are you waiting for? Do you have unmet hopes, dreams, and goals? If so, you are not alone. Me too. Let's take courage together, remember how far we have come and what God has done. It's always a big encouragement for me to look back and remind myself of all God has done. Do you have your goals and dreams written out? It truly is important to do so and *pray into them*. Let God in on your secrets, the good and the bad. Just like we love to give our children good gifts and surprises, so does our Heavenly Father love to do that for us, right along with the training, discipline, and everything else we need for our growth to mature into adults. Back to waiting on the Lord. What do we do while we wait? It depends again on our season of life.

When our six children were small, my life and hands were so full that waiting looked like doing what needed to be done. There was very little time for anything else. Camping was one thing we all loved and did a bit. Getting all of us out into the great outdoors, enjoying God's creation. Waiting, teaching, instructing, Bible stories for our children, and lots of singing were other things we did. Teaching them how to pray, taking them to church, waiting, being faithful, doing what needed to be done. Today our six children are all grown up and on their own; they all love Jesus. All the waiting was worth it. What are you waiting and worshiping through? Be strong. Take courage. It's only a short season before God gives you a new assignment.

Prayer Declaration:
God, You are so faithful. You give us strength and courage for the season You have us in. Teach us how to wait well, to be strong and worship while we wait. Help us to be encouraged and finish the season we are in, impart to us your virtue.

November 30
Eyes on the Prize

"Let your eyes look directly forward and your gaze be straight before you ponder the path of your feet. Then all your ways will be sure," Proverbs 4:25-26. I imagine these verses are talking first and foremost about keeping our eyes on Jesus and our end goal, heaven, not looking to the right or left, comparing ourselves to others, or getting caught up in all the distractions our world offers us. I really want you to be encouraged, especially if you are feeling stuck, in over your head, or if life seems too much some days. I've experienced all of those at one point or another in my life. What I've learned is no season lasts forever except heaven. I've been in long seasons of pregnancies, babies, diapers, mounds of laundry, sleep deprivation, nursing two babies at once (twins), I've had seasons of depression off and on, seasons of sickness, seasons of raising six teenagers and feeling like I'm in over my head.

I've had a season of working two jobs along with my husband, working the third so we could pay our bills. The seasons of not knowing where our next gallon of milk would come from for our children, but by keeping our eyes looking forward and on Jesus, we survived. Not only that, but we are thriving. God is faithful. He is good, even in the hard times. He will be for you too. Lean into Him. Look ahead. Look at Him. Cry out to Him. Tell Him if you feel overwhelmed or need a break. He can handle our emotions. He can even heal our emotions and is still working on mine. It's a daily battle. That's why I don't hold in my feelings. I feel, deal, and heal.

Prayer Declaration:
Jesus, thank you that you care, and you are there in every season of our lives. We will never arrive until heaven, but thank you for teaching us to thrive in the middle of it all. Teach us to reach for You, before anything else, keeping our eyes forward, on You!

December 1
Remain Steadfast

Our time here at the Trump Doral Resort in Miami, FL, has been so relaxing: Connecting with our many friends and team members, eating lots of good food, and lying by the pool. Yesterday I ordered a delectable salad for lunch, and it was one of the biggest ones I've ever had, crisp, fresh, and healthy. This morning I went over to the spa and had my hair done. After an entire year of not cutting my hair, it was time. Last night we had a fabulous meal. At our welcome dinner, we heard from an incredible man. Reminding all of us to stand strong for our America, he reminded us that our freedoms could disappear very quickly under socialism. It was a significant, riveting speech. He ended it by showing a clip of the end of the battle at Gettysburg. It was good for all of us (many from our Amish culture) to see that someone, no, not just someone, but many men fought for our country.

Countless, many men lost their lives fighting for America and the freedoms we enjoy, almost casually, too often. I'm so thankful this speaker reminded us about the observance of our freedom and what it took for America to become and stay its own free country! It also helps me to truly treasure vacations like these, not taking them for granted but being very, very grateful for this business opportunity and all it offers with it. May we never become like Romans 1:21 says, "For although they knew God, they neither glorified or gave thanks to Him. But their thinking became futile and their foolish hearts were darkened."

Prayer Declaration:
Oh, Jesus, don't let that be us, don't allow our hearts to be darkened nor our minds futile. Teach us to remain steadfast, with extreme thankful hearts for all the things You allow us to experience and enjoy. Help us to always keep in mind the sacrifice that was made on the cross and for our country.

December 2
Lean in and Learn

Blue skies, palm trees, sunshine, and an occasional downpour have been our weather here in Florida. Last night, a group of us walked downtown to eat dinner, and on the way back, suddenly, out of nowhere, the wind picked up, and it began to rain. Not just a little shower, but almost more like a mini hurricane. Buckets of rain and wind, making it difficult to see where we were going. We walked, we ran through water up to our ankles, and eventually made it back to our resort, soaked to the skin, dripping, sopping wet. We laughed as we gasped for air and chalked it up as a silly adventure. Sometimes when the storms of life hit us, we might be able to laugh them off too and make light of it.

Other times, though, it can feel like a punch in the gut, and you also fight to keep breathing and keep your head above water. These are the times to remember our lifeguard walks on water, and He always rescues us. Doesn't mean we might not get soaked or suffer for a while first, but He will not let us drown when we cry out to Him. Much like Peter did when he was sinking and in danger of drowning. God is always bigger than any storm we find ourselves in. Psalms 37 talks about this. The Lord loves justice and He will not abandon his Godly ones. They are kept safe forever. What an incredible promise. When we make Him our Lord and Savior, we will be safe with Him for all eternity, no matter what storms we face while we are here on Earth. Cling to Him in it and through it.

Prayer Declaration:
Jesus, thank you that You always rescue us at the right time. Help us to remember that our time isn't always your time. Teach us to lean in and learn until You rescue and deliver us.

December 3
Soak in the Son

Enjoying one last espresso on our balcony in this warm, balmy climate. Back home, the children say we have had snow, sleet, gusty winds, and sun again. Soaking up all the sunshine can and will help me get through the winter better when we get back home. Again, equal to the spiritual aspect of life, the more we rest into the SON, the better equipped we are for what life brings our way. Today, we packed up our room and bags and hired someone to take us over to the port, where we would get on a cruise ship for the next five nights. My husband and I are very different in a lot of things, but we are the same in the fact that we both love a good adventure. We have never experienced being on a gigantic, huge cruise ship in the middle of the ocean with no land in sight, so we are excited and maybe just a tad bit apprehensive. I brought a copy of a friend's new book to read on this trip called Chasing Wonder. Oh, my goodness, it's so good. If you are like me and tend to choose comfortable and convenient, then this book would be for you too.

Do you think Jesus wants us to live boring, mundane lives? Or would he rather we live wide-eyed with wonder, living fully alive? John 10:10 is one of my all-time favorite verses because it speaks about this, living life to the full. Jesus himself says, "I have come, so they may have life and have it to the full." With Jesus, our Heavenly Father and Holy Spirit, I do believe our lives should not be boring and stagnant. We can co-partner with Him every day to live our best life and bring life to those around us.

Prayer Declaration:
Jesus, help us to never become lazy, stagnant or negative, but constantly filled with fresh revelation, wonder and life from You. We appreciate your spirit, overflowing out to others. Teach us to go after your heart and live from your perspective.

December 4
Hidden Wonders

Waking up on a cruise ship this morning was definitely a new experience. It was calm for the most part, but occasionally you could feel the waves rocking us to and fro, to and fro. We got on the ship and ate lunch while we waited to check into our rooms, so much food. Wow. It was almost overwhelming with all the food and people. We got off to explore the island of Nassau today, which was interesting and fun. We took a glass bottom boat to go see some coral reefs, beautiful fish of every color and size. I can't even see things like that without marveling at the detail and creativity of our God. He was extremely creative and some of this exquisiteness is always underwater where you actually have to go to extra measures to see it, like with this boat or snorkeling, which is also a lot of fun. Some even enjoy scuba diving.

Being on the top level of the ship and seeing water all around us is quite an experience. No land in sight, just water as far as the eye could see. Psalms 24 1:2 reminds us, The earth is the Lord's and everything in it, the world and all who live in it, for He founded it upon the seas and established it upon the waters. The wonder of it all is more than I can grasp! This is why I so enjoy experiencing new and different aspects of God's creation. It deepens and broadens my vision and gratitude for being able to see things like this. Have you made your bucket list yet? Perhaps something you want to achieve not necessarily before dying but by a certain time or age? You can start today. It's never too late to pursue new experiences and new opportunities in different places.

Prayer Declaration:
Thank you, Jesus, that you care about our everyday lives. Thank you that you love to let your children experience your wonders every day, but also in new ways. Teach us to never stop seeing the beauty and the wonder everywhere we go.

December 5
Blessings and Struggles

A lovely coconut coffee to start my day right. We woke up and docked close to Half Moon Cay Island. They had to water shuttle us onto the island, where we spent the day. Oh, my goodness, the beauty was breathtaking. The white sand was the finest I've ever seen. It literally felt like baby powder under our feet, so soft and therapeutic. The water was some of the most beautiful Aqua Blue I've ever seen. We swam and enjoyed the water with our friends who were on this trip with us. We both share the same anniversary date, so occasionally, we go explore new places together. We relaxed on the beach mostly today. The sun was perfect and felt amazing. They served us lunch on this island also, such a treat, perfectly relaxing, wonderfully healing, and brilliantly beautiful. Yet by evening, I started getting sick and went to bed very early. In life, there is almost always good and not so good intertwined. I'm learning to be more patient and embrace the times I don't really enjoy at all, like tonight. Instead of enjoying the evening festivities, I took a hot shower, bundled up in layers of clothes, drank hot tea, cuddled under the covers, and let the boat rock me to sleep.

I felt safe, cared for by my husband and God despite my discomfort and disappointment, missing out on an entire evening. My husband always reminds me, honey, we aren't in heaven yet. Even so, tonight, my heart declares. "Many, O Lord my God, are the wonders you have done, the things You plan for us. No one can recount to You. Were I to speak and tell of them they would be too many to declare," Psalms 40:5.

Prayer Declaration:
Jesus, thank you that you do great and mighty things for all of us. Inspire us to look deeper than our discomfort and disappointment, to declare your goodness in the midst of it. Help us all to truly believe that Uou are always good.

December 6
The Silver Lining

Sleeping in this morning after a rough night, felt wonderful. Falling ill while looking forward to an adventure was definitely not in my plans. Today was a low-key day. We could not get off the boat at Grand Turk Island because we didn't meet their vaccination requirements; what a disappointment. However, we still had a wonderful day, deeply relaxing with lots of people off the boat. We went all the way to the top deck, where we could at least see the island. I was also able to go get a facial at Cloud 9 Spa, which was a luxury and a treat that doesn't happen often. We watched another magnificent sunset on one side of the ship as a big full moon rose on the other side.

My heart and soul can hardly drink it completely, all this vast beauty and God's creation, no matter where we are. The sea alone is so massive and mysterious. Life is never perfect, and yet there is always limitless wonder and sublime beauty to be found if we are open to see it. Being sick yesterday made me much more content not to get off the ship; otherwise, I may have raised quite a ruckus.

Instead, I lay quietly and quite meekly in the sun most of the day. By evening, finally, I felt better. It also gave my body a chance to process and catch up with all the food we have been enjoying and, at times, too much. Even though I would never have chosen to be sick today, I was able to find some positive and silver lining in it. You know the saying; every cloud has a silver lining? The next time your plans get interrupted, try to find it! You may be surprised by what God shows you. Lamentations 3:25 says, "The Lord is good to those who wait for Him to the person who seeks Him."

Prayer Declaration:
Jesus, may we always wait for You, specifically when our plans are interrupted. Motivate us to seek You in those times. Mainly help us to find the good in every day, particularly if it doesn't go like we had hoped or planned.

Celebrate Uniqueness

The wind is whipping through my hair. The sun is shining down on me. With the breezes keeping me cool at the same time, it does feel so heavenly. The sea is shimmering in the sunlight, big fluffy white clouds in the blue sky. It all feels majestic. It is not hard at all to see, feel, and definitely smell the goodness of our God and all He has created for us as his sons and daughters to enjoy. Today, I don't want to miss a single thing. I'm feeling better, had a wonderful night's sleep, and it is our last day at sea. By tomorrow morning, we will be back on land at the dock in Miami. Going on a cruise has been on our bucket list for quite some time. It's been amazing for the most part. Other parts we didn't care for as much but isn't that, again, just life? Your experience of something will be completely different from someone else's. It again goes to show how we as people are different even though God created us all equally. We do not all look alike, but we all have the same God-given DNA.

Just like the sunsets are all a little bit different, so are we, His children. We climbed up as high as we could, on the very top of the ship, to watch our last nightfall at sea. It was breathtakingly beautiful. My husband teases me sometimes about how excited I get over every sunset. Don't they all look alike, he asks? I continue to exclaim and tell him sunsets don't appear identical. Let your uniqueness be seen and glorify the God who gave it to you. Use it for His honor and glory instead of hiding it or feeling embarrassed. Remember, there was a time I didn't want people to know my background (Amish), Matthew. 10:31 tells us, "The very hairs on our head are numbered," just wow, that seems impossible!

Prayer Declaration:
Jesus, thank you for how strategically and specifically You fashion each one of us. Influence us to live as individuals and not duplicates. Help us to be thankful towards our own uniqueness.

December 8
Home for the Holidays

We are back in the Miami airport, waiting on our flight home. We were awake early and watched all the lights of Miami as we came into the cruise ship port this morning. We packed everything up and went upstairs for one last breakfast and coffee. After seeing nothing but a few remote islands and water for days, the city lights of Miami look pretty neat. It beckoned us back onto land. I can't believe I'm saying this, but I'm ready to be back where it's a tad bit colder after 11 days of vacation, in warm and sometimes hot temperatures. I'm ready to transition from sun, sand, sea, and palm trees to snow, cold, and Christmas at home! This has been an amazing and relaxing vacation; however, after living out of a suitcase for 11 days, home sounds very delightful. Our daughter picked us up at the airport, and we stopped for dinner and caught up on each other's lives.

The next stop was our son's house to get my car and see them and the grandsons. Oh, what a grand reunion. Zion, age 4, jumped up and down when he saw us. Zander, age 2, asked if I could stay there. Goodness, we missed them. We can travel the world, but I'm convinced more than ever there is just no place like home with your family. Another of our sons stopped in to see us and catch up after we got home. I can't wait to rest this weekend. Tonight, my heart is filled with deep gratitude for so many things, especially God's mercy, protection, goodness, and blessings. So tonight, let's hug our families and say an extra thank you prayer for them. The wonder of the world doesn't compare to the heart relationships of home and family. Psalms 86:12 says, "I will praise you, O Lord my God, with all my heart I will glorify your name forever."

Prayer Declaration:
Jesus, this is my heart towards you tonight. Let it be this way always, teach us to live in thankfulness every day. Stir us to glorify You all our days. Help us to treasure our families.

December 9
Live Adventurously

Waking up in our own bed this morning, making my own cup of coffee, all peaceful and quiet. There's a little bit of snow on the ground outside. It looks and feels extra special and wonderful. Do you know that old country song? *Don't know what you got until it's gone!* I think that can be us, with the blessings of our everyday lives. We get used to them, and we might stop seeing the wonder in it. It is so good for us to shake things up a bit and sometimes do something out of the ordinary. Somehow it always puts things back into perspective. Think about what it could look like for your life? For my husband and I, it is traveling. While we both are homebodies at heart, we also love to go see new places and explore places we've never been to before. We both like adventure. He is often more daring. Although for a girl who can't swim much, I'd say living on a ship for five days is on the brave side, wouldn't you agree? Adventure not only breaks the monotony of life, but it often gives us a fresh perspective. It helps us see things in a different light, sometimes even the very people and things under our noses that are easy to miss.

Adventure doesn't have to be travel; it can be anything that pulls you out of your comfort zone and expands your horizon and your thinking. I encourage you to plan one for yourself today. What is it that you have been wanting to try and yet you haven't? Whether we visit the poorest villages in Africa, or the richest island in the Bahamas, both can teach us something if we are living in wide-eyed wonder. I long to live as Luke 5:26 tells us. "Amazement seized them all. And they glorified God. And we were filled with awe saying, we have seen extraordinary things today!"

Prayer Declaration:
Yes, Lord, thank you for letting us see and experience the supernatural and extraordinary things even while on this earth. Teach us to live in childlike wonder, to step out in faith and create wonder and amazement in your name.

December 10
Proclaim His Birth

It's a perfect cozy wintry day. Getting to be home alone most of the day is exactly what I needed after being with people for close to two weeks straight. I love people, but again, even too much of a good thing can be too much. Just like Jesus needed to be alone at times, solitude is so good periodically, at least for me. I'm catching up on laundry, mail, and odd jobs. Being back in my routine is wonderful. Walking to the mailbox and breathing in the fresh air, doing a light workout and stretches. Vacation is wonderful and a blessing, but so is our everyday routine that keeps us grounded and on track with our goals in life. As this year is ending, it puts me into that reflective mode. What have we done this year? Did we use it for God's glory? This is also the month we get to celebrate the birth of Jesus! My prayer is always for us to truly rejoice in Jesus, to genuinely make it about Him, and not just casual happy holidays. As always, I like to ask myself what can I do? One thing I love doing is sending out cards to family, friends, and neighbors, cards proclaiming His birth. It may seem like a small thing, and it is.

Even though it's very time-consuming, it's something that is natural and enjoyable for me. Try something that comes easy for you. It doesn't have to be difficult. What about you? What do you enjoy? Maybe you enjoy caroling. We used to do that when we had just left the Amish, and I loved it. Maybe it's sharing treats with friends and neighbors with a simple handwritten note attached. There are so many ways we can help spread the good news of His birth. Let's do it together. "He will be a joy and delight to you. Many will rejoice because of His birth" Luke 1:14.

Prayer Declaration:
Jesus, we do rejoice that You came to earth as a baby to save us from our sins. Help us to gladly and fearlessly spread the good news of You. Prepare us to actually celebrate You, this season and always.

December 11
Humility

Oh, come, let us adore Him. Oh, come, let us adore Him. Oh, come, let us adore Him. Christ the Lord! This is one of my favorite Christmas songs. It's not only a Christmas song but also a worship song. It is honestly meaningful and never gets old! My husband and I rode to church with our oldest son and his girlfriend this morning. We met up with another son, wife, daughter, and her boyfriend. After church, we went out for lunch to one of our favorite places to eat. These are some of the most precious times to me, discussing the message and just being together. It never gets old. My dream, hope, and Mama's heart are to be able to be together for all eternity. Does a mother ever stop praying? I really don't think so. I'm so very thankful for a solid Bible-based church our children enjoy going to. Today's message was on humility. What a timely message for the age and era we live in. It was so good, convicting, and encouraging. Based on 1 Peter 5:5-6, Humble yourselves under God's mighty hand that He may lift you up in due time.

The opposite of humility is pride, of course. I'm sure we can all think of people we have dealt with who were either humble or prideful, but now what about us? What do people feel or pick up from us? Jesus was one of the greatest examples of humility we will ever have, born in a barn, dying on the cross, and in between, washing his disciple's grimy feet at the Last Supper, yes, even Judas' feet. The one who would betray Jesus that very night. One meaning of humility is simply being free from pride and arrogance: Doesn't that sound inviting? What area in our lives do we need to cultivate meekness and humility?

Prayer Declaration:
Jesus, will You show us where we are proud instead of humble? Will you gently convict each one of us? Instruct us to live out humility in our relationships just like your word teaches and also by the example You left for us.

December 12
Our Yes Matters

It truly is so wonderful to be home. Wait, I've said that several times now, haven't I? My mind is once again on Christmas. I'm genuinely thankful we celebrate our Savior's birth. Even though we don't know for sure that it was this very day He was born, on the 25th, it's not about the exact date. The Christmas story to me never gets old; when I try to apply it to our culture today, I can't even. I feel like people would believe it even less than they did back then. The nerve of Mary, I can just hear the talk. This is one thing I so love about Jesus, the unlikely way He chooses to show and reveal himself to us still today.

Mary's answer to the Angel who came to tell her that she would be pregnant with Jesus always inspires me. She simply said, "Truly I am the Lord's servant; may it be as you have said," Then the Angel left her. Luke 1:38, what a beautiful, humble response. I like to put myself in her situation. Would that have been my response? Would it have been yours? Or do you think we would immediately have thought about what people are going to say and think?

We don't know what Mary's thoughts were or what she went through bringing Jesus into this world, but I'm extremely grateful she said yes to God! We went to see a live nativity scene at a friend's farm last night. They do a wonderful job of bringing the Christmas story to life, complete with a large angel in the tree, live sheep, shepherds, and a cross lit up in the distance at the very end. From the manger to the cross, it's all too much to grasp with the human mind sometimes. That is why we simply believe!

Prayer Declaration:
Jesus, thank you for this timeless, wonderful Christmas story. We receive the demonstration of your power and believe it in all of its glory and beauty. Help us also to say yes to what You ask of us. May we reflect the humility of Mary and Jesus this Christmas season.

December 13
The Tree

The wind is whipping up something out there. I'm secretly hoping we will get some snow. The Christmas season doesn't quite feel right without it, and it makes everything pop out. The many beautiful lights people put up this time of year are a delight to me. The little girl in me lights right up with them. Of course, growing up Amish, we didn't do any kind of decorating at all for Christmas. Those first years after we left, I actually realized it's not a sin for us to put up a tree. The children were still young, and we would all traipse out in the woods together to find the perfect tree, cut it down, drag or drive it home and then decorate it together. The very first time we did this, we turned the lights on, and our children burst out singing spontaneously, *Happy Birthday to you...Happy Birthday...dear Jesus.*

It was a very special moment and now a memory. Did you know that the Christmas tree symbolizes:

- The spirit of the Christmas season. To Christians, it's everlasting life and the sacrifice of Jesus Christ on the cross. Jesus' cross is often referred to as a tree in the Bible.

- The lights and decorations are symbolic of the wonder and glory of His birth and resurrection.

- The stars and angels most people put on top of their trees were both present on the night of His birth.

- The presents under the tree are a continuation of the tradition of gift giving as God gave to humanity, Jesus, His only beloved son, as a gift. It's also symbolic of the wise men bringing Jesus gifts.

- Finally, Jesus gave us the gift of trading His life for the eradication of sin on the cross or tree. The tree definitely has spiritual significance and it's a wonderful family tradition. "He came to rescue us from our enemies and enable us to serve Him without fear," Luke 1:74. Hallelujah.

Prayer Declaration:
Jesus, thank you once again for coming to Earth as a baby. Thank you for dying on a tree for all humanity. Teach us to honor and serve You all the days of our life. By faith we receive your precious gift of salvation.

December 14
Bitter or Better

My wish for snow is happening right now. Beautiful, big white, fluffy flakes. It looks extraordinary. I realize if I had to be out in it, my tune would change. I feel like I know what it's like, though. I had many years of doing various chores outside on different farms growing up. Even after we were married, we lived on three different farms where we did chores. After our Amish life, it was scraping ice and snow off my car in the early cold mornings to either get the children to school or for me to get to work on time. I'm truly grateful for every one of those experiences because without them, I would not fully appreciate what I have now, a heated garage, and the steering wheel on my car even heats up. I love it! No more freezing hands.

Life shapes us and makes us into who we are. We always have the choice to let our circumstances make us bitter or better. My mom did not always have an easy life, yet she made the best of her life, especially for us children. I will always be thankful for her example of strength and endurance. Today, at 80 years old, she still lives a vibrant, healthy, active lifestyle. She didn't let her trials conquer her; you shouldn't either. There are many examples in the Bible, but Mary is on my mind this Christmas season. Mary, the mother of Jesus, arose to the occasion, even when it was difficult and uncomfortable for her to bring our Savior into the world. I love how the angel told her she is highly favored and the Lord is with her in Luke 1:28. Again, verse 30 says, "Do not be afraid Mary, you have found favor with God." How comforting these words must have been for Mary, knowing many would not understand or believe her. Because Jesus was born, we, too, can find favor in Him and through Him. We don't have to be afraid. When we rise above and push through the hard places in our life, we never know what paths or examples we are opening for others. Ask Him for His strength and favor with whatever you're going through right now.

Prayer Declaration:
Jesus, thank you for all the people who have said yes to You. Help us to be those people who rise above and go beyond what is easy or comfortable. Teach us to know You, above all, your voice and your leading.

December 15
The Flipside of Beauty

Every branch, every ledge, every surface is covered in wet, white, pure, cottony snow this morning. It is completely beautiful! Social media is flooded with pictures of the stunning beauty this morning. Our power has been on and off as the power lines struggle under the weight of the snow. We have candles and an oil lamp or two stowed away if we need them. I'm always grateful that we were taught how to live without power if we ever need to again. My husband is very good with anything motors, so he would probably have us up and running one way or another. Some people are completely without power and have been since early morning. What can be so beautiful to one person can also be the cause of a lot of work and chaos for another. I'm thinking of the power companies this morning and the people responsible for clearing the roads. My guys have been plowing and shoveling here at home for hours, but we wished for snow, and here it is, in all its glory and all that comes with it. Schools are canceled, and I hope people will take this opportunity to make memories with their loved ones and children.

Try lighting candles and tell your children the true meaning of Christmas. Perhaps you can make some cookies, if you have power, and share them with your friends and neighbors. These are special days to treasure, in my opinion. Snow days with our school children almost always turned into a fun day, like an unexpected gift! Time is so fleeting! Build your legacy for the next generations. In Luke 1:50, Mary prophesies, "His mercy extends to those who fear Him from generation to generation." Let us fear, revere and honor Him today.

Prayer Declaration:
Jesus, thank you for this beauty and the baby you sent over 2,000 years ago. Help us to live a Godly legacy. Teach us how to make memories and traditions that will empower the next generation and the next and the next and the next. Amen.

December 16
Christmas Musings

Hark the Herald angels sing glory to the newborn King! Sitting in my office, looking out into the snowy white woods and world, it is quite easy to feel the Christmas spirit. The above song is one of the beloved Christmas carols that also never gets old, in my opinion. Singing Christmas carols together as a family with relatives on Christmas afternoons or at our annual school program are among some of my favorite Christmas memories. Going to school in a small one-room schoolhouse was actually a lot of fun, for me at least. Every Christmas, we would make some kind of homemade gifts for our parents. We also practiced and put on a really good Christmas program for our parents, friends, neighbors, and whoever wanted to come. We memorized and recited long poems and many songs too. Afterwards, we had snacks and candy of every description! Even though presents were very limited in our home, the spirit of Christmas was alive and well. Once again, I'm truly grateful for that. We learned the true meaning of Christmas, Jesus! Santa Claus was definitely not a part of my childhood. To this day, I don't understand teaching your children about someone who isn't real.

Call me old school; maybe I am! One of my favorite parts of the Christmas story is where the angel came to tell the shepherds that Jesus was born. "Do not be afraid, I bring you good news of great joy, that will be for all people. Today in the town of David, a Savior has been born to you. He is Christ the Lord," Luke 2:10-11. Can you imagine just being about your daily chores like the shepherds were, and suddenly an angel appears and brings you such exciting and marvelous tidings? News that changes everything, news that is for all people. I can only imagine the shepherd's surprise, and yet they instantly believed.

Prayer Declaration:
Jesus, thank you for this wonderful, beautiful, precious season. Help us believe and really grasp what it is all about. Help us to be certain of it like the shepherds were. Thank you that you still speak to us today, and that your birth is still good news!

December 17
Perseverance and Rewards

The alarm jolted me awake quite early this morning. We attended our church Christmas party last night, fighting snowy, slippery roads all the way home; it was a late bedtime. As I slipped into the shower to wake up, I was suddenly filled with joy. I remembered why we were getting up so early. One of our twin daughters is graduating from college today as an RN after 4 ½ years. Her pinning ceremony for nurses is early this morning, an hour away at her school. We make our coffee for the road and head out on more snowy and treacherous roads, but we make it in time. We met up with the rest of the family, except for one son, who had already had other commitments. My husband and I both go up front to place the pin on our daughter when the time comes. The pin represents the cross and a rose, among other things. The ceremony was heartfelt. At one point, the whole class lit a candle and recited the nurse's pledge together. It was beautiful. The family went out to celebrate together. We went to eat brunch at one of Lorinda's favorite restaurants to celebrate her achievements. Later in the day, we went back to school to be a part of her actual graduation from college. Nursing school is not easy, and we are very thankful and proud of our daughter to have reached her goals.

She is an example of hard work and persistence paying off. Many exams, presentations, and hours of driving to clinics were not easy for her. Many times, she would ask for prayer before a test or exam. She persevered, and she did it. It was very special to be together and celebrate her success today. 2 Chronicles 15:7 speaks of our labor being rewarded, "But you take courage. Do not let your hands be weak, for your work shall be rewarded." What hard goals are you working towards today? Let the above verse give you strength and encouragement. You can do it!

Prayer Declaration:
Jesus, thank you that You yourself reward our diligence and perseverance. Thank you for our daughter and the future she has as a Christian nurse. Bless her and all nurses indeed, help them to do everything out of love and honor for their patients and You.

December 18
God's Presence

A cold frosty morning. It is close to zero degrees again. Once again, my bed beckons me to stay cozy and snug under the covers. Again, I push them back, get ready, and head right out into the cold. The roads are clear this morning; thank you, Lord! The church is well worth the effort once again, as it always is. Isn't anything that takes some effort on our part usually worth it? Especially when our flesh pulls in one direction but our heart in the other. The worship team sang some of my favorite Christmas carols, then went into a more spontaneous time of worship. God's presence was so strong I was glad I was in it. Have you experienced His presence?

Does this mean we always have to go to church or be with others to experience God's presence? I would say no, we don't, but for me, that's something I truly love and enjoy, being in His presence with other believers. There are other places I experienced His presence, too, like in my car or office or out on a walk. We will never be able to put Him in just one place. He is way too big and omnipresent for that. One chorus we sang today is stuck in my head. *You are Alpha and Omega. We worship you Oh Lord. You are worthy to be praised.* Psalms 145:3 also says, "Great is the Lord and greatly to be praised, and His greatness is unsearchable." What exactly does that mean? I believe it means there will always be more of God to discover and experience if we want it. I, for one, want that, do you? Are you with me? Let's simply ask God for that.

Prayer Declaration:
Jesus, we want to experience all the facets of You and your glory. Will you reveal more of yourself to us? Will you cleanse us from all unrighteousness to make room for more of You and Your unsearchable greatness in us? Help us to let go of old belief patterns and systems that no longer serve us. Teach us your ways, your will. Teach us to look for You in the right places and help us to find You more, as we seek You.

December 19
Wise Men Still Seek Him

Just as the wise men set out to seek and find Jesus over 2,000 years ago, so are we very wise who still seek Him out today. They followed that bright, shining North star all the way to Bethlehem, which took faith just like it takes faith for us still today. Like the wise men did, we, too, have our star, a true north in the Bible we can follow. I love how Jeremiah 29:13 declares, "You will find Me when you seek Me with all your heart." I also love how the wise man tricked the evil King Herod and went back home another way after they had found and brought their gifts to Jesus. They must have sensed that Herod had evil intentions. Can you even imagine living in that era when Herod had such a horrendous law passed that all baby boys two and under must be killed? By doing this, he hoped to also kill the baby Jesus, whom people were saying was the king of the Jews. Herod's jealousy led him to make horrific choices.

I cannot imagine the grief and the horror the moms and dads must have gone through, but Jesus wasn't killed. Not then, His time was not done on Earth yet. He still had a lot of work to do. Mary and Joseph's grief would come later. They had warnings at times. In Luke 2:35, Simeon told them, "A sword will pierce your own soul too." I don't know if they realized what this meant at the time, but I do know everything changed that night in Bethlehem when Jesus was born. Hope was born that night! People knew it and felt it, and some believed it, and some didn't, just as it is still today. Do you believe my friend? If not, then you don't need to wait any longer. Open your heart today! Reach out to a trusted friend if you need help. He came for ALL of us!

Prayer Declaration:
Jesus, thank you for coming to Earth for us. This Christmas season, will you soften and open more hearts to you than ever before? Let the wonder of your birth and your sacrifice sink deep into all our hearts this season. Teach us how to glorify You in greater measure.

December 20
The Ultimate Price

The sun came up in bright reds and oranges this morning. It was a picture to behold against the white snow-laden trees. Because it has turned extremely cold, it snowed heavily, the trees are hanging on to it, and it's incredibly beautiful. It's tremendously perfect for this time of the year, in my opinion. Much of the world is in a tizzy right now, getting ready for Christmas. I love that, but then I also wonder, at times, is everybody really celebrating Jesus, or are they just caught up in the excitement and missing the true meaning of it all? I hope not. Once again, it starts with us. With you and me, what or how are we celebrating this season? Is it all about the shopping, the presents, and the treats we love to make this time of year? Are we allowing ourselves to stop and reflect and truly express our gratitude? I can't stop thinking about those dear mothers whose babies were killed because Herod wanted to kill Jesus.

We can read this account in Matthew 2:18, "A voice was heard in Rama, weeping and loud lamentation, Rachel weeping for her children. She refused to be comforted because they are no more." It's consequently heartbreaking. What if today such an order would be issued? Much happened behind the scenes of our beloved Christmas story. Often in the reality of life, someone pays the price or makes way for us to enjoy our blessings. Jesus paid the ultimate price for us. Can we grasp this? He made a way for you and me! This Christmas season, may we keep Him in the center of our hearts and homes, our festivities, and celebrate Him well. Let's give Him all the honor and glory He deserves.

Prayer Declaration:
Jesus, thank You for what You've done, for whosoever will accept You, draw sinners and saints alike to You this Christmas season. We want to learn as Christians, to reflect your light in a way that draws the world to You. Let it start with us!

December 21
Hold On to True Joy

What a cold morning, 11 below zero, to be exact! They're calling for a winter storm, more snow and wind. What if we were all snowed in for Christmas? For some, that could be a delight for others, a dilemma. I would probably be somewhere in between if our children could get here. Doesn't it sound cozy? This season can be joyous and delightful, especially when we celebrate the true meaning of it all. Yet I know friends who are also struggling and sad, like a family who lost their mom and wife just last week. She was only 42 but died from a heart attack. Our neighbors lost their home in a fire and are currently living in a hotel; they also lost their family pets. Many people are reaching out to them in kindness, but still, this can't be easy for them. Another friend is struggling to keep her house as the court is trying to evict her. Those are only a few examples of grief and sorrow around my small world. I'm sure you could name a few of your own. Yet we still sing, *it's the most wonderful time of the year, because maybe it still is.* Maybe it comes back to being able to feel and experience joy and sorrow at the same time.

Remember, true joy doesn't come from our circumstances but deep inside, from the source himself, Jesus. "For unto us, a child of Hope is born, a Son is given, and the government will be on His shoulders. He will be called Wonderful Counselor, Mighty God, Everlasting Father, and Prince of Peace," Isaiah 9:6. This is one of my favorite Christmas songs and the reason we can rejoice and have joy and hope no matter what is happening around us.

Prayer Declaration:
Jesus, thank you for coming and making way for us. Help us to relate to You in each one of your names. Wonderful, Counselor, Everlasting Father, Prince of Peace, Mighty God, teach us to always hold on to hope and joy. Even in our sorrow and sadness. Help us to be able to hold both in our hearts at the same time, when sorrow visits, you trade our sorrows for joy, sweet joy.

December 22
Prepare the Way

A fascinating story in the Bible before the Christmas story is found in Luke 1. You can read the account yourself in verse 11 all the way through 25. Zachariah was visited by an angel. The angel told him his wife Elizabeth would bear him a son. This was also a miracle, as Zachariah and Elizabeth were well past their childbearing years! Verse 17 tells us more about who this little one would be. "He will go on before the Lord in the Spirit and power of Elijah to turn the hearts of the fathers to their children. And the disobedient to the wisdom of the righteous to make ready a people prepared for the Lord." This baby boy, the angel was prophesying about, was John the Baptist. Yes, the same John who would later be beheaded in prison. He was the voice crying out in the wilderness, preaching, baptizing, and preparing the way for Jesus. John was the one who baptized Jesus. He played an important role in the first coming of Jesus. He was faithful, humble, and also obedient unto death, much like Jesus was.

People of old, of Bible times, prepared, believed, hoped, and prayed for Jesus the Messiah to come. Are we doing the same for his second coming? Are we waiting in anticipation? Are we living in hope and looking forward to that day? Are we praying for the world, the unsaved, and sharing the good news of not only His birth but also the resurrection? Are we doing what we are asked to do like John the Baptist did? What has God called you to do? From the cradle to the cross to the grave, and finally, back to his home in heaven, it truly is the most wonderful story ever to be told. Let us not be shy in sharing it. Be that voice crying out even like John the Baptist did, even when it costs us something. Obedience can be costly, but the rewards are eternal. Let us be brave, bold, and behold our king.

Prayer Declaration:
Jesus, thank you for people like John the Baptist and the many prophets of old who have shown us the way for over 2,000 years. Give us heavenly-minded missions to have obedient, willing hearts, proclaiming the good news of the gospel.

December 23
Believe in Miracles

Merry Christmas Eve! Okay, I know that's a little extra, but my grandsons and I are literally counting down the days to Christmas. Today, it's officially just two more days. The weather is raging outside, way below zero and windy. The one church we attend occasionally has already canceled its Christmas Eve service tonight. I'm hoping the other one won't, but then you know what, being snowed in also could be kind of fun as long as the family could still make it home. We must wait and see what tomorrow brings. Sometimes waiting is the hardest part. Do you think they had to worry about extreme temperatures back in Bethlehem? Let's go back to the story of Zachariah and Elizabeth for a bit. If you think about it, Zachariah and Mary both had angels coming to them in person, bringing them the good news of the baby boys that would be born. Yet their responses were quite different. We already talked about what Mary's response was. However, look at what Zachariah's response was in Luke 1:18, "He asked the angel, how can I be sure of this?" I am an old man, and my wife is well along in years." You would think it would have been easy to believe something coming from an angel. Doesn't this show us they were also human beings, just like we are prone to doubt, fear, and unbelief? He had a good point.

They were well past their childbearing years. It would take a lot of faith to believe something like this could still happen for them, like Abraham and Sarah. How I love when God says it's time, anything can happen. Audacious, extraordinary miracles change the trajectory of our whole world. I want that, don't you? Do we dare ask Him for that, or at least have open hearts to it? If you are willing to let God shake up your ordinary world as you know it, pray the prayer below with me.

Prayer Declaration:
Jesus, we give you permission to interrupt our hearts and lives in ways that will make our lives better for us, for our families. We glorify You! Jesus, thank you for all you have done. We say 'more Lord,' finish what you started in us. We want to keep our hearts open to miracles and whatever it is you desire. Your Kingdom come; your will be done!

December 24
No Room in the Inn

It's finally Christmas Eve, cold and windy, but the Christmas Eve service is on. This makes my heart happy. There's just something about gathering as a family in a packed-out church service, singing Christmas carols together, and hearing the story once again. It's beautiful and precious and never gets old. This church we attend is an hour away; our twin daughters live there. We needed to leave soon after lunch, for their service was at three. What better way to spend Christmas Eve afternoon? I think of Mary and Joseph on their way to Bethlehem. Mary riding on the back of a donkey in her 3rd trimester and Joseph walking. They were probably both weary and worn from the journey, and all they wanted was a room to rest and sleep. We all know there was no room in the inn, which is why our Lord and Savior, Jesus Christ, was born in a barn! Luke 2:7, Mary gave birth to her firstborn, a son. She wrapped Him in clothes and placed Him in a manger because there was no room for them in the inn. This alone is something to ponder. Was this maybe a prophetic picture of the humble person Jesus would be? Even though He was the son of God, He was the most humble and kind man to ever be on Earth. He originated in a modest barn, His cradle was a manger, and He humbled himself to the point of death on the cross for the sins of the world, for you and me and anyone who believes. For anyone who accepts what He has done for us.

Last night, as my husband and I planned our Christmas Day, we discussed the importance of including the Christmas story to truly include Jesus as the guest of honor in our celebrations. He deserves it. He is the greatest gift any of us ever has or will receive. If you haven't already read the story, this would be a good year to start!

Prayer Declaration:
Jesus, thank you once again for your gift of life and salvation this Christmas season. We humbly include and honor you. Open even more hearts to your love and salvation. Thank you for coming to us. Thank you for saving us, until your second coming, we wait readily.

December 25
Merry Christmas!

It's Christmas Day, the day we had been preparing for all month long. The food is prepped. The gifts are wrapped and under the tree. The Christmas Eve service was wonderful last night. Later in the evening, family time around the island, eating, talking, laughing, and finally watching a movie, was special. Everyone found a place to sleep, and no one ended up in the barn. We stayed up way too late. We started our day with homemade cinnamon rolls, fruit, coffee, and Christmas music. Next, we took turns sharing a portion of the Christmas story all around the room. It gets quite animated and interesting with all twelve of us sharing our viewpoints and input. Our youngest son Jon Lamar always tells his portion from our current or modern-day perspective; it is very intriguing. One of my favorite parts of the story is in Luke 2: 10-11, where the angel came to the shepherds and declared, "Do not be afraid. I bring you good news of great joy that will be for all people today in the town of David, a Savior has been born to you. He is Christ the Lord!" In verse nine, it tells us the angels were terrified, one more response to when an angel comes and speaks to man. It is interesting to read all the different responses, the shepherds, Mary, Zachariah, and Joseph. What do we think our response would be?

I'd like to think it would be amazing and heavenly, but I can also imagine it would be intense and maybe even terrifying, like it was for the shepherds to see angels. I'm also struck by the fact that Zachariah couldn't speak until their baby John was born because he questioned the angel. How many times do we question God, but then again, Zachariah was still human, just like you and I.

Prayer Declaration:
Happy birthday Jesus! Once again give us bigger vision and hearts to believe for the supernatural to happen for us too, whatever it is you have for our lives. Like Mary, may our response be humble and willing. Let it be unto us as You say, Lord. We want to ask, 'what do you want from me, instead of questioning why?'

December 26
Double Blessings

The gifts are all open, the food is mostly gone, the dishes are finally done, and my motorized robot is cleaning the floors. My son-in-law gave me the best gifts for Christmas yesterday; that was one of them. Yes, I was delighted; it had been on my wish list for some time already. It's our twin daughters' 23rd birthdays today. Nurse Lorinda had to go to work today. 'Mommy-to-be' Luanne and her husband stayed over last night, therefore celebrating her this morning. We made her a special breakfast, brought coffee to her in bed, and gave her gifts. We talked about the night they were born. They came into this world very quickly on a cold, icy December evening. We made it to the hospital in the nick of time for them to put me under and deliver our twin girls by C-section.

They were born a month early, so this was unexpected. From that moment on, our lives changed tremendously. Up until then, we only had three small boys. Having daughters was exciting and double everything for the next 20 years. Now they are all grown up, have homes of their own, and still bring us much joy. However, parenting twins was not always easy. There were plenty of times we felt like we weren't sure what we were doing. God is faithful. He always is. He was faithful to Mary. He will be faithful to you, too, even when it's a responsibility we don't always feel qualified for. I love how at different times, it tells us in the Bible that Mary treasured things in her heart and pondered on them in Luke 2:19,51. I love that she pondered. I rather like that word. I often pondered and wondered why God entrusted twin daughters to us. I will be forever grateful He did. Even though many times I felt underqualified. Celebrate those special assignments and gifts God has entrusted You with; even if it takes lots of effort, it is worth it!

Prayer Declaration:
Thank You, Jesus, for giving us our precious daughters 23 years ago today. Thank You for giving us baby Jesus over 2,000 years ago yesterday. Thank You for blessing us beyond what we could dream of. Thank You that you never give us more than you're not also willing to help us with! Teach us to lean on You when we are overwhelmed, and focus on our blessings!

December 27
Believe by Faith

It's been a wonderful slow morning which I needed after all the Christmas and birthday activities. It's time to get back to healthy eating and a routine. Christmas has come and gone for another year. The greatest gift that has ever been given is here for all of us, so we truly don't have to fear; just like the angels said, fear not. When Jesus was born, everything changed, not only for the people back in that day but for all of us who hear and believe. I love the story of Simeon and Anna. They were waiting for Jesus to come for many years. Luke 2:29-32, Simeon says, "Sovereign Lord as You have promised, You now dismiss your servant in peace. For my eyes have seen your salvation, which You have prepared in the sight of all people, a light for revelation to the Gentiles, and for glory to your people Israel."

Simeon knew the moment he saw the baby that it was Jesus because of verse 26. It had been revealed to him by the Holy Spirit that he would not die before he had seen the *Lord's Messiah, [other versions say] Christ.* Anna, 84 years old and a widow, saw and believed that it was Jesus. Verse 38 tells us, "Coming up to them, Joseph and Mary and baby Jesus, she gave thanks to God and spoke about the child to all who were looking forward to the redemption of Jerusalem." I can only imagine how this must have blessed Joseph and Mary. Here are two older, devout believers speaking and prophesying over Jesus, His first time brought to the temple at only eight days old. If you don't yet, will you believe in this beautiful, supernatural, miraculous Christmas story that has the power to change your life for all eternity?

Prayer Declaration:
Jesus, give us the faith that Simeon and Anna had; they saw and believed. We hear and believe. Give us ears to hear the good news of Your birth, death, and resurrection. Thank you, Jesus, for Your wonderful and marvelous plan for all mankind if we only believe.

December 28
Wisdom and Favor

Still lingering here in the Christmas story. It seems the older I get, the more intriguing the story is, and I think of different aspects. Imagine it happening in our culture today, the absolute miracle of it all, how Mary became pregnant by the Holy Spirit, angelic activity. It's so wonderful and fills me with hope of the possibilities of serving a God like this. Nothing is too hard or difficult for Him! When we give Him our yes, like Mary and Joseph, Zachariah and Elizabeth, and many others did, God can choose us to do wonderful things for Him too. Where do you need a miracle in your life? Ask God for His favor on your life, your family, and your future. Luke 2:40 and 52, the story continues, "The child Jesus grew and became strong. He was filled with wisdom and the grace of God was upon Him. Jesus grew in wisdom and stature and in favor with God and men." Even though He was Jesus himself, He grew in wisdom and favor. How much more do we need to grow in these very things?

I find myself praying for wisdom quite often. Like this morning, I knew I had a couples counseling session. It's easy to ask God for wisdom in those situations, but how often do we pray for favor? Is it okay to ask for favor? I do believe so. Psalms 90:17 says, "Let the favor of the Lord our God be upon us..." because the more we have God's favor on our lives, the more we will be able to advance His will and Kingdom here on Earth. The more favor we have, the more we will be able to do hard and uncomfortable things. Will you say yes to God with me today and pray for His favor on your life and see what He wants to do in you and through you?

Prayer Declaration:
Jesus, you have our yes. Come, bless us with your supernatural favor and lead us wherever you want, instill the yearning to do your will to advance your Kingdom. Will you help us grow in favor with God and man, just like Jesus did when He was here on earth. Thank you for his humble example.

December 29
Water Baptism

Our weather seems to be back to normal again after frigid, cold, massive amounts of snow and wind. Life, too, seems to have returned to a more normal routine, which, on the one hand, can feel boring or monotonous. It also keeps us grounded and more productive, at least with my personality and perspective. Do you think, as Mary and Joseph left Bethlehem to raise baby Jesus, that they found a normal life? Again, the Bible doesn't tell us too much about Jesus and His growing-up years, but we can imagine what it could have been like for His parents, raising the Son of God. We can read of His baptism in Luke 3:21-22, "When all the people were being baptized, Jesus was baptized too, and as He was praying, heaven opened, and the Holy Spirit descended on Him in bodily form like a dove. A voice came from heaven. "You are my son, whom I love and with You I am well pleased," another supernatural happening. How amazing that must have been for Jesus. More wonder; were His parents there to witness this?

Did others hear the voice too, or was it only for Jesus' ears? I also ask, have you been baptized? Baptism is a public declaration of following Jesus. Maybe you were baptized as a baby. Even so, maybe you have a desire to be baptized now, as an adult, *being baptized on the confession of your faith*, as the Bible says. If Jesus was baptized as a young adult, how much more do we want it? He was blameless and the son of God? He left a perfect example for us to follow. We all long to hear those words one day. "This is my beloved son or daughter, in whom I am well pleased."

Prayer Declaration:
Thank you, Jesus, for once again showing us the way. Leading by example when You were here on earth as a baby, toddler, teenager, then an adult. Teach us how to live like You did. Help us to follow in Your footsteps. Give us soft, repentant hearts that desire Your baptism. Amen.

December 30
Reflect Relax Rest

This year is coming to an end fast. How do you end a year well? Do you reflect and reminisce and maybe repent of things you wish you did differently? I like to do all of the above. Let go of all the old but hold on to and savor all the good, altogether with what we did well and got to accomplish. Now, we start to strategize and dream of the New Year. What hopes, dreams, and goals do you have? Maybe some new opportunities are on the horizon? Above all, I invite you to reflect, rest and relax. Allow Jesus to lead you into the specific steps or endeavors He wants for you. We can get so caught up in wanting to please, we fail to *just be*. Or like a devotional part in my Bible mentions, *we try to go faster than grace*. It's a perfect recipe to crash later in your life; I've seen it happen to others and experienced this myself.

I'm always intrigued by the fact that Jesus started his ministry at 30 years old. Luke 3:23 says, "Now Jesus himself was about 30 years old when he began His ministry." We might wonder why not sooner? Maybe He was learning some very key life lessons. Maybe He was allowed to fully enjoy his childhood without any unrealistic expectations placed upon Him? What are your thoughts? Either way, I think He was being prepared behind the scenes for His public ministry that would come soon enough. We would do well to do the same. We will never have a long-term sustainable public ministry if we don't first get prepared in private, in the secret place with Jesus.

Prayer Declaration:
Jesus, thank You for Your example. Help us to hunger as much for the secret place as we do for a public platform. Teach us to be patient and do only what You ask of us, nothing more and nothing less. You only did what Your heavenly Father asked You too.

December 31
New Year's Eve

The last day of this year has dawned. New Year's Eve is what we call it, which also means it's the last time to write a page for this book. I want to use 2nd Corinthians 13:14 for our verse today, "May the grace of our Lord Jesus Christ and the love of God and the fellowship of the Holy Spirit be with you all." This is my hope and prayer for you as we finish out this year and enter the brand-new year tomorrow. Whatever your hopes, goals, and dreams are, you can accomplish them. Write them down. Make a written plan. Ask God to breathe on them. If you need His grace to accomplish them, ask Him for that. He gives His grace freely when we ask Him. Remember, He is strong where we are weak. I also pray you will grow in His love for you, that you will open your heart fully to the depths of His love that knows no bounds. Fellowship with the Holy Spirit is an adventure. He is our counselor, and He loves to keep things alive and fresh in our lives. Get to know him even better than you already do. Journeying through this "Joy in the Journey" devotional together this year has been an honor and a blessing. We have discussed many things. The wavering mountain peaks and the lower valleys of life are the difference between joy and sorrow.

The fact that we can have joy and sorrow in the same season shows us how to rise above trials and live in the eternal hope of our homes in heaven. We are all human, and we all have our own set of struggles, but we have hope in Jesus! We also discussed how to make Jesus the lord of our lives and to share that good news freely with others. So now I simply want to close out this year and this book with Number 6:24-26. "The Lord bless you and keep you. The Lord make His face shine upon you and be gracious to you. The Lord turn His face toward you and give you peace."

Prayer Declaration:
Jesus, once again we thank You. We simply thank You. Throughout this year we learned: To pivot from sadness to joy. Be real with our emotions. Find rest in Jesus. How to raise a family biblically. Align our thinking with God's mission: And set our goals and sights with heaven in mind. For these things we thank You, Amen.

Acknowledgments

Ernest without you this book would still be in journal form. I want to thank you from the depths of my heart for everything you did to help; your encouragement, your belief in me, your technical skills, the way you walked me through hard things: You don't just do it yourself, you empower me, ever teaching and gently helping me grow. Thank you! *Ernest, I love you to the ends of the earth! You will always be my knight in shining armor.

My beloved children, you have all been so encouraging through this whole process! Thank you for your positive feedback, when I would send you manuscripts to listen too. You all are my world! I dedicate this book to our family legacy. Together we will continue to grow from glory to glory.

Pam my dear family friend, thank you for your belief in me. The hours you spent helping me as well as your positive feedback are greatly appreciated! May God Himself reward you.

Lizzie my dear fellow author and friend. Your encouragement, your feedback, your help in finding the right editor and publisher, and just your genuine, beautiful heart in helping others is so refreshing.

Leanette, my editor and project manager, how do I thank you enough? Your ability to break things down, step by step for me, helping me understand the whole process. You have taught me so much, your affirmation all through the process and your patience. Leanette, you have made this a great experience and I'm so grateful to you.

Thank you Jesus, you are my everything, always have been, always will be.

*Reach Ernest and Laurie, for any ministry event, engagement, or occasion.
Email: laurieschwartz111@gmail.com
Website: simpfaithcounseling.com
Facebook.com/LaurieSchwartzMinistries

Printed in the USA
CPSIA information can be obtained
at www.ICGtesting.com
CBHW071126090124
3192CB00011B/6